TEST RIDE on the
SUNNYLAND BUS

A DAUGHTER'S CIVIL RIGHTS JOURNEY

. . . .

Ana Maria Spagna

UNIVERSITY OF NEBRASKA PRESS | LINCOLN AND LONDON

Library of Congress
Cataloging-in-Publication Data
Spagna, Ana Maria.
Test ride on the Sunnyland bus :
a daughter's civil rights journey
/ Ana Maria Spagna.
p. cm.
ISBN 978-0-8032-1712-6
(paperback. : alkaline paper)
1. African Americans—Civil
rights—Florida—Tallahassee—
History—20th century.
2. Boycotts—Florida—Tallahassee—
History—20th century.
3. Tallahassee (Fla.)—Race
relations—History—20th century.
4. Spagna, Joe, d. 1979.
5. Spagna, Ana Maria. I. Title.
F320.N4S63 2010
323.1196'073075988—dc22
2009034320

Set in Janson by Kim Essman.
Designed by Nathan Putens.

RIVER TEETH LITERARY NONFICTION PRIZE

Series Editors:
DANIEL LEHMAN, Ashland University
JOE MACKALL, Ashland University

The River Teeth Literary Nonfiction Prize is awarded to the best work of literary nonfiction submitted to the annual contest sponsored by *River Teeth: A Journal of Nonfiction Narrative.*

If a young person of this generation came to me and said "What should I do? What should I be doing?" I would say "Find a way to follow the dictates of your conscience. Find your own inner compass and follow it. Do what is right. Be kind. Don't hate. Love is a better way. Don't become cynical. Forget about your own circumstances and find a way to get involved in the circumstances of others." JOHN LEWIS

. . .

Struggle is important and at the same time if it's possible, you try to eke out some corner of love or some glimpse of happiness within. And that's what I think more than anything else conquers the bitterness. BOB MOSES

Contents

Part One

I Think I Can Serve

CHAPTER ONE

In Front of Speed's

The paint-peeling sign above the door is barely legible: Speed's Grocery. I stand on the sidewalk sweaty with nerves. This can't be the place, I think. This is nothing like I pictured. Behind heavy iron bars, darkened windows sport stickers for cigarette brands: Newport, Camel, Winston. Men with graying beards and ball caps pulled low lean against the storefront, paper bags in hand, while I loiter across the narrow tree-lined street, rereading the plywood sign. *Beer Milk Ice* it reads, and below that, *Meats Bread Grocery Lotto.* Beside each line of words coils a hand-painted rattler, the mascot of Florida A&M University, only two blocks east. But there are no students here, no one younger, by the looks of it, than forty. There are also no women. I've been in crowds like that before, plenty of times, but this time it's different. There are no white people in front of Speed's, and I have never, in thirty-eight years, been the only white person anywhere.

I snap a picture and hesitate before I step off the curb and cross the street, walking fast, too fast, in dress loafers and too-hot black jeans, a brand-new digital camera dangling from my wrist.

"Leonard Speed?" I ask. "Dan Speed? Anybody know them?"

The men are silent.

One fellow, his eyes cataract scarred and rheumy, tells me that he's from New Jersey and that he's trying to find work. He stares at me hard.

"I'm a good worker," he says.

I nod uneasily.

Another guy leans back on a car hood and grins wide, gamely pretending to pose for the camera, album-cover style. I smile shyly and pretend to snap a photo.

"This place for sale?" he asks.

"No," I laugh. "I mean, I don't know."

Finally, a third man, more dignified, tall and heavyset and mustached, steps forward. His approach is more direct.

"What are you doing here?"

His age and stature, his bearing—or maybe the mustache—remind me of my father, so I think this might be my chance. I garner my courage.

"My dad used to hang out here fifty years ago."

"Your dad? What's his name?"

"Joe Spagna."

"Joe Spagna?" He draws out the last name "Spaaawn-yuh?" Questioning. Unbelieving. I grow hopeful. He could have known him. He looks about the right age, and it seems like he's recognized the name. "Spaaawn-yuh? A Spanish guy?"

My dad wasn't Spanish. He was Italian. Actually, he was white. Just plain white. And that's what this guy is getting at, I know: what would a white guy be doing hanging around a place like this? That's part of what I want to know too.

. . .

One sunny Saturday morning in January 1957—forty-nine years ago today—my father, Joseph Spagna, along with five other young men, waited to board a bus right here in front of Speed's. Their plan was plain: to ride the bus together—three blacks and three whites—to get arrested and to take their case to the U.S. Supreme Court. But it was dangerous as hell. The morning was quiet, lazy even, and the boys were relaxed, but the atmosphere, nevertheless, was charged. It was not as if they did not know what they were doing.

For starters, the gathering itself was very nearly illegal. Of the six young men, five were college students—two attended Florida State University, and three went to Florida A&M—and social intermingling among students from the white school and those from the black was strictly forbidden. A grad student at Florida State, a friend of my father, had recently been expelled for inviting three students from A&M to a Christmas party on campus. Moreover, this small grocery, of all of the groceries in town, was steeped in controversy. A week earlier shotgun blasts had taken out the front windows as a warning to the owner, Dan Speed, to cut the crap. The crap, as it were, was the Tallahassee bus boycott, a seven-month-long struggle to integrate city buses, which was, at this point, flailing. The boys were there to revive it.

Though the Tallahassee boycott is less well known than the one in Montgomery, Alabama—the one Rosa Parks started and Martin Luther King Jr. led—it took place at exactly the same time and seemed, at first, to be as equally successful. Starting in May 1956, blacks in Tallahassee refused to ride city buses. Through the heat of summer and the cool grace of autumn and into early winter, domestic workers and laborers, teachers and city employees, woke at dawn to walk long miles across the capital city. A group of black citizens, led by the grocer, Dan Speed, and the charismatic Reverend C. K. Steele, organized mass meetings and funded a clandestine carpool. As in Montgomery, the bus company suffered, long-standing discrimination was exposed, and victory seemed within reach. Then in December, the U.S. Supreme Court issued the order to integrate buses in Montgomery, and in Tallahassee all hell broke loose.

The holiday season turned violent. Crosses were burned on

church lawns. Gunfire broke out nightly. Bomb threats accrued. Two days after Christmas, Dan Speed and C. K. Steele and a dozen other ministers met for a planned integrated bus ride, a celebration of sorts of the victory in Montgomery, but they were greeted at the downtown depot by a mob wielding barely concealed weapons.

"I detected how tense the situation was," Steele later said. "There were men from out of town, and most of these were, I guess, Ku Klux Klansmen, buying up hatchets, hammers and carrying them around town."

They called the ride off right then and there.

Soon the city council drafted a new ordinance, Ordinance 741, to maintain segregation in Tallahassee at all costs, and for all intents and purposes the bus boycott was dead.

So Steele called a mass meeting at his church, Bethel Missionary Baptist, a meeting not unlike those he'd called regularly over the past seven months, except that this one was poorly attended. The violence had scared off most supporters. The few who lined the wooden pews that January night were the stalwarts, the true believers, and to them Steele made an impassioned plea. They needed volunteers, both blacks and whites, he explained, to ride a bus together and test the bogus new ordinance. The riders would get arrested and, if necessary, take their case all the way to the U.S. Supreme Court.

Was anyone willing?

The room fell silent.

My father stood. He'd been one of a small handful of white students who had been attending the mass meetings.

"I think I can serve as one of the persons," he said.

The next Saturday six young men met up in front of Speed's. The three white boys—Jon Folsom, James Kennedy, and my dad—arrived in a late-model Studebaker, parked now on a side street while the blacks—Johnny Herndon, Leonard Speed, and Harold Owens—walked the quarter mile from the A&M campus. Together they stood in shirt sleeves on the corner, sweating in the winter sun; they lit cigarettes and sized each other up. Three of them were big guys, over six feet tall, former football players. That might come in handy. They shuffled their feet, drew long on their cigarettes, and looked around, and Leonard Speed, the grocer's son, passed out crisp new dollar bills to cover the ten-cent fare, for as long as it might take.

"I went there to meet some friends of mine," my father later testified. "We had no purpose in mind. We were just going over there—a Saturday morning jaunt, college boys."

He was, of course, lying.

. . .

People who knew my father in 1957 describe a distinctly unheroic character: disheveled, nearly bedraggled, a wannabe beatnik who carried dog-eared paperbacks in the pockets of a tattered coat and slept on a bare mattress in a small rented room strewn with weeks of old newspapers. He was hardly the typical G.I. Bill student. Not that anyone knew he was a vet. No one knew much about him, not even his friends, though he had many. He liked to talk, but never about himself, and never, ever, about his past. He was an English major, fanatic about literature, so mostly he talked about books. Once at a popular café in the center of the Florida State campus, he was in the middle of a heated discussion of *Paradise Lost* when the jukebox got too loud; he marched across the room and yanked the plug.

Though he loved all books, any books, he was especially excited about the new stuff. *On the Road* would come out later that year, and though Allen Ginsberg's "Howl" had been officially censored by the government, it circulated widely in the wake of its infamous initial reading. The trial of Lawrence Ferlinghetti of City Lights Bookstore in San Francisco, around

7

the corner from where my father would later own a bookstore himself, was going full-tilt. My dad, for his part, wrote to Ferlinghetti and got a free copy of "Howl," which he read aloud at parties. I can't imagine my father doing such a thing, but he was young, I suppose, and he was passionate. Not just about literature.

On the streets of Tallahassee within view of the majestic state capitol building sat small wooden homes in rows with rusty tin roofs and clothes drying on the line: the homes of black folks, or the ones left standing after many were demolished a decade earlier to make room for new state office buildings. Just a few blocks south, across the railroad tracks, blacks lived even more poorly. Only two paved streets connected the strictly segregated sections of the city, and the injustice of the situation bothered my dad. That's part of what I want to know, too: *why*.

I mean, of course I know why it rankled—segregation was wrong as rot—but there were plenty of white folks in Tallahassee, and all over the South, who knew as much and didn't do a thing about it, probably didn't think there was a thing they could do about it. I want to know why he did it. Where did he find the courage to stand up at the mass meeting to become permanently and perilously "notorious," as one history book describes him, in that sunny college town? I would ask him myself. But I can't. He's been dead now for twenty-seven years.

After his death, scraps of the bus story became part of Spagna family lore. Here's how it went: once upon a time, Dad sat on the back of a bus in Florida and got arrested, but if he'd gone to jail, at that time, he'd have been killed as a so-called "nigger lover," so the NAACP paid for him to leave the country until the statute of limitations ran out. Where the story came from, I can't say. I never heard it until after he died, and by the time I reached adulthood, I had it figured for bullshit. For one thing, I knew enough, or thought I did, to know that a white man sitting in the black section of a bus was not nearly the crime that a black person sitting in the white section was. He might be an eccentric, even a detestable "nigger lover," but not a criminal. For another thing, while my father had, in fact, left the country for several years—he spent most of the 1960s in Mexico and South America—he'd also supposedly owned a bookstore in San Francisco at some point and built a small cabin on a beach in Marin County. Since immediately after returning from South America, he was married and having kids, well, the timeline wasn't holding up.

I liked the story anyway. I told it often, mostly because it explained why I'd been born in Bogotá, Colombia, better than saying that my dad was working for Catholic Relief Services and my mom was on a Fulbright scholarship. Those two labels—the do-gooder and the egghead—embarrassed me as a teenager. In hindsight, I don't know why I was so ashamed of plain good intentions, but I do know why I wanted to avoid any talk about my dad. He'd died too young. He'd abandoned us. For twenty-seven years, I'd been in no mood to forgive my father or even to think much about him. Until, last January, when I headed off to Tallahassee.

I flew three thousand miles from northwest Washington State, a corner of the country that could not be further, geographically or culturally, from panhandle Florida, especially in January. At home there'd been three feet of wet snow on the ground with more sure to come. In Tallahassee, sun shone brightly on the broad drooping limbs of live oaks. I lugged a bag of thousand-page histories across the Florida State campus, and I sequestered myself in the basement of the library squinting at microfiche copies of the local paper, the *Tallahassee Democrat*. Several crucial issues were missing from the collection, but at first I hardly noticed. I sank happily into the egghead world of research, pencil-scratched notes, and musty old books. Then I emerged into the winter sun and drank espresso on park benches in the sun with my partner, Laurie.

Laurie had accompanied me to Tallahassee as moral support. I'd started investigating the test ride story in the winter of 2004 when, on the nightly news, same-sex couples were flocking to San Francisco to get married. Our own civil rights movement seemed on the rise, and I use the word "our" loosely. Though I'd lived with Laurie for fifteen years, I still shied from the gay rights movement, never seeking out the opportunity to participate. And not just gay rights. Though we lived surrounded by pristine wilderness, I ridiculed environmentalists. I couldn't think of one good reason for the Iraq War, but I never marched in protests. Laurie and I had always been apolitical—part of the reason we could live together, two women, so peaceably in a very small town—but lately I'd begun to change. Or the world had. And it was hard not to notice that those changes were for the worse: terrorism, environmental degradation, ethnic cleansing, sure, but also closer to home, the seeds of it all, paranoia, xenophobia, plain old-fashioned hate. I didn't know what to do about any of it because I didn't really believe anything could be done. Worse yet, I didn't know *why* I didn't believe. Sure, I was weary of self-righteous liberalism—so many causes, so little time—and I was wearier yet of the flag-wagging Reagan fervor that had suffused my high school and college years, but as I followed the saga of the couples lining up in San Francisco over the radio from my cabin, and as I listened, too, to the voices rising in shrill opposition, I began to think the real reason I hid out in the woods was this: I was a coward.

In Front of Speed's

. . .

In front of Speed's, in 1957, an empty bus screeched to a stop. The door opened, and the driver recoiled. He knew that everything, at this point, was up to him. The complicated new city ordinance required that the driver assign riders seats based, supposedly, on weight distribution and the "maximum health and safety" of the riders. He had some time to think as he made change for a ten-cent fare, over and over, from those crisp new dollar bills. Finally, he made his decision: whites up front, blacks in the back. The boys pocketed their change and sat without incident. The driver pulled safely away from the curb and checked his rearview mirror only to see that three of the riders had moved so that now they sat as three interracial pairs.

The bus crawled slowly along the perimeter of the A&M campus, round and round, the boys rode silently, and because the route was entirely on the black side of town and because there was hardly anyone out on a Saturday morning to get riled up, the driver ignored them. So, according to the history books, the boys got off.

Again, they stood on the street and waited until they spied a bus. This one, called the "Sunnyland," was headed for Thomasville Road, across the railroad tracks to the north, toward the white side of town. This new driver was considerably more agitated than the first. He made change hastily and assigned them seats angrily: whites up front, blacks in the back. Again, they dutifully sat. And once again, as choreographed, midway through the ride, three of them stood to switch seats. This time the bus driver caught them red-handed. In other words, he took the bait.

The driver abandoned his route and headed directly for the police station downtown, where the three who had moved—Leonard Speed and Johnny Herndon, who were both black, and my dad, Joe Spagna—were promptly arrested and later released on $50 bail.

That night, C. K. Steele called another mass meeting. This time the church was packed to the hilt. Besides the stalwarts and the supporters and the gawkers, this one was attended by about twenty white students from Florida State and eighteen carloads of black students from Florida A&M energized by this new development. When the young men arrived, they received a standing ovation.

My father stood to speak. "I want to live in a country," he said, "where everyone, regardless of race, creed, or color, has equal rights under the law."

There was more thunderous applause.

The glory, such as it was, was over. The trouble had just begun.

. . .

"You need to go over to that grocery store, Speed's," Laurie said.

I'd talked a good game back in Washington about wanting to find living witnesses, to interview people who might have known my dad, but now the library sounded a whole lot easier.

"Come on," she said. "Let's go."

We drove south on Monroe, the same thoroughfare that the Sunnyland bus had taken. Four lanes wide and traffic clogged, Monroe took us past Thomasville Road and past the bus station, where a small statue of C. K. Steele stood tucked out of view behind orange construction fencing. In the time it took me to climb out of the idling rental car and take a few photographs of the statue through the fence, not a single bus pulled in. In fact, when I'd been planning the trip, I'd considered not renting a car at all but instead using the bus system to get around. People I mentioned this to laughed outright. That won't work, they said. The world has changed in the past fifty years, they said. Sure enough, we saw no buses at all, until farther south, past the capitol building, where a lone gray-bearded white man sat cross-legged on the lawn, draped in the American flag, protesting the Iraq War. Then suddenly buses were everywhere. And everyone on the street was black.

"We crossed the tracks," Laurie said.

I flinched. Fifty years later, I thought, not that much had changed. Not enough. The cars were newer, the businesses looked well kept, not shabby, and, well, the roads were paved. But something felt wrong. I'd been forewarned about crime before traveling to Tallahassee, but under those branchy green trees, on sidewalks lined with camellias in bloom, I'd felt plenty safe. I felt safer, certainly, than I did on the streets near my mother's house in California, where on our most recent visit, Laurie and I passed makeshift memorials to gang shootings at suburban intersections. Compared to that, Tallahassee seemed benign, bucolic even, until we pulled up in front of Speed's.

"Go ask," Laurie said.

I froze. We were two white women in a red rental car. We were, in a word, a spectacle.

"What do I say?"

"Tell the truth," she said. "Now, go."

I climbed out and weaved through the crowd on the sidewalk, nodding vaguely, not risking eye contact, and into the store, harboring a ridiculously bookish fantasy. I would ask about Leonard Speed or Dan Speed, and the matronly black woman behind the checkout stand would say *Oh, he's around back* or *See? That's him unloading the milk bottles.* But the clerk was not a black woman, he was South Asian, and he spoke with a heavy lisp. He'd only owned the store a couple of years, he said, but he wanted to help. He pulled out a street map and pointed to where a couple other Speed's or Speedy's might be out on the beltway highway around the city. I thanked him and walked the gauntlet of loiterers one more time. At the curb, I hopped back in the rental car, and we drove around the block.

"Maybe he's right," Laurie said. "Maybe that wasn't the place."

"It was," I said. "I found the address in the archives. 801 North Floral Street."

Laurie stopped and put the rental car in reverse.

"You've got to get a picture of the place at least," she said.

So I climbed back out of the car and crossed the street with my camera on a string.

. . .

"Spagna? A Spanish guy?" the fellow repeats.

I hesitate.

I look long at the man, gray at his temples, wondering despite myself what he's doing standing outside a seedy convenience store at two in the afternoon anyway. I don't want to have to make a long explanation.

"Yes," I say. So much for the truth.

The man chuckles. I look not the teensiest bit Spanish. I'm either adopted or a liar.

"You from California?" he tries.

"Yes," I say.

This is partially true. I grew up in California, but I don't usually associate myself with the place. The Pacific Northwest doesn't hold California in very high regard, so I generally avoid conversation about my home state at all costs.

"Where at?"

"Riverside."

He nods again, grinning, like he's trying to get me to linger, like I'm big entertainment. I'm obviously no real-estate monger. I'm no journalist or historian either, it turns out. I'm no damned good at this.

"You know where that's at?"

He nods again, but I don't think he knows. I don't think he cares. He has something else he wants to say.

"Well, if you remember Tallahassee from fifty years ago, you know how much has changed," he says. Dead serious now. No small talk. No flirting. He means it.

"No, no. I don't remember Tallahassee. It was my dad. My dad, Joe Spagna, he hung around here back then."

"Your dad still alive?"

"No," I say, honest at last. "He's been gone a long time now. Do you know Leonard Speed?"

"Who?"

I look around at the other guys hoping for a smirk or lifted eyebrow, any hint that this might be a bluff.

"Leonard Speed. He was Dan's son. I guess Dan owned this place."

He shakes his head.

"Never heard of him."

He turns away to stare down the shady street past the well-kept lawns and the modest houses, at something somewhere far off in the distance, and I follow his gaze, shielding my eyes from the sun with one hand, trying to focus. I can't see a thing.

CHAPTER TWO

Never Go Back

On January 19, 1979, twenty-three years to the day after he rode
the Sunnyland bus in Tallahassee, my dad and I sat together
on the couch in the family room in Riverside, California. I was
eleven years old. My dad was forty-seven and already a ghost
of himself, only three months out of triple-bypass surgery, a
brand-new procedure. He had not been back to work at his
job as a psychiatric social worker for the county, and instead
he spent most of his time wood carving in the garage, though
he had no aptitude for carving whatsoever, and the head he'd
been hacking from a six-by-six for weeks was heinously mis-
shapen. He was restless. Smog-orange sun glowed through
dusty windows. It was too cold, by California standards, to
shoot baskets or slam tennis balls against the garage door, so
I sat on the couch with Dad and watched TV.

"Come running with me," he said.

"No," I said.

He'd taken up jogging after I joined a track team when I was
eight. I'd joined because a handsome coach had come recruiting
and because I was a tomboy first degree, and probably because
Dad had got me hooked on the Olympics. He'd bought a color
TV so we could watch the 1976 games, the same TV we were
watching right then, and I'd joined the team, and he started
running and, over time, he'd grown a little fanatical.

"Then you ride your bike, and I'll run," he said.

"No," I said. "The doctor said no."

No one remembers my dad as an athlete. He was earnest and intelligent, warm, they say. No one says that he had a helluva hook shot or a mean serve. His father, a first-generation Italian immigrant, played professional football in the 1920s. Though I never met my grandfather — he died at fifty-two of a heart attack, a fateful omen — we had a scrapbook of his gridiron achievements, including the time he tackled the legendary multisport athlete Jim Thorpe and made him quit football for good. The back of the scrapbook was reserved for my dad's own football career at Dartmouth; it's mostly empty since he dropped out of Dartmouth to join the Marines. Turns out, he wasn't that good at the game. That's not the only difference between my dad and his. In the fading photos, my grandfather appears dapper in tailored suits and hats. My dad wore a suit, too, when he went to work, but he wore it sloppily, the shirt untucked, the belt-slung pants hanging low. Fashion was not his forte. And though he liked sports, they weren't either.

Like many things — cooking, carpentry, gardening — my father pursued sports with a doggedness that was heavy on enthusiasm and light on follow-through. The playhouse he built us leaned and sagged, his oatmeal bread was leaden. The only dish he made with any success was jelly omelettes, a specialty for Sunday mornings that was, for us kids, a scrumptious treat and, for our mother, an atrocious mess to clean up. Dad never did the dishes. The way I see it, his football career probably flailed under this untucked-shirt nonchalance, which makes his single-minded pursuit of long-distance running at the end of his life that much harder to understand.

When he started, he was in lousy shape. At six feet tall, he weighed 240 pounds, smoked a pack a day, and drank beer regularly if not heavily. He would never have taken up jogging, if I hadn't begged him to. I was very enthusiastic about my fourth-grade track team; I didn't want to skip a day even when the team wasn't practicing, so I begged. And my dad, eventually, gave in. He donned a bandanna and plodded along beside me. The possibility that he would grow obsessive about the sport, that he would someday buy a hardcover copy of *The Complete Book of Running* and fork out $50 for waffle-soled Nikes seemed laughably remote. He ran with me, then with the older kids on the track team, then, when none of us could keep up, with a buddy from work. After a while, I branched out on the track team and tried the high jump. He built me a pit for the backyard: cement in paint cans to steady the uprights, a bamboo pole for a bar, and a Goodwill mattress. I was happy, then, to stay home and practice jumping. But Dad kept running.

He ran awkwardly. He had to. The bulky frame that served him well on the offensive line was not made for the Boston Marathon. He sweated profusely and wheezed. Over time, he began to lose weight and gain some endurance, until one year he ran the ten miles of the annual Hunger Awareness Walk. By then, he looked unnaturally thin, and our fridge was packed with Near Beer and egg substitute. By then, it was already too late.

The Hunger Awareness Walk was one of a million do-gooder events in the life of the Spagnas. My parents had a large circle of mostly Catholic friends who were social-justice junkies. They attended guitar Mass, marched at rallies, adopted mixed-race kids, and on weekends, staffed yard sales to raise funds for Friends Outside, a group they'd started to provide aid to prisoners and their families. Some had done stints in the Peace Corps just as my parents had worked for various non-profits in South America. My parents, I understood early, were liberals, like Meathead and Gloria on *All in the Family*, a little older perhaps, less fashionable, but otherwise the same. Once a week, my younger sister, Lisa, and my younger brother, Joey, and I went to sleep to the opening credits, Edith and Archie singing off key at the piano, and we knew, on that night, not to bother asking for an extra kiss or a drink of water. *All in the Family*, like Hunger Awareness, was serious business.

Of course we were taught that racism was bad, but I had no real sense of what that word—racism—meant. The elementary school we attended had been integrated a few years earlier by busing with, more or less, a shrug. We had several black kids in class, though not as many as Mexicans, and I had a black friend, Shirene. We kids knew about Martin Luther King Jr., and we knew from watching *Roots* that black people had once been slaves, but we didn't quite grasp the gravity of it all. At least I didn't. Once I came home singing a distasteful little jingle I'd picked up on the playground, "A fight, a fight, a nigga and a white," and Dad gave me the spanking of my life. Even midspanking, I felt eye-rolling disdain for my parents' overzealousness on such matters. It's just a word, I thought. Gawd.

The same went for war. My parents taught us that war, especially Vietnam, was very bad, but that was hardly a radical position in California in the mid-1970s. You only had to watch the news, as Dad did most nights, forcing us to switch off *The Monkees*, to see that war was bad and that being in the military was stupid. What was harder to understand was how or why my dad had ever signed up to fight in the Korean War and what, exactly, had happened when he did.

This much we knew: after dropping out of Dartmouth, he joined the Marines, and he was assigned to work as a helicopter mechanic at Camp Pendleton, California. It was a job, he'd always say, for which he was ill suited. (Considering his lack of prowess with the playhouse and other minor home repairs, I'd have to guess he was right.) He offered this as explanation for why, one day, he just walked off. AWOL. He said he got sick of praying every time one of his helicopters took off, bound for Korea, that no one would die because of his ineptitude. Who knows what the truth is? Camp Pendleton boasts a fine stretch of California coastline, one that borders bikini beaches to the north and south. There would have been plenty of reasons to go AWOL short of conscience or compassion. If he did go AWOL, he somehow made his peace with the Marine Corps because his discharge was acceptable enough for him to head off to Florida State on the G.I. Bill. But he never talked about the Marines, just like he never talked about Tallahassee, just like he had never, apparently, in Tallahassee, talked about his life before that. He just didn't.

For some reason, in his midforties, my dad took to wearing a saint's medal on a chain around his neck. The medal was, ironically enough, a pewter image of Junipero Serra, the priest who first journeyed up California's Camino Real establishing missions and enslaving Indians. Not exactly your typical liberal icon. I don't think he wore it because of Serra. He wore it for the message etched in the back: *Always go forward. Never go back.*

This had been my father's credo, and he had lived it faithfully from Dartmouth footballer, to Marine Corps deserter, to Florida, to San Francisco, to South America, and to the couch in the family room, the sun sinking low behind the palms.

"Come on," he said once more. "Run with me."

"No," I said.

"Don't tell Mom," he said.

And he left.

. . .

In 1984, five years after my dad died, Jim Fixx, author of *The Complete Book of Running*, died while out running. There'd been history of heart disease in his family, so when Fixx started running seriously at midlife, when he quit smoking and lost weight, the stress of all that change at once, the newspaper reported, was too much for his heart. *Duh!* Like we Spagnas didn't already know about that. There was more than a hint of I-told-you-so in my reaction to the news. *He should have known better!* What was harder to swallow was the flipside of the Jim Fixx story. He died happy, the newspaper said. He died doing what he loved best. That was hard for me to think about in 1984 because I knew even then that it was as true of my dad as it was of Jim Fixx: he ran because he loved to run.

Before Jim Fixx died, he was called a running guru, and "guru" was the right word. The rhythm of feet on pavement is so mantralike. A runner's high, those fleeting ecstatic moments, must be like nirvana. For my dad, I thought, maybe running was transcendental like prayer, liberating like a beatnik road trip, only minus the drinks and the chicks and, well, everything, but the wind in your hair, and maybe when you're over forty and the father of three, the wind in your hair is enough. That, and the fat slabbing off like arctic ice, feet slapping like a metronome, and sometimes, every so often, sunlight slicing through the smog and clarity at last!

I knew all this because I had been a runner too, a too-young runner pretending to be a grown-up, fists balled tight and eyes fixed forward, plotting to be an Olympian as my father and I jogged together around the local playground or on through our neighborhood, while asphalt rippled in triple-digit heat, while our socks soaked in the rain. Together we rode in his Pinto to track meets. Together we flipped through the pages of *Runner's World*. Though I quit running cold turkey after my dad died, I always remembered the plain unrestrained joy of sprinting, kicking hard for the finish, with my chest thrust forward, my head lolling back, surging up one last hill, and then lunging for the ribboned chute where my dad was always waiting.

. . .

On January 19, after my dad went out running, breaded chicken sat in the pan he used to make jelly omelets. I sat on the couch watching *Bewitched*. The chicken had been sitting there for a long time, through *The Monkees* and *Gilligan's Island* and *I Dream of Jeannie*, and though on most days we had to turn off the TV long before *I Dream of Jeannie*, nobody told me to turn it off that night, so I kept watching. I listened hard, and I kept my mouth shut tight, while my mother talked on the rotary wall telephone behind the couch to the police, and then to the hospital, while she went through the details: black hair, mustache, scar down his chest. She was not crying until they got to the medal. After she described the medal—Always Go Forward—she dropped the phone, and the receiver dangled by the wall, cord twisting, mom sobbing, for a long time.

He wasn't dead, Mom told us. He was in a coma.

I continued to go to school while he was in the hospital. The annual spelling bee was a week away, and since I was the defending champ, with only this year left of eligibility, the pressure was on. The night before the bee, as I ran through my word list alone in my bedroom, I overheard my grandmother and my mother talking in low tones.

"It's the right thing to do."

"You have to do it."

I knew somehow what that meant. I'd heard the phrase before—"pull the plug"—probably on TV, and that night it lodged in my mind, though I don't think they actually said it. It played over and over like a skipping record—pulltheplug, pulltheplug, pulltheplug—as I lay awake through the night, the alphabet raining down on me, letters jumbling together in nonsense configurations. I struggled to make sense of them, to spell them into proper order in my mind.

You know that word, I told myself. You can do it. Don't panic.

I knew, in a way, what was to come.

The next day the auditorium at school was dark. By the end of the spelling bee, only three of us remained among thirty cold metal chairs. The microphone squawked, its long cord coiling back and around, then disappearing off the stage, and when the principal called out "adequate," it was as if I'd never heard the word before. I could not imagine where it came from or what it meant, and I didn't bother to ask.

I spelled it: "A-T-T-I-Q-U-I-T."

The principal said: "Sorry."

I lugged home a third-place trophy three times the size of my first-place one from the year before, and when I stepped inside everyone made a too-big deal of it, hugging too long, and my grandma had already begun to cry before they told us: your dad died. Pretty soon, my little brother and sister were crying. But not me.

The next day, even though my mom said I could stay home, I didn't want to. I wanted things to get back to normal as soon as possible. So I trudged off to school and stood outside the classroom waiting for the bell to ring, leaning against a railing, my arms folded across my chest, when Shirene approached.

"How's your dad?" she asked.

"What dad?" I snapped. "Does that answer your question?"

PART ONE

. . .

After my dad's death, the world changed. Reagan got elected president, and *Family Ties* came on TV. I gave up running, and for a few years, I ate a huge bowl of ice cream each afternoon after school. I grew soft and cynical. A radical priest came to our house every few months, and he called me blasé and asked me to fill his bourbon glass, and I could feel bile rise in my throat. Liberal causes, like drug addiction, fundamentalist religion, or marathon training, I thought, were mostly about self: self-aggrandizing, self-serving, self-righteous. In other words: selfish. I'd have none of it. I planned to go to Oregon, to a green pastoral kind of netherworld, where less would be expected of me, almost nothing. If I wasn't going to do much good for the world, at least I wouldn't be doing much harm.

Meanwhile, I carried a hefty burden of responsibility, babysitting Lisa and Joey while Mom went to work teaching seventh grade, a job she detested. I was in seventh grade, and, more than anything, I did not want to be the kind of seventh grader she hated. No, I would be a grown-up instead. I would stay by her side, folding the local newspaper back to the op-ed page in the morning, staying up late to watch *St. Elsewhere* at night, setting the table always—assuring that there'd be four plates, not five, a calamitous mistake Lisa and Joey made all too easily.

Late in high school, I joined the cross country team. I felt guilty for my dad's death—for starting him on his running kick in the first place and for not stopping him that January night—and I knew that running would likely churn up those feelings. I also knew that jogging brought back bad memories in our household, and for that reason, I made sure never, ever, to arrive home late from an evening run. I also knew that, much as I loved my mom, I wanted her to get used to me being gone.

24

Eventually I gave up ice cream for cottage cheese. I left for Oregon as planned, then later to Washington, moving farther and farther into the woods. I felt at home among the mountains and the tall trees, and I found work that I loved, maintaining hiking trails for half the year, making do the rest of the time. For years Laurie and I kept moving, working seasonally around the West, until finally we settled in a dinky mountain town along a glacier-fed lake, a town so remote that there were no roads in or out—you'd have to take a four-hour boat ride or an expensive float plane to get there—a town so remote, in fact, that it did not have telephones, not even cell phones, but it did have Internet access via satellite.

One day I was sitting in my cabin Googling my brother's name: Joseph Spagna. Joey is an entomologist, and I often find his research fascinating or at least more interesting than whatever I am supposed to be doing. This time, I'd already scanned a few abstracts and checked out some video clips of snap-jaw ants snapping and tumbling backward in slow-mo when his name popped in a book titled *Inside Agitators: White Southerners in the Civil Rights Movement*. There wasn't much detail in the online blurb, but one thing was clear: it could not possibly be Joey. It had to be our dad. I ordered the book.

The mention was brief, but it did substantiate that old family myth. My father had, indeed, been arrested for sitting on a bus. What's more, he and two other defendants had taken their case to the Supreme Court. This was beginning to sound interesting. I drafted a letter to the author with several questions. What exactly happened that day? What happened in court? Did he know why my father had jumped bail or where he went or if the NAACP paid for the trip?

The author, Dr. David Chappell, wrote back immediately. He did not know the answers to my questions, he said, but he gave me several leads, and he emphasized the importance of finding living witnesses.

"Track down people who might have known him. Anyone. Talk to them," he said.

He made the story seem, if not huge, certainly worth examining.

Then he said this: "Your father is the kind of person who makes us enjoy our jobs and feel we have some examples of courage and decency to hold up in a world that otherwise is inclined to cynicism and despair."

I felt a wave of pride. *That's my dad he's talking about!* And quick on its heels came shame. Cynicism and despair? *That's me he's talking about.*

I decided to start writing e-mails—some that were answered, many that were not—and to read books and to try to understand. I didn't know if I was doing it out of pride. If I was, it was a shy, uncertain pride. How could I claim this father, after I'd denied him for so many years? Maybe, I told myself, I was doing it as a cure for cynicism and despair.

CHAPTER THREE

The Tallahassee Bus Boycott

I run each morning in Tallahassee. I've been running most days for a year now, to stay in shape and for the sheer rediscovered pleasure of it. My gait is unsightly, one leg swings wide, so I look more like an eager preschooler flailing across the playground, Laurie always tells me, than a thirty-eight-year-old woman. That doesn't stop me. I run the streets of Tallahassee, along wide sidewalks into gutters and out again, looking for any sign of the turbulent history. I see none. Now, after I cool down and shower, I plan to head to Florida A&M University, where the state black archives are housed and where the Tallahassee bus boycott began.

. . .

On Saturday, May 26, 1956—five months after Rosa Parks took her famous stand to start the bus boycott in Montgomery, Alabama, two hundred miles to the west—two young Florida A&M students, Wilhelmina Jakes and Carrie Patterson, boarded a Tallahassee city bus to go shopping downtown for dress patterns and paid the ten-cent fare. Nearly everyone shopped on Saturday, so the bus was crowded as usual, and, as usual, most of the riders were black. There was hardly even room for the girls to stand, so a white woman—a woman who actually *knew* the girls—slid over on a three-person bench to make room for them to sit.

The bus driver watched the whole thing in the rear-view mirror and pulled over.

"Get up or get off," he said.

"I'd be glad to get off," Jakes said. Then she got bold. "If you'll give us our money back."

Ten cents. All she wanted was ten cents.

The driver refused and waited instead for the cops to arrive. The two young women were arrested, charged with inciting a riot, and released on bail.

That may have been the end of it—yet another bus humiliation, yet another bus arrest—except that the next night, Klansmen burned a cross on the lawn in front of the girls' apartment. Word spread across the Florida A&M campus like wildfire, and on Monday morning instead of attending classes, students gathered spontaneously at the main bus depot in the middle of campus and waited for the first bus to arrive. When it did, a handful of spokesmen boarded the bus, told the story of Jakes and Patterson, and urged riders to get off. Most of the riders did, either in fear or solidarity. So the crowd grew as the day went on, and the story was told over and over, until eventually, only empty buses pulled into the depot at A&M.

The crowd cheered wildly.

. . .

When I arrive on the Florida A&M campus, hundreds of ROTC students, all of them black, march in formation around the football field. Students scurry past me, cell phones jangling, as I lug my heavy bag up the sidewalk toward the grassy lawn square. My first stop, I figure, will be the bus depot in the middle of campus. I am imagining the crowds on that Monday morning, fifty years ago, and sure enough, today another crowd is assembled. Maybe it's a war protest, I think, picturing the hippie campus out west where I attended college, but then I remember the ROTC hoards and think again. Maybe it's a band playing, I think, but I can hear no music, no throbbing bass, no squawking mike. Nope. Turns out it's just a rowdy bunch of guys catcalling women, rating their looks on a scale of one-to-ten, commenting on outfits, body shapes, hairstyles.

I pass directly in front of them—there's no way around—and the mood instantly dampens. At first I figure the problem is my race: I haven't seen another white person on campus. But it doesn't take long to figure out that's not the case: it's because I'm old! The students have taken me for a professor, and they're giving me wide berth. I nod and smile shyly as I pass through headed toward the library.

Inside, I sit on a high stool at an antiquated computer and run a search for "Tallahassee bus boycott." Only one slim volume on the subject, published in 1958, appears. I scour the shelves but find all three copies missing. Not checked out. Just missing.

"Do you know if this book has been checked out?" I ask at the reference desk.

The librarian stares at me long and then scrolls slowly through the same series of text-only screens I just scrolled myself.

"No, it's here," she says.

"Where, exactly?"

She walks me down the aisle, following the Library of Congress code numbers, and points to the place on the bottom shelf where the books are missing. I'm thinking she'll take notice. Instead, she turns her back and walks away.

I pretend to search the shelves a little longer, as if I have been helped, as if the books might magically appear, and while I'm at it I check for a copy of Glenda Rabby's *The Pain and the Promise*, an excellent history of civil rights in Tallahassee that my brother bought for me, in dissertation form, for my birthday six months ago when all this was just beginning. It's not here either.

I leave the room and head back out toward the information desk.

"Where are the black archives please?" I ask.

"They are closed," the receptionist tells me.

"Oh."

"But they are usually housed right over there."

She points in the direction of a stately building, currently under reconstruction, nestled between a large palm and a pine. I walk out across the wide green lawn, toward the two big trees, and take a break in the shade to snap a picture for Laurie of the unfamiliar combination. Pine limbs as long as the tree is tall. Palm fronds wide as billboards. Laurie does not plan to return for two more hours. I'm at loose ends. So I wander around the back side of the archives and find a door propped open with a sawhorse. I sneak in through a billowing sawdust cloud and past the high-pitch whirr of a circular saw, into the empty building, and stand dumbly among the mostly empty museum displays.

. . .

In 1956, three days after the spontaneous bus boycott kickoff at A&M, more than five hundred people crowded into Bethel Missionary Baptist Church, where C. K. Steele was pastor. Many blacks in Tallahassee didn't know much about the Montgomery boycott, but C. K. Steele did. Steele had spent thirteen years in Montgomery before moving to Tallahassee in 1952, and he knew Martin Luther King Jr. personally. Fifteen years older than King and never as famous, Steele shared the younger man's vision. And, as time would reveal, the same courage.

The church was abuzz until Steele stepped to the podium to call for a vote in support of the students' boycott. Then it fell silent.

"All those in favor?" he cried.

A unanimous roar erupted in the sanctuary.

After the meeting, black community leaders banded together, preachers mostly, or businessmen, anyone whose livelihood didn't depend on Southern white patronage. They formed the Inter-Civic Council (ICC) to oversee the boycott and announced the same three demands put forth in Montgomery

1. Seating on the buses would be on a first come, first served basis
2. Blacks were to be courteously treated by white drivers
3. Blacks were to be hired to drive predominantly black bus routes.

The ICC also promptly elected C. K. Steele president, though he was neither the unanimous choice nor the obvious one. In photographs, he wears a bow tie and spectacles and sports a tidy goatee, and in written descriptions, he is almost always described as "diminutive." Some in the newly formed ICC would have preferred to elect a local businessman as president, someone from a locally respected family, someone, well, bigger. But they would have been wrong. Over the next year, Steele's home, where he lived with his wife, Lois, and six young children, would be shot at repeatedly, often by off-duty police officers. Twice, undertakers from his own church would arrive at his doorstep to snatch up his body, responding to reports that he'd been killed, only to find him standing fully alive at the front door, no doubt sporting the trademark bow tie. Every time I read about C. K. Steele, I think that a better adjective than "diminutive" to describe him would be the obvious pun: "steely." C. K. Steele was unyielding.

The ICC elected Dan Speed as treasurer. Gregarious and feisty, Speed owned not one but a whole chain of small groceries on the black side of town. ("I was not too dumb in business," he'd later explain to an interviewer.) Because he owned a car and knew others who did, he also headed up the Transportation Committee. He organized a carpool system, much like the one used in Montgomery, to get folks across town. The carpool finances required fancy footwork. If drivers collected fares, the whole operation would crumble. A fee-collecting carpool could be considered a franchise, and white city commissioners had to give any franchise the okay. Instead, carpool riders were to contribute directly to the icc. And donate they did. At its peak Dan Speed's Transportation Committee was able to purchase six brand-new station wagons.

So Steele handled spiritual matters, and Speed handled practical matters, and dozens of other leaders in the black community donated time and money, and thousands of regular folks supported the boycott. When, in mid-July, riders began to grow antsy, Steele implored them, over and over, to stay the course. And, for a while, things were looking pretty good. By August, the bus company had agreed to hire black bus drivers for two of the black routes around Florida A&M. One of the demands had been met.

But the end was still not in sight.

. . .

"Can I help you?" a woman hollers at me from the end of the hall at the black archives like an angry schoolmarm.

I walk quickly through the collecting drywall dust. "I'm looking for information on the Tallahassee bus boycott. My father was involved and. . . ."

She sighs and rolls her eyes. "Everybody's doing something on the *boycott* these days."

Well, that comes as a surprise. So far in Tallahassee I've found no evidence that anyone even remembers the boycott.

"Do you have any documents?"

"Not really."

I can see it on her face: she would like me to leave.

"Do you know *The Pain and the Promise?*" she says, holding up the Rabby book.

"Oh yes," I say, excited now to be on common ground, excited to have found one person, after four days in town, who seems to know something on the subject. "That's the Bible!"

Her face pulls taut, her eyes narrow. I can see I've said the wrong thing.

Not the Bible. A good book, I should have said. A very good book. But not the Bible. I'm busy scolding myself when I realize she's talking to me.

"Pardon me?"

She's holding a photocopied flyer. "Have you seen this?"

The flyer advertises a weeklong celebration of the fiftieth anniversary of the bus boycott. There are several events planned, apparently, this coming May. There are speakers and programs. There will surely be someone who knew my father in attendance, and I begin to ramble, telling her all about my dad, and the test ride, and Leonard Speed.

"Do you know if he's still alive?" I ask.

"I don't think any of them are."

"Not Dan. Not the grocer. His son, Leonard."

The telephone rings, and the woman picks it up, and she settles into another posture altogether, easy, chatty, at home. I am sitting on a wooden bench staring at the flyer, my feet pinched and sore in my dress shoes, thinking about Leonard Speed.

I picture him on the streets on Tallahassee today, having inherited the family business, a man of integrity, healthy but weary, and I have so many questions for him, this man in my imagination. What does he think about the state of his community? His nation? His family? Is he jaded? Is he hopeful? I know that I am projecting, that these are questions I'd like

to ask my dead father, and I also know it is a tad ridiculous
since who among my friends with living fathers asks them such
things? No one does. But I revel in the fantasy anyway. I can't
help it. I keep a running list of questions to ask Leonard Speed.
If he is alive. If I can find him. Fewer, I know, are about *back
then* than about *right now*.

The woman on the telephone puts her hand over the mouth-
piece.

"Do you need anything else?"

"No, no," I say, scrambling to organize my bag and staring
still at the flyer in my hand. "Can I keep this?"

She nods and waits for me to leave.

Back outside, I wander around looking for a pay phone on
campus, harder and harder to find in these cell-phone days,
before I give up and sit to wait on a curbside, like a little kid
squinting in the sun.

Laurie pulls up in the red rental car, and I climb in and try
to show her the flyer, to tell her I've finally found a lead, that
I have a number to call, an actual number!

"Tomorrow, let's go to the coast," she says.

The afternoon is hot, the sun is glary, the traffic dense, and
while I've been snooping around libraries, Laurie has been
hanging out in coffee shops, talking to hairdressers who are
more interested in passing on the latest sordid gossip about
Steele's descendants than about civil rights history, and she's
been studying the vegetation of the area, her own passion.
She's eager to get out of the city and see the countryside. Since
most libraries are closed on the weekends, and since my eyes
are bloodshot from squinting at yellowed microfilm, and since
the story, interesting though it is, seems to have little to do
with my dad, I agree.

"Sure," I say. "I'm ready to get out."

But I am lying.

I don't want to leave the city. In my bookish fervor, it has taken on a dreamlike sheen like Narnia or Camelot. Even the name—Tallahassee—has a lilting, exotic sound to it. When people ask what I'm working on, I always say, simply, "Tallahassee." Sometimes when I am searching through documents by states, I look under T instead of F. I forget that Tallahassee is in Florida. And now I have this flyer with an actual name on it, a person to call, evidence that there's interest in the boycott after all, that there might be living witnesses, people who knew my dad. Maybe Leonard Speed. Maybe even Dan Speed. I do the math in my head: if Dan Speed is alive, he'd be in his nineties. That's not impossible. Unlikely, maybe, but not impossible.

. . .

Throughout the summer of 1956, Tallahassee police hounded Dan Speed's carpool drivers, stopping them daily, sometimes several times daily, every four or five blocks, on minor traffic violations, and in October, they finally found an excuse to shut the carpool down. An illegal franchise, the police concluded, was being operated. They arrested C. K. Steele and Dan Speed and seventeen others defendants, and a local judge, John Rudd, sentenced them to sixty days in jail and a $500 fine each. For the boycott, this was the beginning of the end. Judge Rudd suspended the jail sentences in a gesture of mock empathy, but the $11,000 in fines effectively broke the icc bank. For the next decade, C. K. Steele would travel nonstop, preaching up to six sermons a Sunday in order to pay the backers who bailed them out.

In the meantime, he appeared in public the day after the arrests, steely as ever.

"The war is not over," he said. "We are still walking."

They may have been walking, but they were also losing.

With no funds to support the carpool, all they could do, really, was hope that blacks would support the boycott independently and wait to see what would happen in *Browder v. Gayle*, the case from Montgomery, which was making its way to the Supreme Court. That was, after all, the single worrisome difference between the two boycotts. In Tallahassee, Jakes and Patterson had been arrested for inciting a riot, not for any violation of a segregation ordinance. Moreover, the chief of police had wisely turned over the girls' case to Florida A&M officials. There was no chance for a test case to take from Tallahassee to the Supreme Court. At least not at first.

Autumn settled in. The weather cooled, and tensions, for a short while, subsided. Students returned to school, my dad among them, but his mind, apparently, was not on his studies. According to his transcripts, his grades were dropping precipitously. According to court documents, he was attending ICC meetings regularly.

Then, on December 20, 1956, after city buses in Tallahassee had been running nearly empty for seven months, the good news came down. Nine justices had lived up to their titles—justice at last!—in *Browder v. Gayle* by upholding the lower court's ruling that segregation on privately owned municipal buses violated the Fourteenth Amendment. Even federal judges in Florida grudgingly admitted that this decision represented the final nail in the coffin of segregation. In Montgomery, boycott supporters reveled in the victory. In Tallahassee, on December 22 C. K. Steele and the ICC immediately announced an official end to the boycott, and they planned their mass integrated ride to show that the Supreme Court's decision applied everywhere, that their boycott, too, had been an unequivocal success.

That's where most timelines end.

. . .

Back at the La Quinta, where we've been staying, Laurie heads for the ice machine while I sit on the bed and hold the photocopied flyer with the number for Reverend William Foutz, the president of the local branch of the Southern Christian Leadership Council (SCLC), the organization started by Martin Luther King Jr., C. K. Steele, and others in February 1957. Reverend Foutz is, apparently, organizing the fiftieth anniversary celebration. His number is given as the contact, but I am stalling. I pull out my notes one more time to make sure I get this next crucial part of the story straight.

The Klan shut down Steele's integrated ride, and the moderate governor of Florida, Leroy Collins, a Tallahassee native, pled publicly for peace to no avail. On New Year's Eve, the windows at Speed's Grocery on Floral Street were shot out. Two days later, a cross was burned on the lawn of C. K. Steele's home, and shotgun blasts peppered his living room windows nightly for a week, terrifying his six children and leaving bullet holes in the blinds that the Steeles would leave hanging for years. Few people, white or black, dared board a bus, so the bus company itself, in desperate financial straights, filed its own appeal in court to ask for a final determination: were they required to integrate or not?

Finally, city commissioners came up with a crafty solution. On January 7, 1957, they passed Ordinance 741, which gave bus drivers within the city of Tallahassee the right to seat riders—not according to race, no, that *might* be unconstitutional—in such a way as to provide for "maximum health and safety." The ordinance was an obvious smokescreen for continued segregation, a last-ditch effort, pitiful, really, from the perspective of history. At the time, the *Tallahassee Democrat* heralded it as a reasonable compromise.

An editorial in the Sunday paper read, "We are confident that this thing will turn out all right for everyone if the Negroes will use the bus to ride to a destination instead of as a vehicle for agitation and if a few white people will settle down and quit looking for trouble." It's hard to know, in that climate, if "white people looking for trouble" meant the hatchet-wielders or the agitators like my dad. Probably both.

When, at the ICC meeting later that week, Steele asked for volunteers to try once again to ride the bus integrated—blacks and whites together—to test the bogus new ordinance and take their case, if necessary, all the way to the Supreme Court, everyone in attendance must have thought he had lost his mind.

That's when my dad stood up. At this point it's hard to tell from the historical accounts whether the boycott was dead or still limping along, whether the ride was staged or spontaneous. But I know this much for sure: what he did took guts.

The least I can do, fifty years on, is make one lousy phone call.

I dial the number, hear a woman's voice on the other end of the line, and begin talking too fast, anxious and squeaky— "Hello? Ma'am? May I speak with Reverend Foutz?"—before I realize it's the old message-machine trick we used to pull as kids. There's no one there. Just a recorded voice repeating: "Hello? Hello?"

I laugh and relax and wait for the tone. Then I leave a quick message saying who I am, that my father was involved in the boycott, that I'm at the La Quinta, and looking for Leonard Speed, and that, though I'm leaving town for a couple of nights, I'll be attending Reverend Foutz's services on Sunday at his church.

When Laurie returns from the ice machine, I tell her my plan.

"You said what? You told him you'd go to church?"

"Well, I need to meet the guy, and. . . ."

The phone rings, and I leap.

CHAPTER FOUR

The Acquaintance of Grief

"How's it going, Mama Sue?"

The voice on the phone at the La Quinta is not Rev. Foutz returning my call, as I'd expected, but my ailing mother in California.

"I'm really tired," she says. "I sleep all the time." Her voice slurs and lilts upward, a half-octave too high, and nearly quivers.

"Are you eating? Do you eat enough?"

"I try."

There's a long silence.

"How is Florida?" she asks.

"It's beautiful," I say. "The sun shines every day. Do you think you should call the chemo nurse? Should I call Lisa and have her call the nurse?"

She ignores my question. "What are you learning?" she asks instead.

"Oh, lots," I say. But I'm afraid it's a lie. I'm afraid that I'm not learning anything, nothing that matters, and I'm starting to panic besides.

"Are you sure you're okay, Mom?"

"I'm just so tired," she says.

My mom was my age, thirty-eight, on the day my dad went out running and never came back, and her world shifted for good. She was widowed, devastated, left alone with three small kids to raise. Over the next twenty years, she kept us fed and housed and educated, managing money frugally, extremely frugally, shopping at garage sales and clipping double coupons. She went to church on Sunday and to school during the week. She quit her job teaching seventh grade after one miserable year and applied to grad school, where she'd stay for a decade. The year I graduated from college in Oregon, my mother graduated, too, receiving at long last her PhD in Spanish literature from the University of California, Riverside. Mom and daughter grads, she used to brag, tickled by the plain coincidence. After that, she tried teaching at the university, but she had, by then, wearied of the snobbiness, she said, the privilege, the ivory tower bullshit. Instead she settled into a tenured job at a community college in a neighborhood so rough I once had my car stereo stolen while parked for ten minutes in the gated faculty lot. There she taught beginning Spanish to immigrant students with a dozen different native tongues from Tagalog to Mandarin. You get my point: no one ever said Sue Spagna had it easy. But in the months before my Tallahassee trip, things had turned particularly bad.

She'd had bladder cancer for years, but urologists had always been able to nip her tumors off tidily in outpatient surgery. Now, they announced, they'd have to remove the bladder and the female organs too, for good measure. There'd be no choice. I traveled south in October 2005 to see her through the surgery. My sister, Lisa, and I figured she'd be in the hospital for a few days, and then I could hang out with her at home, helping with the shopping, maybe, or cooking.

We checked Mom into City of Hope, a fancy cancer-cure hospital on a lush, sprawling, flower-rich campus near Pasadena, sixty long miles from Riverside, and I sat dutifully through the ten-hour surgery with one of her many friends. My mother never remarried, never dated even, but she'd always had a gift for making and keeping friends, and she held them tight, so that now, in her midsixties, she no longer had a circle of friends but a whole series of interlocking circles like Olympic rings: church friends, university friends, activists, neighbors, card players, garage salers. With her friends, she went out to lunch often—splitting the bill, always, to the penny—and to garage sales weekly, to church functions, and, occasionally, to political fundraisers. When my brother married and a shower game required my mother to give her new daughter-in-law advice for marital bliss, she wrote only this: *surround your-self with friends*. Mom was never as lonely as I worried that she was. But worry I did. Always. In high school, I passed up social invitations if she had no plans for the evening. Now, as an adult, I sat beside her in intensive care, sipping cold coffee from Styrofoam, rereading the *L.A. Times*, waiting for her to wake up long enough to say: I'm here. I'm right here.

In the evenings I drove twelve lanes of snarled traffic back to the house where I grew up on Burnside Court. The photos on the walls have been in place since my childhood: me setting the needle on my first record player, toddler Joey sipping beer, Lisa smiling up at Dad—beaming, actually, so clearly smitten—on a trip to Disneyland. Cheap paper mats frame snapshot memories of birthday parties, first communions, graduations. In my old bedroom, books I read in high school line the shelves. *The Color Purple. The Compleat Beatles.* Outside, neighborhood cats hunker in the juniper bushes. Though my mother detests cats, her petless yard provides haven from the neighborhood dogs. The neighbors themselves are mixed race and stolidly middle class: truck drivers, teachers, probation officers, a local hardware-store owner. My parents bought the house in 1972 for $11,000; it's a three-bedroom rambler on a dead-end street off of a dead-end street off of a dead-end street, a classic 1950s cul de sac, a safe place to raise kids—a safe place still, my mother insists, never bothering to lock her front door—where we ran as a pack, loud and rambunctious, every summer night, until the streetlights came on. When I was a kid on Burnside Court, I did feel safe, but staying there alone while my mom was in the hospital, I felt downright scared. A few years back an elderly woman was murdered in her sleep just a few blocks away. I double-checked the dead bolt each night before bed. The night she moved from intensive care to a regular room, the phone rang late in the night.

"I'm scared," Mom said. Her voice was garbled.

"Of what?" I said.

"I'm scared," she said, "that I'm going to die." She drew the last word out long, more short *A* than long *I*, a high-pitched tone, nasal and Midwestern, that sounded exactly like her own mother's, my Irish grandmother who died when I was nineteen, and drove home the sense that generations were shifting fast here, shuffling like playing cards, and I was not ready.

"You're not going to die. You're at a very good hospital. The nurses are right there."

"I'm scared," she said. "Can you come sit with me?"

"I'm not going to drive right now to Pasadena," I said, a sleep-deprived edge of denial creeping into my voice. "I'll be there in the morning. Is that okay?"

"That's okay."

After that, I camped in the parking lot of the hospital in my sister's fifth-wheel trailer.

"Thanks for what you're doing," my sister said as she and her husband hooked up my sewage.

"It's no big deal," I said.

And I meant it. Lisa taught elementary school full time and had a teenage stepson, and on top of everything, she and her husband had recently decided to try to get pregnant, to have a baby of their own before her biological clock, slowing now at thirty-six, might decide to rattle to a stop. She couldn't just drop everything to camp at the hospital, and I could.

A year earlier, around the same time my mother retired, I'd quit my job working for the National Park Service to focus on my writing, and since writing didn't pay the bills, not even close, I'd begun teaching classes online. Over the past year that decision had sometimes seemed like a terrible mistake. I went days without talking to a real live human being, my muscles withered, my confidence flagged. But now, with my mother sick, my career switch seemed like a stroke of extraordinary luck. A year earlier there'd have been no way, realistically, I could be here. Now I could work anywhere, which freed me up to stay at City of Hope, sitting by my mother, filling in crossword puzzles, nagging her to do her physical-therapy exercises, and getting to know her anew.

My mother takes her personality from her parents transparently. Her German father, Clem, who owned a successful Catholic supply store in St. Louis, was frugal and unerring, inflexible, smart as hell. Her Irish mother, Virginia, no less smart, was more playful and easy to laugh. When Virginia came to visit us, annually, she climbed the steps of the plane onto the tarmac wearing a pair of bright-red pumps two sizes too big. They were, my mother explained, her flying shoes, a proud garage-sale purchase. Looking back, I might be able to divide my mother's character precisely in half, placing each trait in the proper column: this one Clem, this one Virginia.

When I starting babysitting, the kids I watched wondered what to call my mother. She was nearly, but not quite, old enough to be their grandmother. She was warmer and closer than "Mrs. Spagna," but they were too young and too polite to say "Sue," so at last she became "Mama Sue." And in time she became Mama Sue to us kids, too. She gained weight and softened around the edges, like a less showy version of Virginia in her red pumps. Still, I was scared of my mother's Clem side, more distant and stoic. I craved her approval of my Tallahassee project, but I wasn't at all sure what she'd think of me snooping around in my father's freewheeling past.

"Did he tell you anything about it?" I asked.

"He told me he could never go back to Florida, that he'd been arrested," she said. "I didn't like the sound of that, a man with a record. That might be why he never talked about it."

I wasn't buying it. Of all the possible reasons he'd kept the story a secret, protecting my mother didn't sound to me like the most likely. Besides, I knew that the way my mother liked to see herself, as the straight-laced foil to her radical husband, wasn't the whole truth. She was modest and hard working and conscientious to a fault, but she was also braver than most people suspected. She graduated college, applied for a Fulbright scholarship the first year they existed, and flew off to Venezuela on a DC-3 from Miami. She was twenty-three years old and completely alone.

She met my father in Maracaibo, an oil-rich metropolis on the shores of a large lake, a cosmopolitan city, as I imagine it, fairly brimming with machismo. In that setting, I don't know if my Italian father appeared swarthy and mysterious or warm and friendly, bookish or worldly, earnest or wizened, or all of the above. He was eleven years older than she was, and by then he'd been in South America for several years. Within three weeks, they were engaged. Mama Sue never told us kids much about the whirlwind romance, but she loved to repeat another story about when the news of the engagement reached St. Louis.

"What is her fiancé like?" the parish priest asked my grandmother gingerly.

"He's Catholic," Virginia answered.

"Yes, good, good. But what is he *like*?"

My Irish grandmother hesitated. She knew exactly what he was asking—whether my father was Latin American—and she had no high-minded ideals about multicultural tolerance, but she didn't abide meddling priests.

"Father," she said, "he's blacker than the ace of spades."

My mother loved the story, not only because she loved her mother's sense of humor and her blunt confrontation of prejudice, but also, I think, because she saw marrying my father as the greatest rebellion in her life. And maybe it was. But it certainly wasn't her greatest act of courage. Everyday survival as a widow—paying the bills, dressing for church, refilling the chip bowl late at night—took far more courage than marrying a dark stranger. Who knows? Maybe it took more courage than riding an empty city bus in Tallahassee.

After three weeks at City of Hope, finally, Mama Sue was ready to go home. And I was, too. Even though I grew up there, the whole hyped-up culture of Southern California, like an old vinyl record played at 78 rpm instead of 33, depressed me. Every time I visited, I left feeling unmoored. Every time I left, I said, I'm never coming back. And every time I got on an airplane to leave, I cried. I looked down on the mass, tile-roofed cul de sacs swirling like aboriginal art, freeways intersecting like ant-farm tunnels, trapped between the oceans and the mountains, and I was so grateful to have escaped that I could hardly control the sobbing.

But this time was different. Despite the horror of the situation, the endless bored hours while my mother slept, the green-bile vomiting and the yellow-pus dressings, I had liked sitting with my mother. I knew I would cherish the memories, at least some of them. Often I'd read aloud the hardest crossword clue, and though she hadn't moved a muscle in hours, she'd spit out the right answer and then lift one eye to see if she had impressed me. And, of course, she had. Once, an aging chaplain had charged into her room to say the rosary with us. He grasped our hands vicelike, mine and my mother's, and he said the ten fastest Hail Marys I've ever heard, in a burbling Irish brogue, followed by an Our Father and three Glory Bes in rapid-fire succession, before he scurried out of the room as quickly as he'd arrived. My mother looked as though she'd slept through the entire visit.

I sat alone in the silence for a few minutes.

"That was kind of funny, huh?" I said.

Mom lay motionless on her back, as she had for days, but she smiled for the first time since surgery, and nodded slowly.

I was glad I could take these memories with me. I was relieved, and more than a little self-satisfied, to have survived. Then, just days before my scheduled flight, my triumphant leave-taking was ruined. The results of a biopsy, the surgeon explained, showed that cancer remained. The malignant cells may have been removed in the biopsy, but there was no way to know. Chemotherapy, he said, would be a preventative measure. I remembered this word distinctly: preventative.

Now, in January, she hardly eats and she's tired all the time. Except for a short visit at Christmas, I haven't seen her. I've been hiding instead, ostensibly from cell phones and freeways, in my piney woods, or now chasing shards of my long-dead father among the live oaks.

"Do you want me to come down there?" I ask over the phone from the La Quinta.

"Oh no, honey. My friends visit every day. You stay there and do your work."

After I hang up, I lie on the bed, thinking about how distance can fuel denial but can also make the worry grow large and unwieldy, out of proportion to the situation. Or in this case, maybe not out of proportion.

"How is she?" Laurie asks.

"She says she's okay."

"Is she?"

"I don't think so. I think the chemo is killing her."

"But is it working?"

"There's no way to know."

I lie awake much of the night.

In the darkest early-morning hours, I switch on the wall-mounted lamp beside the bed and tip the shade away from Laurie, who shifts in her sleep and turns away from the light. Outside I can hear semis shifting and groaning along Interstate 10, charging east to Jacksonville, west to Mobile. I pull out my notes, scribbled on a wide-ruled spiral notebook from the microfilm copies of the *Tallahassee Democrat*, and I try once more to piece the story together. I want to see it as it happened, so many years ago, back before semi-trucks or interstates, before Kennedy was president, or civil rights was a movement, or beatniks were hippies, back when my mom wore a Catholic schoolgirl uniform in St. Louis and my dad showed up in a municipal courtroom in a rumpled suit to face his sentencing from the mean-spirited judge, John Rudd.

"Let's try to settle this in a Christian spirit," Judge Rudd says as he opens the case. His disgust, even from fifty years on, is palpable.

The courtroom, according to the *Democrat*, is "crowded to capacity for the brief session with ICC leaders, students from Florida A&M, and students from FSU."

I've read those lines a dozen times over, but lying on the hotel bed, pillows propped uncomfortably against the wall, I finally get it: the courtroom would normally be segregated. Judge Rudd has decided to try the white boys together with the blacks, as a slap to the whites, a humiliating blow. But he's misjudged, and everyone in attendance knows it. Students who one month earlier couldn't attend a Christmas party together without risking expulsion are now sitting side by side. My dad and his friends set out to integrate a city bus, and without even trying—voila!—they've integrated the Leon County Courthouse. Later, a TV cameraman will capture footage of the integrated crowd and the mixed-race defendants leaving the courthouse, further infuriating Judge Rudd, who will promptly confiscate the camera and slap a charge of contempt against the reporter.

Meanwhile, a young black NAACP lawyer—the *Democrat* calls him a "Negro"—Francisco Rodriguez, from Tampa Bay, a Cuban émigré who would later defend hundreds of civil rights activists through the 1960s and beyond, steps forward to enter pleas on his clients' behalf.

"Innocent," he says.

This is not what Judge Rudd had hoped for. Maybe a plea bargain. A simple admission of guilt. Not an out-of-town lawyer pleading innocence when these boys have *purposefully* broken the law.

Judge Rudd's patience shatters. He denies the lawyer's request for a speedy trial and instead refuses to even set a trial date. He names the other three riders—Jon Folsom, James Kennedy, and Harold Owens—as material witnesses. Then he launches into a tirade, scolding my father and his friends for trying to be "modern fly-by-night martyrs."

I stop and reread the line, "fly-by-night martyrs," as Laurie shifts again in her sleep, and morning light begins to seep through the heavy drapes. It's a nice turn of phrase, I think, one scripted for a movie where John Rudd stars as the consummate bad guy. The line betrays so much: that Judge Rudd knows exactly what the boys are trying to do, that he knows the boys believe in the rightness of it with fervor, and that their fervor is utterly abhorrent to him. The "fly-by-night" part reeks of rotten old name calling: outside agitator. As for the "martyr" part, well, in that climate, I remind myself, martyrdom was a real possibility.

The end of the *Democrat* article emphasizes that fact. Another black attorney stands and warns of "the possibility of reprisals" against the three white youths. Judge Rudd refuses to comment. Even Francisco Rodriguez seems unfazed. The *Democrat* reports that he promises to protect his clients, but it also reports that Rodriguez is headed straight back to Tampa, three hundred miles to the south, the very next day. How, exactly, he plans to protect my dad from there, I can't figure.

I put down the notebook, feeling vaguely nauseous and unsettled. I dress quietly and step out blinking into the ever-present sun. There's only one answer at this point: coffee.

. . .

A few hours later, with the car already packed and ready to head to the coast, I ask Laurie if we can make one last stop, this time at the R. L. Gray building at the state capitol. The security guard at the door checks my ID and shows me to the archive room, where documents are catalogued in meticulous order, and cherry wood tables are arranged in tight formation, and a small handful of newish computers take you straight to the state archive Web site: MyFlorida.com. The Web site sports the same half-dozen photos from the Tallahassee bus boycott that I've seen over and over in my research: C. K. Steele, bow-tied as ever, posing in front of his church with a charred cross; stock portraits of Wilhelmina Jakes and Carrie Patterson looking pretty and girlish, like the embodiment of that uniquely 1950s word, "co-ed"; and one of John Boardman, the expelled FSU grad student, looking boyish and, well, geeky.

On the computer, I find the number of the file I need, and one of three eager employees brings me a manila folder with transcripts, and there he is: my dad, age twenty-five, the fly-by-night martyr being interrogated by a group of good ol' boy politicians. It's the kind of interrogation that flourished in the era: the unabashed, sometimes ludicrous, efforts to root out Communists in the mold of J. Edgar Hoover or Joseph McCarthy. In late 1956, Florida state senators had started a special committee to look into so-called subversive activities. This was a distinctly Southern brand of McCarthyism. Instead of going after artists or bureaucrats, the Florida Legislature Investigative Committee—the "Johns Committee" it was later called, for the senate leader, Charley Johns—went after civil rights activists, a fact that, when I first started my research, was a little hard for me to fathom. After all, the easy version of the civil rights movement, the one I learned in the 1970s, when we sang "We Shall Overcome" sitting cross-legged in a circle, only covers the hatred activists faced from purely evil foes, Klansmen in capes. It never mentions the more pervasive and insidious kind, the kind they faced from paranoid bespectacled bureaucrats and armchair patriots, even distrustful neighbors and church folk. To them, activists weren't just misguided or kooky like our guitar-strumming camp counselors; they were sneaky and foreign like the bad guys in a James Bond film, and the catch-phrase was "outside agitators." It was code for "communist."

Among the first witnesses the Johns Committee called were Wilhelmina Jakes and Carrie Patterson, but it didn't take the Southern gentlemen long to decide these two young co-eds could not possibly be troublemakers. After a few minutes of questioning, the senators escorted the girls on a grand tour of the capitol grounds. My dad and his codefendants were not so lucky. To the Johns Committee, they looked mighty suspicious. All but one hailed from outside of Tallahassee, and none of them needed to ride the bus that day. As the senators would soon remind them, the three white boys had ridden to Speed's grocery in a Studebaker. They had no alibi. Their feet were not tired. The bus was not crowded. They were, it must have seemed, the plainest sort of outside agitators.

Several pages of testimony are dedicated to those crisp dollar bills Leonard Speed passed out. My father steadfastly denies ever having been handed one. He likewise denies that Francisco Rodriguez's services had been procured for him before the ride. Whenever the day of the bus ride comes up, my dad pleads the Fifth Amendment so as not to incriminate himself. In forty pages, he invokes the Fifth Amendment no fewer than eight times. He denies planning to test Ordinance 741, and he sticks to his story.

"What was your intent in riding the buses that way that day?"

"To go sightseeing."

"Just to go sightseeing? Didn't you have an automobile out there that you got out of to get on the bus? Why didn't you go sightseeing the car?"

"We just wanted to go sightseeing on the bus."

"Isn't it true that you were determined to get arrested, to make a test case out of that ordinance?"

"No."

"You never had that kind of understanding with anybody?"

"No."

The legislators grow frustrated with him, and one interrupts to ask him specifically about Leonard Speed.

"Don't you know that boy was born and raised in the city limits of Tallahassee?" *That boy!* This is how state senators discuss a grown man? I expect the words in a Faulkner novel but not on this polished cherry wood table, in this carefully cataloged file, in this official state building. *That boy.*

"No."

"Can you imagine why a fellow that old, who had lived here all his life, needed to get on a bus to go sightseeing?"

"No," my father says.

"Do you have any reasonable explanation for that at all?"

"No."

The hearing room, I imagine, grows tense with anger and frustration. I've conflated the two settings by now, so that it is a sterile room, silent, air conditioners whirring, polite Southern women typing. Transcripts of Johns Committee hearings did not become public until the early 1990s. They were, apparently, considered top secret, the stuff of spies and traitors and wily anti-Americans.

The state senators have had it with my dad.

"I would like to say one other thing, if I might. I would appreciate your showing some proper respect to counsel and to this Committee and I would appreciate it also if you wouldn't have so many 'yep' and 'yips' and 'nopes' and that sort of thing."

"I'm sorry," my father says. "I wasn't aware of that."

Yip? It is hard to imagine anyone saying "yip." But if the sloppy way he dressed and kept house and left sentences dangling, unfinished, in midair, is any indication, there's half a chance that he wasn't aware of those yips. *Half* a chance. The other half is more likely. Maybe all that yipping and noping was meant to bug the hell out of those senators. Because they were bugging the hell out of him.

The interrogation, at any rate, is winding down. And the next question gets to the heart of the matter.

"Where are you from?"

"I live in St. Petersburg."

"I understood your testimony earlier, I believe, to say that you had been in Florida since 1950?"

"That's right."

"Where was your home? Where did you come from?"

"I was born in Philadelphia."

They want to prove he's an outside agitator. But his story is not so simple.

"Do you live in St. Petersburg or does your aunt live there?"

"My aunt lives there, and I live there with her."

"Where are your parents?"

"I don't have any parents."

I drop my pencil. For all that I ever knew about my father, from books and from memory, all that I admired and all that I disdained, I had somehow missed this central fact: he was, like me, well acquainted with grief. Maybe more well acquainted than I am since I—at least for now—have my mother. His mother had skipped out when he was a toddler and died when he was a young adult. I'd known this fact, vaguely, all my life, but my mother didn't talk about it much, probably because my dad didn't talk about it much, or because I didn't want to hear it. None of us cared to cavort with the past. But sitting in the R. L. Gray building, I feel a deep kinship with my young father, and I realize that this, and not the way the syllables in Tallahassee roll off my tongue, is the reason I've come three thousand miles, the reason I don't want to leave town, not even for the weekend. I realize this in the space of a moment and then come to my senses. I remind myself that Joe Spagna is a character on the page, the same as Jakes or Patterson or Steele or Speed. My interest is purely academic. Really, I tell myself, it is. My own capacity for stubborn denial drives me as crazy as my dad's drove his interrogators.

"And you still say you all had not decided to ride that bus integrated when you left Dan Speed's store, Spagna?"

"I do."

"Let this witness go."

It's time for me to get out of town.

CHAPTER FIVE

The Forgotten Coast

We leave Tallahassee, straight from the clicking heel echo of the state archive building onto the highway heading south toward the Gulf Coast. Trees line the narrow two-lane road tight and tall. No horizon. I feel both at home, as I do in the dense forests of the Pacific Northwest, and suffocated, as I do on any lush flat terrain, where the lack of relief, geographically, feels like there's, well, no relief. Let me out! More than anything, as we shake off the Office Depots and La Quintas, the four-lane traffic, the safe distracting clutter between me and the past, it's the young father I never knew that I can't escape. He's a smart ass, I know, full of bravado and his own stubborn cleverness—a copycat of James Dean, Holden Caulfield, Jack Kerouac—though god knows the Johns Committee deserved his disdain.

He's also unmistakably sad.

"I have no parents," he said.

I feel deeply sorry for him.

Once in high school a Driver's Ed teacher hollered at me as I crept white-knuckled down a wide, palm-lined street. He was a despicable part-time instructor, who chomped loudly on his PBJ, spun the radio dial on static to distract us, and hollered indiscriminately. Rumor had it that he'd once called a girl, at our Catholic school, an abortion reject.

"This is all wrong," he cried. "It's incomplete and unacceptable. Completely unacceptable. Why didn't your father sign this?"

I'd turned in an application for a learner's permit with only one signature: my mother's.

"Because he's dead," I hollered back, all smart ass and bravado, as I stared straight ahead at the slow-moving city traffic.

"Good reason," he said.

Feeling sorry for my young father comes dangerously close, I realize, to feeling sorry for myself.

Laurie and I pull over at a road junction where an old Ford pickup sports a plywood sign advertising Tupelo honey, a product I've never heard of outside of the Van Morrison song, but we can use a break from driving, and we're suckers for roadside produce and for Van Morrison.

"Best honey you can buy," he says. Or at least that's what it seems like he says. The accent is a little thick. He gives us each a taste on our index fingers—it's fine and sweet and rich—and sells us plastic bottles from the back of the pickup, his belly huge and his laugh easy.

"You gotta hit the hives in April," he says. "First the Tupelo, then later on the baking honey. This here is eating honey."

As we leave, the kindly fellow offers a photocopied treatise with a colored-pencil bear and a honey jar on the outside, and on the inside, a dire warning that if you don't accept Christ as your savior, you will burn for eternity in the fires of hell. What this has to do with the honey bear, I don't know, but I am unnerved by the message, which I take as a reminder of the sinister political stereotype of the small-minded Southerner that I have been trying hard not to think about.

Suddenly, it's not hard to imagine these woods full of hate and lynchers. I've lived in the woods long enough to understand people who take government into their own hands, sometimes for good reason, but thinking about it here in the South, in terms of the boycott and the whole sordid history, it seems like anyone could become this way, good, easy people, full of God talk and Tupelo honey. Not for the first time, I'm relieved that I don't wear my sexual identity on my shirtsleeve, that it's not as obvious as, say, skin color. I've said it before: I am a coward. Lately I've begun to worry that my dad was too.

After they appeared a second time in front of Judge Rudd's courtroom to be sentenced to the full sixty days and $500 fine, Spagna, Speed, and Herndon never appeared in court again. They waited, instead, for a long year while their lawyer, Rodriguez, took the case through a dizzying legal labyrinth. No judge seemed willing to take responsibility for calling the city's obvious bluff, so the case ricocheted, like a pinball, from federal court to state and back again. Federal judges wouldn't review it until the state did, and vice versa. When, finally, Judge W. May Walker ruled in federal court that there'd been no denial of constitutional rights, the door was open to the U.S. Supreme Court.

This was what they had hoped for, the moment of truth, when justice would reign again, as it had for Rosa Parks, and the precedent would be upheld: segregation was illegal, not just in Montgomery, Alabama, but anywhere, everywhere, in the entire nation! But that is not what happened.

Instead, in February 1958, more than a year after the ride, the nine justices of the Supreme Court claimed to have no jurisdiction in the case. No one had seen it coming. My dad and his friends had believed they were right. Hell, they'd *known* they were right, but, as would happen over and over, in the next decade and beyond, civil rights cases were decided not on right versus wrong, but by legal wrangling by states' rights defenders and scared politicians and plain by-the-book judges. The Supreme Court told Francisco Rodriguez and his clients that the Florida Supreme Court would have to decide this one. And decide they did by refusing to review the lower court ruling. Leonard Speed and Johnny Herndon went to jail. My dad, meanwhile, eluded police. Newspaper editorials were unequivocal: "Justice demands that the third defendant be brought back from wherever he is to take his medicine like the others."

Fifteen days later, Judge Rudd suspended Speed and Herndon's jail sentences. He suggested that the two young men "were not the real culprits but were the victims of circumstances and acted under the influence of persons or organizations who gave little or no consideration to the public interest or the interest of the defendants." He meant, in large part, in his unabashedly bigoted way, that the black men were too dumb to decide to test a law on their own. Which made the business of my missing white father even stickier. Would Judge Rudd have characterized him as the bad influence? Or would he have claimed that he, too, had been duped? If my father had stayed, I can't help thinking, the whole incident could have made a bigger splash, a bigger difference.

As Laurie and I drive further in air conditioning (in January!) and in silence toward the ocean, sea smell in the pines along the curvy road, and now, through tall grass and estuary sloughs at St. Mark's Wildlife Refuge, I think about my young father. How easy it was for him to ditch town, I think, to leave it all behind.

"I have no parents," he'd said.

We stop for an alligator in the road. The cool air hangs weighty. The alligator sits stone still, unblinking. I've never seen such a thing. Before the afternoon is over, we'll see, in total, six alligators and an armadillo, egrets swooping white against the smoke plume from a nearby prescribed burn, and finally, the wide blue expanse of the Gulf.

. . .

The father I knew loved the beach more than any place else. We spent a week or two a year at Crystal Cove, a ramshackle assembly of unmaintained shacks on the Southern California coast, tucked between the millionaires in Newport Beach and Laguna. The shack owners had tenuous ownership of the places, so they hardly bothered with upkeep. As a result, the shacks were imbued with a timeless funkiness, a temporary slapped-together kind of charm. Friends of friends owned one particularly shabby cabin and rented it surreptitiously, since the rules prohibited it, and we came every summer, without fail, because it was cheap and because my dad loved it so much.

My mother didn't love it quite as much. At least not at first. She was a Midwest girl, born and raised in St. Louis, who never saw the ocean until she was an adult, a fact that baffled us kids, Californians to the core. She slathered us in sunblock and then sat on the cabin porch, playing solitaire and eating Cheez-Its, the sea wind in her hair.

My dad didn't grow up near the ocean, either. He told us bedtime stories about his boyhood on a farm in rural Pennsylvania that we called "When I Was a Little Boy," simple tales of romps in the woods and loyal dogs and a best buddy named Bruce. The tales delighted us like Sunday Night Disney Specials, and we preferred hearing them to being read to, partly because of his enthusiasm for them, how he turned goofy and animated lying beside us on the bottom bunk, and partly because he so obviously made them up on the spot, bestowing boys and dogs with supernatural powers, and melding elements of *Little House on the Prairie* with Paul Bunyan. But woodsiness did not cling to my dad. Beachiness did.

Once I went out alone with him at dawn at Crystal Cove, and we set up our fishing rods alongside the crusty old fishermen in lawn chairs on the beach. Almost immediately, my line pulled taut. Together my father and I reeled in a rare multicolored fish, like an aquarium variety, that the others admired. The crusty fishermen congratulated him, but he gave credit to me, and the salt sprayed on my sweatshirt, and I shivered. Proud. The fish had almost certainly been illegal. Civil disobedience came naturally to my dad and crossed many lines. He could be daring and courageous, foolhardy and plain foolish.

Dad taught us to be bold.

Meanwhile, we kids spent hours in the ocean, our skin wrinkling, pickling, burning, always burning. The surf was very gentle, usually, but we were very small children. Waves pummeled us and pounded us into the sand. Mucusy salt water might run down the back of your throat after washing up your nose. But you did not run crying. You rinsed yourself in the deeper, cleaner churn, yanked your bikini bottoms back up the slender shaft where hips would someday be, then marched back out into the surf, triumphant to stand alone late into the afternoon, staring straight into the sun at the boats on the horizon and the kelp swaying on the swells, standing on your tiptoes at the very place where waves crested, turning occasionally to float down the backside as the wave rolled onward, curling over, then breaking, charging for the land.

When it was time, my mother was the one to teach us to swim in the waves. How she learned herself, I was never sure, but she was a quick study at almost everything and a water lover, and when it came time to teach us, she was brutal, as perhaps she had to be. Lie still beneath the churning surface, she told us, because if you try to come up for air, you will be pummeled again.

Mom taught us to endure.

After dad died, we'd sit together, Mom and me, at the kitchen table, while she struggled to take care of us, and I struggled to take care of her. She played solitaire while I read the newspaper, and she was attentive, usually, and involved—always on top of things—but every now and then, I'd tell her something about the cross-country team or about a newspaper tidbit, and her mind would be elsewhere.

"Mom? Did you hear me? We have a meet in Elsinore tomorrow afternoon," I'd say.

She wouldn't look up from the cards.

"That's nice, honey," she'd say.

I knew, then, that she was thinking about my dad and that she was sad, and I knew there was nothing I could do about it, not me and not anyone, and there is no more helpless feeling in the world. At those times, the only thing I knew how to do was to keep sitting there, pretending to read the paper, staying the course. My mom had taught me how to do it: lie under the churn, and then stand up again.

. . .

On the Florida coast, Laurie and I drive into the setting sun, following shiny suvs headed for white sand beaches on St. George Island or further on in Panama City, in Pensacola. But we've already decided, without discussing it, that we won't be going that way. It's not the destination or even the setting sun that has us mesmerized. It's the shanties along the offshore side of the highway, modest and flat-roofed, half-dilapidated, as if here in hurricane country there's no point in making things more than temporary. The ethic is familiar from Crystal Cove and from the tiny mountain town that I call home: living in balance with nature is living off balance with nature. Catastrophe threatens? Shrug and put up with it. Everything is temporary. Only four months after Hurricane Katrina, very few of the shanties have been repaired, though at a few newer, larger homes there is a flurry of activity. Construction workers stand on the rooftops silhouetted against the blue gulf.

As we pass through Eastport, Laurie spies a billboard, obscured by trees, of a fisherman leaning hard against his line, the fish leaping, the paint fading. The Sportsman's Lodge, the sign reads, and it points not toward the ocean but inland down a ragged, postholed road where we rent a room in a tree-shaded village of cabins, cedar shingled and set back away from the estuary, facing west with a wide, uneven lawn and rickety picnic tables by the water. Across a small river slough, a former restaurant leans off broken piers that jut out of the dark water like a mouthful of jagged broken teeth. This, we decide, will be perfect.

While Laurie unpacks, I dial my mother's number. She sounds slurry again and not particularly good.

"Are you finding out good things?" she asks.

"Sure," I say, not sure at all. Then I pause, trying to think of something to say. That I feel sorry for him? That I'm worried that maybe he had been a coward after all?

"We saw six alligators," I say.

"That's nice, honey," she says.

. . .

One weekend, when I was eight, Aunt Rose showed up at our house in Riverside. A tall woman with a heavy accent and a bright-plaid pantsuit, she kissed us sloppily on the cheeks with desperate grandmotherly passion. We were startled. We did not know we had an aunt on my dad's side.

"She's not your aunt," Mom told us later. "She's your dad's aunt. She raised him."

Raised him? Like an elevator or a crane? I was confused. I looked at this tall gray-haired woman with Cat Woman glasses. She looked strong, but not strong enough to lift my two-hundred-pound father.

"Huh?"

"She was like a mother to him."

This hardly made more sense. Why have someone "like a mother"? Wouldn't it be better just to have a mother? Aunt Rose stayed a few nights and cooked in my mother's bland Midwest kitchen, exotic smells of garlic and spices permeating the house. She drank whiskey in her coffee.

"My medicine," she called it.

Where had this woman come from? And why hadn't we heard about her before? My dad seemed to take her presence entirely in stride. He bussed her cheek in the morning and complimented her cooking. I'd have none of it. I'd have been a lot happier if Bruce, his pretend boyhood friend, had appeared out of the dark woods of his bedtime stories. Because this woman seemed to expect something of us.

Sitting at a picnic table staring out at the wide mouth of the Apalachicola, I see the pieces begin to fall into place. Florida must have been where Dad learned to love the ocean. Those summers with Aunt Rose, the ones he never talked about, were spent at the beach. He fished and swam and ran home sun-baked and elated in time for garlicky pasta and motherlike love. Then, when he jumped bail, he left her for good.

I realize, for the first time, that when he left Florida in 1958, my dad did have something to lose. I try to imagine what he told Aunt Rose, if anything. Did he tell her that he'd broken the law, that he was planning to jump bail, that he'd be leaving the state, and that he would never, ever, return? In a collection of letters my mother kept, there's one from Aunt Rose dated 1960, by which time my dad was in San Francisco, running his bookstore.

"Received your letter and always so glad to hear from you

and especially that you keep well. After all, I am all that you have now that is interested in you and naturally I worry when I don't hear."

A couple pages of family news follow along with a bit of browbeating over him not yet being married.

"Hope to hear from you soon again," the letter concludes. "Missed getting a card from you for Mother's Day. Still have the ones you sent me when you were a little boy. Love always, Ma."

. . .

After my dad died, we didn't go to Crystal Cove for a couple of years. When we returned, I walked along the beach, dragging a driftwood stick along the hard sand below the high-water mark, toward the tide pools: the first rocks, we called them, and the second rocks, and the third, and so on. I stopped between the surf-sculpted outcroppings and ran my fingers through sand and pebbles to parse out the shells, hermit-crab discards swirled lilac and gray, that my mom saved in peanut butter jars in the garage, shelves and shelves of them. Then I ventured out. Usually, to go out on the rocks, you had to wear tennies because the rocks were covered in mussels with their sharp shells pointed upward and painful, but I didn't care. I walked barefoot, and I stooped to look for starfish and abalone on the undersides of the rocks and to brush a hesitant finger across the suction-cup tentacles of anemones. I looked down to see my own reflection—greasy hair and pimples, a teenager in the works—and I gazed back up to where the breakers crashed, to where my father used to cast his line into the surf. He'd stand still for hours, sunlit and shirtless, wearing a Gilligan hat and smoking while we kids waited for him to return and bait our hooks with mussels, the orange meaty innards, so we could dangle a line in a smallish pool, almost perfectly circular, into which the surf swirled with some degree of force depending on the tide. At high tide it ripped into our pool and sprayed over our heads. At very low tide, it trickled in to barely wet the sand. Most of the time, it was somewhere in between: knee or waist high on me, the oldest. I sat beside the small pool and tried to remember if I ever caught a fish, or even how often my dad got lucky, but I could not. All I could recall was that once we had found an octopus in our fishing pool. It had seemed sickly, on the verge of death, and my dad told us not to touch it; he held us back, and we watched our octopus make the slow barmy lap and retreat.

· · ·

Laurie and I eat mounds of oysters, for less than the cost of a beer in Seattle, on paper plates. We sit in plastic chairs on the outside deck of a small oyster shack, shivering, the dark Apalachicola stretching out before us, until we give in and sit inside under fluorescent lights and read a local paper about this last rural stretch of Florida coastline—the Forgotten Coast, they call it—savoring the history of the place, built for bear hunters in the 1950s who came for the bears that used to come down for the plentiful fish, before they were killed off, before the fish were fished out. Now it's mostly oysters. Not that we're complaining. The next day we walk long on the beach on St. George Island, beyond the megahomes on the empty, protected shore, in the sun and the wind, and stop to buy prawns from a self-proclaimed Florida cracker to microwave in our room at the Sportsman. We sit cross-legged on the deck while peacocks beg at our feet.

"We don't have to go back, you know. We could just stay here," Laurie says.

The sun is bright, the sky blue, the breeze cool with the faint smell of fish. I can hear water lapping from the river estuary onto rocks. She's right. I could leave this complicated bus saga behind. Maybe I should. But I still want to know so many things: why he acted, why he left, what happened, in the end, to him, to all of them.

"We could," I say.

"No. You need to do this." Laurie peels a pink prawn shell, shakes a splash of Tabasco onto the meat, pops it in her mouth, and smiles. "You're going to church tomorrow morning bright and early."

Before we leave, our plan is to explore one more peninsula—St. Joe's, it's called, a seemingly auspicious name—and we can't help but be excited, remembering the magic alligator afternoon only the day before in the tall grass of St. Mark's. But we've crossed over from the protected to the developed. From wildlife refuge to white sands. We drive the winding road out the peninsula, wishing we'd stayed at the Sportsman, but we've gone off looking for more, like the bear that went over the damned mountain, trying to see what we can see. And now we see it. More megahomes, newly painted beachy pinks and blues, the size of six Crystal Cove shacks stacked one on the next, with solid foundations intended to be hurricane proof, not hurricane flimsy, line the beaches, barely ten feet between them. And there is plenty of insurance money out here, apparently, plenty of reconstruction, much of it cosmetic: repainting and gutter replacement. Where such money comes from, and why it must be spent here, and who, exactly, is spending it, these questions rankle, and as we drive slowly looking for a place, any place, to pull over and watch the sunset, the sun slips down behind the megahomes, and Laurie is disgusted. She is angry about so much that seems so much bigger than us, about how injustice endures.

"Stop right here," she says.

Laurie jumps out, and I can see by her posture that she is seething. That she would start the revolution this minute if she could. She stands in front of a new home addition under construction, a stack of plywood higher than our car, brand new and neatly stacked, in the driveway. We'd heard that plywood prices had tripled since Katrina, that in New Orleans there was a genuine shortage. She drops her pants to pee in the yard, right beside the plywood. This is as far as the revolution will get.

"Come on," I say. "There's nothing we can do about any of it."

Something More

Rain starts slow as we pack the rental car and settles warm and hard as we pull away from the Sportsman's Lodge, the skies gray and the highway empty on a Sunday morning. Along the coast the clouds hang low, and waves swell and crest toward a thin strip of beach and the two-lane road as we wind along, away from the gulf and into the woods. Small, white clapboard churches—Primitive Baptist, the signs read—appear at intervals amidst the pines, more churches than I've ever seen anywhere, their lots filled with pickups and long-hooded sedans, scenes from another era, and I'm relieved to think that in a city church I won't be as conspicuous as I might be out here.

What had been a four-hour drive on Friday night takes not quite two before we are back on the outskirts of Tallahassee. At Rite Aid, a multipierced white girl sells me a city map. I couldn't find Reverend Foutz's church on the one from the rental car place, or the one from the Chamber of Commerce, and I worried that this might be a bad omen, that I wasn't meant to attend.

"Buy a map," Laurie said.

She had long since decided that she wouldn't be going to any church.

"Because it's wrong to go as a tourist?" I asked. "Because we don't really believe? Because the past is dead?"

Laurie shrugged. "Because I don't have the clothes for it."

"Can I borrow yours?" I asked.

I'm more like my dad in his sloppy coat than I like to admit.

I usually cry when I have to put on makeup, rarely, for a wedding, say, or a family portrait. If Laurie was concerned about wardrobe, there was probably a good reason, but her clothes were nicer than mine, and I was determined to follow through on this. When I told a friend back home that I might attend church in Tallahassee, he'd nodded exuberantly.

"I might feel out of place," I'd said.

"Any church worth its salt will make you feel welcome," he said.

I had to agree.

Now we weave through a residential neighborhood, checking curbside numbers, until we see it: a tiny white clapboard building, the familiar simple lines, the unpaved parking lot, empty for now, and the small sign: Primitive Baptist. I'm afraid that means the congregation will be very small, and potentially closed minded. I try to steel my resolve. They will make me feel welcome, I tell myself.

I ask Laurie to pull over at the curb, and I wait for her to encourage me, to goad me on, as she had back at Speed's Grocery.

"I wouldn't do it, either," Laurie says. "It's okay."

Along the empty street, a lone black man, around my age, in non-church clothes walks fast staring hard at us, hands stuffed in his jacket pockets, as he approaches the car, and I am instantly afraid, and I am instantly ashamed of being afraid. Then he passes.

I step out in the rain to read the sign.

This is the place. *Reverend Foutz*, it reads. *Services every 1st and 3rd Sunday.* I check the calendar in my head. Today is the fourth Sunday. I'm off the hook. But I don't want to be. I'm already dressed and ready as I'll ever be.

"Let's try Bethel Missionary."

Bethel Missionary Baptist Church was where C. K. Steele

preached, where the mass meetings were held, and there's the chance, once again, of running into Leonard Speed. Interviews with Steele had mentioned that both Speeds, Dan and Leonard, had been church members, so I check the times out front on the marquee, the same one Steele stands in front of in that famous photo where he holds the charred cross. The service won't start for an hour, and FSU is only a block away.

"Want to go to the library?" I ask.

"Sure."

Rain continues, and if nothing else, the library will be dry. Besides, other than a Wendy's across the street, windows still painted for Christmas, no place else is open. The library is deserted. Work-study students at the checkout desks yawn over unopened textbooks with hangover lethargy. I check my e-mail: a few notes from friends back home about the lousy ski conditions—we aren't missing much—and an angry note from my sister about my mom's chemotherapy. The doctor, Lisa says, isn't taking her concerns seriously; she wants more information. Something in me thinks that there is no more information, that chemotherapy is for surviving, that we just have to sit tight and wait. My sister never mastered that skill. If she were here in Tallahassee, I think, she'd have no qualms about charging into churches or offices or archives. She ought to be the one sleuthing about, not me. I decide I'll write and tell her as much, but first I decide to check Laurie's e-mail account, and once again, the world shifts.

I find her in an armchair with a book about the flora of the Gulf Coast and lean down in the library quiet to tell her the news.

"Grandma Ethel died."

She nods and tears up and stands to go read the note from her dad.

Laurie's Grandma Ethel, her father's mother, had been 105.

Born in 1900 on a farm in North Dakota, she'd married late and been widowed young, and she exuded independence and graciousness and, toward the end, weariness.

"I've lived too long," Ethel would say often, in recent months, when we visited her in the nursing home near Laurie's parents' home.

It was hard to argue with her but harder still to think of life without her. Years earlier, when we worked seasonally, Laurie and I spent our winters in Flagstaff, Arizona. On weekends we'd drive two hours south to visit Grandma Ethel in a trailer park outside Phoenix, to sit and drink strong Folgers and watch Lawrence Welk or sometimes TV golf, to help feed chickadees and plant nasturtiums. Every spring when we said goodbye, we thought it might be the last time, but it never was. Grandma Ethel just kept on keeping on. Until now.

"You still don't want to come to church?" I ask.

I'm thinking it might offer her some solace.

She shakes her head. "You're wearing my clothes," she says.

So we leave the library and head separate ways, Laurie for the Christmassy Wendy's, and me toward Bethel Missionary Baptist, where, by now, the parking lot is jammed and clumps of umbrellas stream toward the stately brick building. I scamper across a rain-spattered street, awkward in heels, and onto the white columned porch. From within I can hear the sounds of voices merging, praising, glorifying. Before I've even crossed the threshold, I begin to cry.

Bethel Missionary Baptist is packed to the hilt. There are maybe three hundred people in attendance, maybe five hundred, and I am one of a half dozen whites. I am also, as Laurie predicted, the most underdressed by a long shot, and now I am blubbering openly, blotting my face with wadded Kleenex. A large swaying choir belts out a cacophony of joy. Young men in pressed shirts study well-worn prayer books. The hard-backed church pew feels right, the place for sinking into the familiar buzzing numbness of loss.

The minister steps forward. He is a very tall man with a linebacker build and a booming voice. He leans into a huge microphone, the top the size of a grapefruit.

"God is good," he begins.

"Yes, he is," replies the congregation in unison.

I cry harder. I'm crying for Ethel, of course, and for Laurie, and because I miss my father. Mostly I miss going to church.

. . .

When I was very young, my family attended Catholic Mass at a seminary located on a historic California ranch in the hills outside town. Stone buildings, cool even in the searing heat of summer, housed the would-be priests, and stone staircases crisscrossed the grounds, former desert foothills terraced into a semblance of English gardens, tucked among acres of orange groves. Often as not, Mass at the seminary was celebrated outdoors, and for little kids like us it was a rollicking good time: the music was upbeat, the liturgy lively, the crowd blue jeaned and ponytailed. It was Kumbaya Catholicism at its best. We kids listened a little, especially to the energetic guitar strumming, and we wandered a lot, amongst the unfamiliar lushness — goldfish ponds and oleander hedges and orange groves—and after Mass, each week, Dad took us out for donuts, a full dozen, chocolate sprinkles for us kids, jelly for himself.

At Bethel Missionary Baptist, the preacher takes the pulpit to read from scripture, and the churchgoers follow along in black-bound Bibles. I sit silent and, for now, content. To misquote Mohammad Ali: I have no quarrel with Jesus.

My dad may have, though. For the young white activists, existentialists well versed in Camus and Sartre, all the Jesus-talk of the civil rights movement must have been unsettling. For my father, there was culture clash besides. The only Jesus he had known was the Italian Catholic one. Both his father and Aunt Rose had crossed the Atlantic as children and attended Mass, well, religiously. My father had been baptized and confirmed, he'd been to confession and communion, but by the time he started reading "Howl" aloud at parties, he must have, like any good second-generation immigrant kid, shirked his Catholic identity, at least until he went to those mass meetings.

"I don't recall ever having gone to an ICC meeting without a prayer, reading scripture, and singing religious songs," Dan Speed later explained in an interview. "And mostly we used spiritual songs."

After the boycott, in fact, Speed became a Baptist minister himself. And my dad rediscovered Catholicism. By the time I knew my dad, he was deeply religious in another fashion, the lefty Catholic version. Portraits of Daniel Berrigan and Cesar Chavez hung on our living room walls. Radical priests slept on our couch when they returned stateside after long stints in South America. The years my parents spent south of the border, where they met in the late 1960s, had coincided with the rise of leftist regimes and of liberation theology. These priests were activists on behalf of the people they called "the poorest of the poor." I saw pictures of brown-skinned children, so many of them, in brightly colored Maryknoll magazines on our coffee table and in faded slides in a box in the hall closet. My father had been godfather to dozens of them, and he and my mother were godparents, in a way, to these wayward priests, these true believers who were nearly kicked out of their orders for practicing what they preached: that Jesus came down from heaven to comfort the afflicted and afflict the comfortable.

Shortly before my dad died, my family stopped going to Mass at the seminary. There weren't enough new priest recruits coming up through the ranks, so the seminary closed, and the Spagnas were left back at our regular diocesan parish, Our Lady of Perpetual Help, back in the workaday world of Sunday Mass mumbled to the floorboards. Forty minutes max. That is, until Father Dominic DePasqualie came along. Father De's name translated to mean Easter, my mother never failed to tell me. Easter, she said. Like resurrection. And I knew why: because for us, Father De represented just that.

After Father De arrived, Mass at Our Lady lasted an hour, sometimes longer. Fresh flowers were placed about the sanctuary, and a huge tapestry of the risen Christ, vaguely cubist in sunlight shades, was hung behind the altar. Father De insisted that the resurrection outshine the gruesome life-sized crucifix that hovered, suspended by wires, over our heads. Life-death-resurrection. Father De harped on this metaphor. He started a committee to offer classes to parents of children to be baptized or to adults who wanted to become Catholic—evangelization taking a foothold in those heady days—and my mom joined, and life-death-resurrection became the oft-repeated theme of telephone conversations with her fellow committee members. The timing was impeccable since, shortly after Father De's arrival, my dad fell on the street, not a half-mile from the church, leaving my mother with that burden of nearly insurmountable grief. What a relief it was to eavesdrop on her everyday parables, small-scale resurrections, recounted into the telephone while she drew long on her True Blue cigarette.

Father De's politics were clear. The congregation raised money for No Nukes, sponsored a branch of Beyond War, and prayed, always, for world peace. But his main message was closer to home. Community. We must become a community. People should depend on each other, care for each other, actively and outwardly, center their lives on faith and upon each other, not kneel like wet rags—like hypocrites, he might as well have said—through forty-minute masses. And I believed him. I possessed a romantic unerring puerile faith, the kind of swooning piety that kids a generation earlier might have reserved for saying the rosary or saving pagan babies.

. . .

The minister's message at Bethel Missionary Baptist is simpler. His baritone voice, rising and falling, follows a cadence familiar to me from a half-century of recorded civil rights speeches.

"Will an iPod give you what you want?"

"No!" the crowd responds.

"Will an Xbox?"

"No!"

Will money? No. Education? No.

"Who gives you what you want?"

"Jesus!"

The voices of the congregation rise with enthusiasm, with certitude. I think about my dad and how he was able to reconcile with Jesus. When did he decide to change? And why? From the notorious agitator and the reader of Allen Ginsberg to the pious Catholic, godfather to dozens of children. Or did it merge effortlessly, one thing into the next? I bow my head and pray genuinely for a merging of my own, for grace and understanding.

The service has now lasted well over an hour. At this point, when I would very much like to go home, the minister begins to call people forward to be saved.

"Give your life to Jesus," he cries.

Here in this church was where C. K. Steele had called for volunteers to ride the buses integrated, a different kind of call is going out.

"Take him in your heart," he says. He is sweating and shaking. He means it.

74

The pianist plays a background riff, something appropriately gentle and coaxing, something you might hear on the soft jazz station in a dentist's office. People begin to pour forward, one at a time or two by two. The newly saved are very young women mostly, dressed modestly and well. They stand in a row before the congregation and weep silently.

"One more for Jesus," he hollers. "Just one more."

A few more people walk forward and stand tall. Before the piano stops, there will be more than two dozen.

The minister moves toward them.

"Where do you go to school?" he asks.

Florida A&M, most answer, though a few are from FSU. Their majors are ambitious: chemistry, physics.

"What is your home church?"

They reply without hesitation, speaking clearly, leaning into the big mike.

"Bethel AME in Valdosta, Georgia."

"First Baptist in Gainesville."

The reverend nods and smiles, familiar with these congregations, with the pastors there. This confuses me: if they already have a church back home, why do they need to be saved? While I was attending Our Lady, a new church opened in Riverside. At Calvary Chapel, the choir played rock 'n' roll, and a hipster preacher called people forward like this to be saved. I'd gone to revivals at the local city park and watched young adults and teenagers stumble toward the huge amplifiers on stage in their cutoffs and sandals. I knew some of them from the neighborhood: they were drug addicts or petty criminals, misfits every one. What is your home church? That question would have set those lost souls running.

These young women are more firmly moored. They would never say: "I have no parents." What this rite seems like, more than anything, is joining a community. I try to tell myself

75

this: Father De would be proud. I try to tell myself that these young women have the same youthful idealism that my young father did. Times have changed, and no matter what, stepping forward in a room of strangers to express what you believe is a brave step, one steeped in commitment and integrity. I desperately want to give these young women credit. They could have been here fifty years ago, I tell myself. They *would* have. It's no use. I am not convinced. They are utterly comfortable in this culture, the culture of their parents. I admire that. I'm maybe even a little jealous of it, but I don't think it makes you likely to want to change anything. What's the point of religion, anyway: comfort or courage? I suppose it ought to be both.

When, at long last, the service is over, I stand in the crowded aisle, red eyed, asking attendees: Leonard Speed? Dan? Do you know them? They shake their heads politely. I stay until the church is nearly empty, hoping to ask the minister, but he is preoccupied with the newly saved, welcoming them into the fold. I step onto the porch and watch rain fall in silvery sheets. I came here to be comforted, and I'm leaving afflicted. I can't help but think my father would be pleased.

Laurie pulls up at the curb, and I adjust the too-long skirt to climb into the passenger seat.

"Well," she says. "How was it?"

"The music was good."

She's waiting for more, but I can't think of anything to say. The rain beats down hard, skipping off the waxed hood of the car. Helplessness gnaws at me. I keep picturing Ethel, bony and curled, on her nursing home bed. "Who are you? Who are you?" she demanded the last time we saw her. She didn't recognize Laurie anymore, and Laurie didn't mind. Laurie stroked Ethel's hand steadily. Someday that hand would be mine. Someday that would be me curled on the bed. I can see why people are attracted to religion, the kind that narrows like the tunnel that people say they enter when sliding toward death, because maybe this is it, all there is: a body shrunken small breathing one last time through an oxygen tube, a six-foot frame under a smog-orange sunset smacking hard on the sidewalk. That can't be all there is, I think. There has to be something more.

That afternoon, we walk together in the rain among the live oaks one last time and then check in for the night at the Super 8, cheaper than the La Quinta next door, and Laurie makes the requisite phone calls to her family, making plans for the funeral. I organize my notes once more, underlining the name of the case so that I can write again to the courthouse to request the transcript. *Joe Spagna, Leonard Speed, and Johnny Herndon v. the City of Tallahassee.* That's when it hits me. I've been so obsessed all week with C. K. Steele and the Speeds, the heroes, the big names, that I haven't considered the obvious.

While Laurie speaks softly to her father, I pull the phone book from the Super 8 drawer.

There it is: Herndon, Johnny. My heart is racing. We leave first thing in the morning. It's too late to go meet him, but I could call at least. But I'm scared. What would I say? I am sorry my dad left you behind to go to jail?

"What are you looking at?" Laurie asks when she hangs up.

"Oh, nothing," I say.

I copy the phone number and address, close the book, and put it back in the drawer.

Another day and three thousand miles away, we drive the snow-white rolling farmland of eastern Washington State, Laurie and I, past empty fields and small towns, past gas-station neon and water towers, brick-walled high schools in session, windows yellow lit. Snow falls dry as desert sand, swirling white over the road, obscuring the center line until the road

77

itself vanishes, indistinguishable from the fields or the fence wire. We slow to a crawl, rising and falling on the unseen road, the sensation not unlike air turbulence, and suddenly a huge white form swoops in front of the windshield and hovers close, a large snowy owl, and we both know without a doubt that it's her, Grandma Ethel, the bird lover, the North Dakotan. It is, as much as anything I've ever experienced, something more.

Part Two

A HIGHLY PERSONAL THING

CHAPTER SEVEN

Handwriting

Back home in the tiny mountain town, winter settles hard. I sit by the woodstove, night after night, reading civil rights histories, hoping to put my dad's role in perspective. I spend so much time in the 1950s, I joke to friends, that pretty soon I'll start wearing pill-box hats. I do it because want to understand the past, sure, but also because I desperately want to escape the present. In California, things are going from bad to worse. The community from Our Lady has organized a meal chain for my mother. Someone stops by each day with a small casserole or a child's meal from a fast-food joint. Nothing appeals to her. Not even chocolate. Even I know that means trouble. My sister continues to try to alert the oncologist, but she never gets her calls returned. Lisa has begun to hear rumors around town about this oncologist. She is so infamous, it seems, that she even has a nickname: Dr. Death. *Do you want me to fly south?* I ask Lisa in an e-mail. *No,* she writes. *You already did enough. Joey will come.*

She means I did enough in October, when I stayed at the hospital, but she also means more: that I did enough when I was a kid, when I was the too-responsible oldest and she was running wild. Ever since I'd left home, we'd had an unspoken agreement that if and when Mom got sick, Lisa would take charge. She lives in Riverside, after all, and she knows how to manipulate the system, any system, and maybe she owes it to all of us.

So I hide in the 1950s in Florida. I'd always hated the fifties in the pop-culture sense: poodle skirts and root beer floats and Elvis; and in college I learned to hate the era in an academic historical sense: sprawling suburbs and repressed housewives and McCarthyism. I culled the prejudice, in part, from my mother, who left the 1950s Midwest and never turned back, who had nothing but disdain for sock hops and Latin Mass. Now I see the era differently, as I imagine it through my young father's eyes. And ears. Once as a teenager, I found an old copy of Miles Davis's classic album *Kind of Blue* that had belonged to him, and I listened to it often before selling it off with the rest of my LPs in college for a quarter each. The histories of the early civil rights movement remind me of that sound. The late 1950s offer a kind of cool jazz protest, a reasoned and disciplined rebellion, complete with young men in suits, young women in heels, predictability, solidness, security. I long for this. I slip back in time while the fire burns and the cat lounges and yellow light through the glass-front stove casts a small shadow around me. In the daytime, I go out running. I am up to six or eight miles, and I cannot let the progress slip. The ice is treacherous, so I plod gingerly; it feels productive, like I might be getting somewhere, and there's patience in it, too, a sense that if you just stay with it—the short runs getting longer, the thousand pages turning—you will be rewarded.

I spend much of my time reading the first of the Taylor Branch civil rights trilogy, *Parting the Waters*, and I fall in love with Vernon Johns, the pastor of First Baptist Church in Montgomery before Martin Luther King Jr. He was plain-spoken and contrarian, an unabashed, overall-wearing farmer who sold watermelons from the back of a pickup after Sunday services. Compared to Vernon Johns, Martin Luther King Jr. was a dandy: fastidious in dress, obsessed with church finances, intent on increasing collection-plate donations. And as I read about King, I realize that a lot of my assumptions about civil rights were dead wrong. I'd convinced myself that my dad, at twenty-five, was too young to have known what he was doing in Tallahassee. Now I find that King was only twenty-six when he led the Montgomery boycott. I'd even decided that maybe my dad was an outside agitator, straight out of Philadelphia and Dartmouth. Though a Southerner, King was from the big city of Atlanta and had just finished graduate school at Boston University. A PhD, no less! Turns out, there are no hard-and-fast rules for heroism, no blueprint, no age or residency requirements.

There are, in other words, no excuses.

Occasionally I hound myself to get in touch with Johnny Herndon, but conveniently I can't. The tiny mountain town is so isolated that it does not have telephone service. The possibility of phones had, in fact, united the valley in protest only a few months before. I'd written two dozen letters to public officials. I'd even been quoted in the *Seattle Times* about my opposition. Now I feel a little silly about that. I mean, my dad opposed segregation and I opposed . . . phones?

Late one night, I tell myself: no more excuses. I pull out a ballpoint pen and a sheet of printer paper and sit at the kitchen table watching snowflakes flutter lazily in the slop-over glow from the indoor light. I could have typed, but I like the rawness of writing for real. I also think that a man in his seventies might trust handwriting. You can judge a person by the steadiness of their script, and here, for once, my Catholic-school training might serve me well: the nuns had made me spend tedious hours practicing. Still, my hand shakes as I try to keep my cursive uniform, my tone proper:

Dear Mr. Herndon,

My name is Ana Maria Spagna. I believe you may have known my father, Joe Spagna, when he lived in Tallahassee in the late 1950s. My father died in 1979 when I was eleven years old. I am writing to you now because I am interested in any memories you may have of him or of your experiences together during the bus boycott.

I grew up in California—a long way from Florida—and I never heard about my father's involvement in the bus boycott until long after he was gone. When I read about it in a book last year I decided to make a trip. Last week I visited Tallahassee for the first time. I found your name and address in the phone book, but I could not bring myself to call out of natural shyness and, moreover, because I understand that both you and Leonard Speed served jail time while my father did not. I suppose I felt a bit ashamed. I very much admire your courage, and I am humbled by it.

I have many questions for you—about your memories of that time, your impressions of my father, about how you decided to ride the bus that day, about why you served time and he did not, and finally about whether you and Mr. Speed kept in touch and involved. (Is he still alive?)

I realize that the 50th anniversary of the boycott is approaching and that many people may be pestering you about your memories. Whether you would be willing to talk to me by telephone or drop me a note at this address below—for the record or off the record just for my personal interest, I'd very much appreciate it.

I currently live in a very remote area of the Pacific Northwest where we do not have telephones, but if you wrote and suggested times I might call, I could travel to do so.

Respectfully yours,

For good measure, I also write to Reverend Foutz, to apologize for missing his church service, to ask about Leonard Speed, and to ask about the fiftieth anniversary celebration. Why not?

I'm on a roll. There's comfort in the slowness, the permanence, of the ballpoint looping across the unlined page while snow falls and the fire crackles. In the morning I address the envelopes and stamp them. I seal the letters in a Ziploc bag and run six miles to the boat landing in the chain tracks of the snow plow, to drop them in the mail.

Back home, I pull out a squeaky twenty-year-old cassette to relisten to a recording made by a couple friends of my dad. I'd heard about the tape from my mom after he died, but I'd never listened to it. I'd never seen it. I'd never even asked about it. There'd been so many tributes. My dad's funeral procession had snaked for miles, it seemed, behind our car along the palm-lined streets of Riverside, the San Bernardino Mountains snow-capped in the distance, and me so young and flummoxed: who *were* all these people? And why were we parading to the gravesite to toss shovels of dirt on a concrete box? And who would make a cassette of reminiscences for kids who didn't know them, and maybe didn't care, just hoping that someday they might? Well, good people would. And did.

The story went like this:

In the late 1970s, Bob White and Joe Amato, two middle-aged college professors, were driving back from Sioux City, Iowa, to tiny Marshall, Minnesota, where they lived and worked. To pass the time, the two men began to talk about people who make an impression in your life, the kind that stand out among all those you've known, even if you only knew them a short while. Amato began to describe a friend he'd known in Riverside, California, while Bob White described a college buddy from Tallahassee. As the miles rolled on, and the road flattened out, splitting the cornfields of Iowa, the two stories began to sound suspiciously alike.

"What was your friend's name?"

"Joe Spag-Nuh."

"Yours?"

"Joe Spawn-Yuh."

Same guy, they figured. Different pronunciation. (My dad changed it himself, actually, sometime after college, opting for the smooth Italian pronunciation rather than the short *a* hard *g* Americanized version.) Not long after the road trip, they found out that he'd died, tragically and young, leaving a widow and three young kids. So they got together with their wives for beers to tell the story of their trip and the unlikely coincidence, and to tell stories about this man they had both respected, while an early-model cassette recorder turned in the background. They sent the tape to my mom.

And my mom put it in a drawer. She was not a past-dweller. Turns out all that time when, as a teenager, I struggled valiantly to keep her from being sad, she was doing the same for me. We were tiptoeing around the huge chasm of grief on Burnside Court, taking baby steps back to normalcy. The abyss was too deep to look into. It would be twenty-seven years before my mother sent me a copy of the tape, not after I turned twenty-one, or even thirty, not after I'd built my house and settled down, not until after I called to tell her I'd booked my trip to Tallahassee.

"Oh," she said. "I have something you might be interested in."

I'd listened for the first time shortly before Laurie and I left for Florida. The tape is where I heard about the beatnik with the tattered sportscoat, about the clandestine copy of "Howl" and his college pad with the newspapers strewn over every inch of the floor. On the tape, Bob's wife, Posie, tells of how local bookstore owners cowered when he walked in. He's "an inside-out nigger," they warned her. If not heroic, this version of my father sounded vibrant, almost funny, a caricature completely unlike the guy who lay on the couch watching *Monday*

86

Night Football while we kids ran amok. The tape is also where I learned that my dad had been an English major.

Now I listen again for a more specific piece of information. I sit alone on the couch, Laurie at work, the cat prowling, whining for attention, trying to figure out where these ghost voices are from, strangers in her house, talking, laughing, beer caps twisting. I rewind to be sure I've heard right. I have.

"I only knew Joe from September to about May," says Bob White, "when he was advised by his legal counsel, I think, to split, to get outta there because it was not gonna come through for him, and, uh, they were gonna take a loss and it would be in his own best interest to git."

His own best interest? What about Johnny Herndon's best interest? What about the greater good? I suddenly wish I hadn't written those letters.

But it's too late.

The first reply arrives via e-mail from Cynthia Williams, a friend of Rev. Foutz and a member of the SCLC committee working on the boycott.

We have been diligently searching for your father. Reverend Foutz received your telephone message when he returned from an out of town trip. When he returned you had checked out of the La Quinta Inn and the desk clerk could not give him any information. We searched the Internet and found several Spagnas in the state of Washington. However, there were no telephone numbers given.

Why hadn't I thought of this when we moved motels in Tallahassee? It hadn't once occurred to me that Reverend Foutz would try to return my call.

Ms. Williams also sends a snail-mail packet that includes a series of newspaper articles, many that I never saw in Tallahassee. I can't figure it out. Are these the missing dates from the microfilm? No, these were from the black paper, The *Florida Star*, a statewide publication out of Jacksonville. When would I get it straight that everything—everything!—had been segregated? The *Tallahassee Democrat* as the establishment newspaper had been, more or less, the white paper. And, I'd later learn, in early 1957 when tensions pulled razor-wire taut, white community leaders pressured the *Democrat* editors to scale back coverage of the unrest. No wonder the test ride story was understated, oddly characterized. Seemingly no big deal. In the *Florida Star*, it is a very big deal. Huge.

There's even a front-page photo snapped outside Judge Rudd's courtroom. In it, the three defendants—Speed, Herndon, Spagna—look young and, in their suits, dapper, not triumphant, but not scared either. They look, in a word, steadfast. This is the first photo I have ever seen of my father at this age, and in it, he looks less like a beatnik than a young Marlon Brando: slick-haired, pouty, and defiant. ("Man," a cousin of mine would remark later, looking at a fuzzy photocopy of the photo, "your dad was hot!") There's something gentler, too, a kind of penetrating sadness wholly different from earnest bravado or revolutionary fervor. Johnny Herndon, in a sweater vest, has a similar look, though more triumphant, a half-smile without the trace of a smirk. Leonard Speed's expression is harder to read.

In her letter, Cynthia Williams says that Mr. and Mrs. Herndon were "delighted" to receive my letter and that they will be writing soon. It's clear, too, that she has read the letter I wrote to Johnny Herndon because she weighs in:

> You have no reason to be ashamed that your father left town after being arrested. We are only sorry that we will not have the opportunity to personally thank him for the courageous stance he took. Those were difficult times in

Tallahassee for African Americans who protested, and we know that it must have been very difficult for your dad to not only speak out, but to act against what he perceived as an injustice. We only have admiration for him.

I reread the paragraph over and over, sitting cross-legged on the floor, photocopied articles and draft agendas for the fiftieth anniversary celebration strewn around me. I appreciate Ms. Williams's reassurance: *no reason to be ashamed.* I know she means well, but I am not convinced. She doesn't know the truth. Johnny Herndon does.

. . .

The days grow longer. Varied thrush call at dawn: one long whistle, shrill in the leafless forest. The snow freezes hard overnight and glitters in the sunlight by day, coaxing me outside, craving the smell of dirt, when it is still too cold. At night by the woodstove, I read about the Freedom Riders of 1961. The riders, blacks and whites together, had been journeying through the South testing the laws prohibiting segregation on intrastate buses, laws that had been on the books for thirteen years and rarely, if ever, enforced. On Mother's Day in 1961, just outside of Anniston, Alabama, the Greyhound bus they rode was attacked by local whites—thugs and Klan members and everyday upstanding citizens—who intended to burn the Freedom Riders alive. "Fry the goddamn niggers," they cried as they tossed gas-soaked rags in through the bus windows. The riders managed to get off, only to be met by baseball bats and steel pipes as they disembarked. I study the pictures, the crowds of white women and children, dressed still in their Sunday best. I reread a paragraph, flip to the photo section and back. Vigilantes and spectators alike look gleeful, exuberant, their lips curled like mules, their upper gums showing hideously, like their mouths can't hold the laughter, like the epitome of evil. I close the book. I feel nauseous. And angry. This is what lies beneath those pill-box hats, those starched shirts. This is the discord beneath the easy rhythmic piano plinking at the beginning *Kind of Blue*. This is, I'm pretty sure, why I learned as a small child to hate the 1950s: because my parents distrusted prim civility and tried to instill that distrust in us. It worked.

The next afternoon, I listen to Coretta Scott King's funeral, a special CNN radio broadcast over the Internet. She died shortly after our return from Tallahassee, just as Rosa Parks had died in the fall. I feel a wave of panic. People who lived history are dying, leaving their stories for those of us who weren't there to tell. What if we don't get it right? I desperately want to retell history as honestly as possible. No spin. No agenda. So I tune in to watch the funeral service from a megachurch in Atlanta where King's youngest daughter, Bernice, is an elder. The four-hour service is broadcast over the Internet, shot 24,000 miles into space from a church balcony, and back down, to a lone satellite dish perched on galvanized pipe in my yard among dark-trunked firs. I listen to speechifiers from a broad swath of American politics and culture—George Bush, Jesse Jackson, Ted Kennedy, Oprah Winfrey, Jimmy Carter, Maya Angelou—and I grow depressed. Time has rendered civil rights benign and benighted enough to embrace tottery George H. W. Bush and preachers stooped with bling. The entire ceremony feels too safe, bereft of any ties to protest or rebellion, choreographed not to offend anyone, but not to defend anyone either. While she was alive, Coretta Scott King supported gay rights and famously claimed that her husband would have too, had he lived. But inside the church there is not one peep about that during the four-hour service.

Later I will read that, outside the church, followers of Reverend Fred Phelps from Westboro Baptist Church in Topeka, Kansas, picketed. These are the crazies who had picketed Matthew Shepard's funeral, the young gay man beaten to death along a barbed-wire fence in Wyoming. They'd picketed at the funerals of Iraq veterans for fighting for a country that supposedly supports homosexuality. They'd even picketed Mr. Rogers's funeral claiming that, as a Presbyterian minister, he had a responsibility to renounce homosexuality on his children's show. Gay-coddling, according to Reverend Phelps, is responsible for September 11 and the Columbia space shuttle disaster. His is an all-purpose hate, like the KKK, more actually like a *Saturday Night Live* spoof of the KKK. By supporting gay rights, Reverend Phelps said, Mrs. King had been "giving God the finger." And in four hours of commemoration of the courage of the civil rights leader, not one speaker, not *one*, has to guts to acknowledge these haters on the street.

I shut off the computer. I can't decide if I'm heartened or distressed by the whole regal spectacle. I am somewhere in between. I am somewhere on the streets of Montgomery or Tallahassee, somewhere in the middle of a very long book, somewhere between winter and spring, staring at an old photograph, three young men: two black and one white. Waiting.

A week later, Laurie and I sit on a scrap of black insulate pad leaning against a one-hundred-year-old apple tree. We sip champagne from an icy minibottle to celebrate our fifteenth anniversary together. We clink our glasses and toast our easy quiet life, and I return home, climb upstairs to my desk, planning to spend the afternoon pecking away at a slew of e-mails. The first message is good news: Lisa is pregnant. Pregnant already after trying for two months! Then I scroll down to the next highlighted message in the queue, click twice, and my easy quiet life begins to slowly unhinge.

The story is harrowing. During Joey's recent visit, severe

dehydration finally knocked the last wind out of my mother. She'd stumbled from her bedroom, loosing her bowels on the hall carpet, scaring the bejesus out of my little brother, my not-so-little brother, who lifted my not-so-little mother to her feet and dragged her to the car. Lisa and Joey took her to Dr. Death, who claimed she could do nothing to help. (Nothing? Nothing?) Dr. Death suggested they take her to the local emergency room. Forget that, Lisa thought. She called City of Hope instead, and they said: come quick. And they did. Joey drove his mother sixty miles on the freeway, fast, to City of Hope, where they were met at the door by technicians with a gurney. Code blue, they called out. The scene, Joey would later tell me, was straight from a TV drama. I am thinking: I need to fly south. I am thinking: Oh Jesus, I do not want to fly south. I did my heroic act back in October. Can't I just skip town? Hasn't someone posted bail for me?

Should I book a flight now? I type. *Could you take the trailer down again?*

No, Lisa types. *There's nothing you can do.*

The next day the letter arrives. The careful handwriting on a yellow legal pad is the kind you can trust—even nuns can't teach sincerity—and the words are generous.

Dear Ana Maria,

I do wish you had contacted me while you were in Tallahassee. However, you did the next best thing by writing to me. I am very happy to hear from you. For many years I have wondered what happened to my friend, Joseph Spagna. Because of you, I know now. You inquired about Leonard Speed. He died in 1991. We remained in contact until his death.

Your father was a very brave man. As a white man he forfeited his right as a privileged one, in that day and time,

92

in order to stand up for the rights of blacks. We are indebted to him.

Let me know when it is convenient for you to call me. Mornings, afternoons or evening are okay with me. Give me a specific date and approximate time and I'll be here.

I am eager to hear from you.

Sincerely,

Johnny Herndon

I read the letter and reread it by the woodstove. A very brave man, he says. Your father was a very brave man. I fold the yellow sheet carefully in thirds and return it to the envelope. I climb the stairs and turn on the computer and watch the screen flicker in the dark. Outside moonlight limns the snow-burdened trees. Whatever I'm learning, it's not about protest or politics; it's about courage. And it's not about my dad; it's about me. Laurie has not yet returned from work at the orchard, so I can't ask her about my decision, and I know what she'd say anyhow: it's up to you. I pull out my credit card and set it beside me on the desk. It's time to go back.

CHAPTER EIGHT

Herndon

Dawn skims the tops of the snowy peaks surrounding us. In winter, our ferry boat runs only three days a week, so I've hitched a ride on a smaller ranger boat, now bucking wind swells and slamming down, tipping precariously to one side then the other. I hold tight to an overhead rail, straining on my tiptoes, taking the swells with my knees like moguls on a ski slope, trying to avoid leaning my hamstring against the red-hot propane heater as winter sun beats in through the windshield. When at last the dock comes into view, I head immediately to a small downtown motel, the Midtowner, where they offer a special rate for travelers from the tiny town, set down my bag, pull out my notebook, and dial Johnny Herndon's number.

His wife answers. "Oh, he'll be so sorry he missed you. He's out fishing for the day. Can you call back in a few hours?"

Lamplight in the motel room filters dust. Traffic on the street is sparse. I sit on a plastic lawn chair bundled in a work coat, the sun hitting on my face, the temperature around forty. I rehearse my questions and then page through my notebook. After getting the reply from Johnny Herndon, I'd grown brave. I spent hours on the computer searching for people with the right name, around the right age, in or near Florida, and writing letters. So far, I've written to Harold Owens, Jon Folsom, James Kennedy, even Emory Elkins, the bus driver. But I've received no more replies. The addresses filling up my notebook look purposeful, like progress is being made, though what kind, exactly, I can't say. I pace the parking lot. The restless hours pass.

Finally I dial again.

"Mr. Herndon? How are you? How was the fishing?"

"Caught the limit," he said. "Can't complain. Can't complain."

His voice is warm, his accent gentle, unmistakably black and Southern, understatedly formal, something like Morgan Freeman meets Jimmy Stewart. I like him immediately, immensely. We chat for a while about fishing, how often he goes—daily now that he's retired—and where. Turns out he most prefers a spot beneath the St. George Island Bridge, at the mouth of the Apalachicola, a short distance from the Sportman's Lodge where Laurie and I stayed so happily a month ago. I am almost giddy with excitement. I picture his bass boat in the wide blue gulf off the Forgotten Coast, his line in the water, and I feel a deep and easy bond.

"Mr. Herndon," I say at last, "I wonder if I could ask you a few questions."

But he doesn't need my questions. He is ready to tell his story, and he tells it in a way that suggests that he's been asked before. He is humble and careful, precise in his word choice. His is not the story I am expecting.

"The bus," he says, "was very crowded with a mix of white people and mostly black, and the seats were arranged such that there were three on one side and two across the aisle on the other side. Leonard and I and your father found a vacant seat in the white section with room for all three of us."

I try to make his story mesh with the one I've learned.

"There were other fellows with you as well that day, right? Folsom, Kennedy, Owens? I read about them as material witnesses."

"No, just Speed, Herndon, and Spag-Nuh."

"Did you ride more than one bus?"

"Oh, no. Just one."

"And the bus was crowded?"

"Very crowded," he says.

I feel a wave of panic. The story he's telling, I'm afraid, is the Rosa Parks story. After fifty years maybe he's confused the familiar media-hyped story with his own.

"Listen," he says suddenly. "I want you to know, your father was already gone by the time we went to jail. He had graduated, you see. Leonard and I, we didn't have any idea the police would come for us. We thought the case was dead."

He pauses.

"I see," I say. I don't know what else to say. My voice is unnaturally high, my manners uncharacteristically formal. "He was already gone, you think? I see. I see. I had the wrong idea, Mr. Herndon. I was just certain that he had left because of the threat of jail."

"Not at all. You see? It came as a complete surprise. Now, this paints a different picture for you, doesn't it?"

"It does. . . . It paints a *much* different picture. Like I said in my letter, uh, that's why I didn't call when I was there. I just couldn't figure out why he would do that, leave you and Leonard Speed to serve your time, then, uh, he didn't do that?"

"He did not."

Johnny Herndon goes on to say he grew up in Valdosta, Georgia, a place worlds worse than Tallahassee in terms of race relations.

"Vicious," he says. "Those small rural towns were vicious." I can hear him shaking his head.

He moved to Tallahassee after high school to attend Florida A&M and got involved with the bus boycott. He was studying political science, but after the bus incident, with only a term left to go, he had to quit. No one would hire him to work—he lost his job on a construction crew—so he could not afford tuition. Instead, eventually, he started his own business.

"What kind of business?" I ask.

"A taxi cab company."

I laugh. "Really? Right there in Tallahassee?"

"Yes, yes."

I laugh. "Well, that makes sense."

"Pardon me?"

"It kind of goes with your bus story a little bit to be running a taxi company, doesn't it? Another transportation company?"

"I suppose so."

The conversation is settling easily now, moving into the past and back to the present. As we speak, I think about Johnny's story, how it does and doesn't agree with the history books. I think about how much he reminds me of my neighbors in the tiny mountain town, where stories are not forgotten, where you live with the past, your own and everyone else's. He has stayed in Tallahassee, after all, for more than fifty years, longer than my dad lived anywhere by a long shot, longer actually than my dad lived.

"Do you remember where you met my father or when?"

"We met at a meeting concerning the bus situation. A committee called the meeting and asked for volunteers. He was one who volunteered. And Leonard. And me."

"I was sorry to hear about Mr. Speed," I say. "Was he a friend? Did you stay in touch?"

"Leonard and I were friends for many years. We went to the same church."

"Bethel Missionary Baptist, where C. K. Steele was pastor?"

"Yes."

"I was just there a month ago."

"At the eleven o'clock service?"

"That's right."

"Well, I'll be. I was there too. It's a small world, isn't it?"

"Yes, it is. What was C. K. Steele like? Did you know him?"

"I knew him well, very well, nearly all his life."

Even though the naysayers during the boycott had called C. K. Steele a suitcase minister—an outsider, in other words, a transient who could pick up and leave at any time—in the end, he was anything but. C. K. Steele was committed to Tallahassee. Though he served as vice president of the national Southern Christian Leadership Council for years, he never wanted to be president, not even after King's death, because such a post would require him to be constantly on the move. Steele refused to abandon his congregation. He stayed on as pastor at Bethel Missionary Baptist Church until his death at sixty-six, from bone marrow cancer, in 1980. Now Johnny Herndon tells me what I already know: that Rev. Steele was powerfully charismatic, inspirational.

Mainly, he is eager to return to his story.

"In spite of legalities," he explains, "the city had passed an unconstitutional ordinance." He and Leonard and my father had challenged that ordinance, he says. They were arrested and released. After that, the city was in an uproar. The boycott was reinvigorated. He *is* telling the Tallahassee story, I realize. Who knows? Maybe Johnny Herndon is right, and the history books are all screwed up, I tell myself. There is integrity about this man that makes me want to believe him very badly.

"The police were very cordial during the arrest. They knew our objective. They wanted to discourage us, to get us to say 'sorry' and let us go."

The threat of violence, he says, after that was strong. The incident had been covered in the newspaper, and angry whites were looking for the students. The articles had mentioned that Speed and Herndon lived on the A&M campus in the dorms, which wasn't true—they lived in an apartment downtown. But this hardly limited the threats they received. In the packet of information, Cynthia Williams had sent me a letter addressed to Johnny Herndon in February 1957.

Neatly typed, it contained a number of quotations from Abraham Lincoln suggesting his support of segregation and ended with a few ideas from the anonymous letter writer himself:

> It seems Mr. Lincoln was not a communist. We also have so many who make and inforce [*sic*] our laws, not as laws but the soviet ideas. Just why a group of cannibalistic niggers is more powerful than our Anglo Saxon, am unable to say. All nations who mix whites and blacks soon fall, America is on the way down. Keep America white.

The only handwriting on the letter was scrawled at the bottom: *Why do you niggers want to ride with white girls? Back to Africa.*

"Did you receive other letters like this one?" I ask.

"Many more. And many personal insults. Your father did, too, I know. But he could handle it." He pauses. "Your father was a very brave and great man."

"You are a very brave and great man, Mr. Herndon."

"His path," he says, "was more difficult than mine."

"Because he was white?"

"Because he was white. Most white support was behind the scenes, you see. Retaliatory measures would have prevented them from coming forward."

I believe him. I have learned, finally, from reading, that it's true: a white man sympathizing with blacks was a bigger threat, and therefore a bigger target, to Southern rednecks than a black man was. On May 20, 1961, four years after Johnny Herndon and my dad rode the bus—and only six days after the bus burned in Anniston—Freedom Riders descended from their bus in Montgomery into a mob of starched-shirt thugs. It was the third time in three days that local police in Alabama had given Ku Klux Klansmen fifteen minutes of free time to "have some fun" before appearing on the scene. This time the first two riders to descend from the bus were John Lewis, a nineteen-year-old black seminarian, and Jim Zwerg, a white divinity student from Wisconsin. The crowd was on Zwerg in a flash, beating him unconscious with pipes, breaking three of his vertebrae in the process. Lewis, too, was beaten severely—not for the last time—but Zwerg, everyone agreed, took the worst of it.

Later the same year in McComb, Mississippi, a group of Student Nonviolent Coordinating Committee (SNCC) volunteers followed a group of school kids, led by a local fifteen-year-old girl, marching on city hall after an unsuccessful library sit-in. A crowd of furious local whites descended at once. Bob Zellner, the only white person among the marchers, took the brunt of the crowd's fury. He clutched his Bible to his chest while white attackers gouged at his eyes and kicked his face repeatedly. When the authorities finally arrived, he wasn't sent to the hospital, but directly to jail to await trial on charges of disturbing the peace.

"We were lucky," Johnny Herndon says. "We had a strong governor, Leroy Collins. He said, 'if you don't stop I'll call in the National Guard.' If he didn't. . . ." Here Johnny's voice trails off. I can sense that he's trying to regain composure. "If he hadn't, well, we would have had another Selma in a matter of days." He pauses. "Do you know what happened in Selma, Alabama?"

"I do."

There is more silence while we both picture the spectacle on the Pettus Bridge in 1965, at the height of the movement, when the same John Lewis, a hardened activist at twenty-three, wearing an overcoat and a small knapsack, led hundreds of blacks out of Selma on a march for voters' rights. The moment they hit the bridge, with no escape, no cover, Alabama state troopers set on them, beating Lewis within an inch of his life.

Johnny Herndon is emphatic now. His voice is firm in its softness. "Leonard and I had no idea the police would come for us. None," he says. "Your father would not have known neither."

"Did you talk to him?"

"No, not after our last day in court."

"Did you ever see him again? Do you know where he went?"

"No, no."

"Did he ever talk about his past? His family?"

"Your father was, uh, a very friendly and determined person. He had strong convictions." He speaks gently, slowly. "But we weren't friends. We couldn't have been, you see? Not the way things were. I didn't know him well."

I toy with the phone cord, twisting it round my hand.

"I understand."

The conversation lightens. He invites me, as Cynthia Williams has already done, to attend the fiftieth anniversary celebrations in May.

"I'd like that," I say. I think about my mother's cancer and the one-way ticket to Los Angeles I have in my bag. So much could change in the next three months. "I'm not sure if I can make it, but I will try."

"Thank you," I say. "For everything."

"Thank you for calling," he says. "Please keep in touch."

And it's over. I set the receiver in the cradle, collapse back onto the pillows propped against the wall, and stare at the empty television screen.

PART TWO

After my dad died, I dreamed regularly that he was still
alive. He'd appear vague and indistinct, playing a bit part: a
balding man with a mustache but no speaking lines, sitting
somewhere in the background of my life—in a high school
biology lab, say, or sitting on the living room couch, feet up,
when I got home—and I'd be gravely embarrassed. Oh no, I'd
think, I told everyone he was dead. I mean, I let people think
he was dead, when I knew all along that he wasn't. Like a kid
who fakes being sick to miss school or church, I felt caught,
like the truth was leeching out for everyone else to see. When
I woke up, I never lay in bed scrunching my eyes tight wishing the dream would last a little longer. I leaped up thinking:
Phew! Sure am glad that's over!

At the Midtowner I have the same feeling, that I am in a
dream where my father sits quietly in the scratchy upholstered
motel chair in the corner, his hair slicked back, his loafers
scuffed. I try to reread my notes, to fill in the blanks, but the
presence feels too close and unsettling. I decide to go running
before dark. I run a narrow road shoulder, among the orchards
and past the small-town store fronts. The cold numbs my fingers, my legs move steadily, my lungs burn, my mind drifts.

I had wanted Johnny Herndon to give me a definitive answer:
your dad left on such and such a date. I wanted him to say he
left because it was too dangerous. Or because he was a coward.
Period. I wanted to know that he went to Saint Petersburg to
collect his things and kiss Aunt Rose goodbye. I think, secretly,
I wanted to know that he'd gone to South America, that he'd
had to go, that the NAACP had paid for him to go. But I knew,
even before I talked to Johnny Herndon, even though I may
not have admitted it to myself, that there was very little chance
of that. The NAACP was under too much scrutiny. Even before
the Tallahassee bus boycott they'd had to move their Florida
enrollment records, in crates, out of the state under the cover

1. Reverend C. K. Steele in front of
Bethel Missionary Baptist Church.
Courtesy of State Archives of Florida.

2. (*Left*) A photographer captures
Reverend C. K. Steele and Dan Speed
attempting to ride in the front of a
Tallahassee bus, December 1956.
Courtesy of State Archives of Florida.

3. (*Above*) Morris Thomas showed up
on the wrong day for the planned mass
integrated ride, but his image came
to define the Tallahassee bus boycott.
Courtesy of State Archives of Florida.

4. Leonard Speed, Johnny Herndon,
and Joseph Spagna, January 1957.
Courtesy of The *Florida Star*.

5. The Spagnas, January 1979.

of darkness to protect the innocent. After the boycott, the Johns Committee never stopped hassling the NAACP, grilling their board members, scouring their financial records, looking for any meager evidence that they'd been fomenting unrest. Funding outside agitators like my dad would have been like funding the Kremlin directly. No way.

I'd asked Johnny Herndon if he'd stayed active in the civil rights movement after the incident, when Tallahassee became a hotbed for activism in the early 1960s, when A&M students held sit-ins at restaurants, movie theaters, and swimming pools.

"Did you take part?"

"No, no," he said.

He had to earn a living, he said. He had to build his business to support his young family. He had done his part, he said, and he had gone on to live his life and to keep his nose clean. And I know the truth: my dad had done his part, and he'd gone on to live his life too. I even know exactly where he went.

CHAPTER NINE

The Cloven Hoof

San Francisco to a kid from Riverside had always stood like an overachieving older sibling. Sure, Los Angeles had glamour and money, but that hardly mattered. For one thing, L.A. was sixty long miles away—we usually went only once a year for a school field trip to the Museum of Science and Industry—and besides, in our house, glamour and money didn't count for much. San Francisco had a bookish glow and texture to the landscape, hilly streets instead of flat freeways, and colors, so many colors: rainbow sails on the bay, yellow-orange flowers lining Lombard Street, the dramatic red-orange of the Golden Gate Bridge. In my imagination, San Francisco loomed large: seductive and intimidating. In reality, I'd rarely been.

We drove there once before Joey was born. Mom and Dad loaded Lisa and me into the back of the vw Beetle in the pre-dawn dark, hoping we'd sleep most of the way, but we were wide awake before Bakersfield. Are we there yet? we cried. No. Dad's big, hairy forearm rested on the car door, his elbow jutted out the open window. His cigarette dribbled ash on the steering wheel. Are we halfway there? No. Are we halfway to halfway?

"Nope," Dad said. He smiled in the rearview mirror wide enough that the hole showed where he was missing a molar. "Not even close."

Hot air blew in our little girl faces. I couldn't think of another question.

We were going to see Clayton Barbeau, a man whose

bearded face I'd seen on Christmas cards pinned to the hot-water closet door, posed with a passel of kids in front of a big, multicolored Victorian house. (Because of that picture, I'd be confused years later when I saw my first photo of Jerry Garcia, so similar. *Hey*, I thought, *isn't that Clayton Barbeau?*) I remember the grueling monotony of the drive north and the anticipation in the backseat, and I remember eating at an Italian restaurant in North Beach, but I don't remember much else. I don't even know if I met Clay Barbeau.

A few years later, after Dad died, Mom drove us north again, this time to visit a priest friend who was pastor of a parish in Oakland. We stayed with him over New Year's Eve and listened to gunshots at midnight, and I lay awake in this drafty, wooden-floor house in this hard, broken-down neighborhood wondering why we were not visiting Clay Barbeau, why no restaurants in North Beach. But by then so much had changed. The next day our priest friend drove us out a long gravel road to Muir Beach, a smallish cove north of the city, where, Mom said, our dad had once lived alone in a cabin on the beach. The January day was far too cold for us to put our toes in the water, and I couldn't imagine the allure of living in such a place. Not yet.

· · ·

I returned to San Francisco in October, before I'd ever heard of Johnny Herndon or visited Tallahassee. I was there to visit Joey and his wife and small daughter, my goddaughter, on my way south to help Mom through what looked to be a routine surgery, and I was taking my first tentative steps toward figuring out my dad's story.

I knew this much: after my dad jumped bail, he didn't go directly to South America as I'd liked to believe for so long. No, that came later. He left Tallahassee and headed directly to

San Francisco to open a bookstore. With the cassette tape from Minnesota, my mom had sent me a packet of my dad's papers. There were several college essays, and a few short personal letters, dated between 1958 and 1961, that proved once and for all that he lived in California during those years. And there was a single business card: The Cloven Hoof Bookshop. 1315 Grant. Books. Prints. Original Art.

Now I clutched the card in my hand as I walked fast to stay warm. The streets were steep and shaded, and soon I was away from the hurried center of town, the ringing bells of cable cars, the entreaties of the homeless, and onto narrow side streets where Asian women swept sidewalks and pigeons pecked at crumbs and strips of blue bay halved the horizon between vertical building sides.

I passed a white-bearded man in a canary-yellow three-piece suit with a straw Panama hat. If he hadn't been a beatnik, I thought, he should have been. I nodded and smiled.

"Beautiful morning, isn't it?" I offered.

"Because of people like you," he said. He doffed his hat and held it against his chest, head bowed, as I passed.

I couldn't help it, I was utterly charmed.

In no time I was there: 1315 Grant. The narrow storefront was a four-minute walk from City Lights Bookstore, Lawrence Ferlinghetti's famous Mecca, around the corner from St. Francis Church, not far from Coit Tower, and it housed a trendy new restaurant—Ristorante Ideale—boasting acorn-squash pasta and organic wine. I stood in the morning light, leaning in with hands cupped against the glass, to look at the brick wall, the preset tables for two, the yuppie ambience. I could not, for the life of me, imagine what it had been like in the late fifties. I had nothing to go on.

If I ever had anything, I knew, I'd have gotten rid of it.

The last gift my father ever gave me was a box set of *Anne of Green Gables* books for Christmas 1978 that I never, ever, cracked. Sometime in the year after his death I tossed the handwritten gift-tag bookmark—*to: Ana Maria. Love, Dad*—into the kitchen garbage.

My mother found it there.

"This was from your father," she said. She was shaking with fury.

I shrugged.

"You don't want this?"

"No."

. . .

Of all the people I'd write to months later, after my success with Johnny Herndon, Clayton Barbeau would turn out to be the easiest, by far, to chase down. He's the author of dozens of books, mostly on psychology, a family therapist and a devout Catholic. He's an inspirational speaker with his own Web site. When I painstakingly handwrite my letter, he promptly replies via e-mail, a long missive, the first of many.

"Your father," he begins, "was a man with a heart as big as his whole body, which was not small." My father was dozing behind the desk at the Cloven Hoof on the day that they met, and he describes the bookstore as "very neat and very well stocked with the latest titles," with a tiny backroom where my dad let transients crash. The bookstore was frequented by writers and artists of all stripes for whom the uniform was long hair and beards, sandals and sweaters, a decade before the look came into fashion. It was a place, Clay Barbeau says, where things were happening.

Once they invited a Catholic anarchist to read at the store, a huge draw since, according to Barbeau, most Beats thought all Catholics were "Franco Spanish Fascists." During the reading an angry drunk came in brandishing a knife, and no one could calm him down. (Drunken recklessness was not, apparently, the kind of anarchy the bookstore folks were interested in.) Finally, my dad persuaded him to step outside. "Within about five minutes," Clay Barbeau writes, "the gentleman had closed his knife, pocketed it, and Joe was shaking his hand and wishing him well." Clay Barbeau tells the story with clear affection. He's enthusiastic, ebullient even, about my dad, about the past, about life in general. His beloved wife is dead now—she died in 1979, same as my dad—and his kids have dispersed. He no longer lives in Haight Ashbury, where his large family weathered the late sixties, but in an apartment in San Jose from which he sends frequent bulk e-mails, political jokes or news items mostly, that use an epigraph from A. A. Milne, a different *House at Pooh Corner* quote at the bottom of each. When I picture Clayton Barbeau now—I can't help it—I picture the man in the canary-yellow suit.

Clay Barbeau has also, apparently, heard more about my dad's past than most other people. In one e-mail, he tells a story about my dad's father, the original Joe Spagna, my pro football grandfather, making my dad eat massive meals, weighing him and measuring his arms, then pulling strings to get him into Dartmouth to play football. Then one day, according to the story my dad told Clay Barbeau, he went out for a long pass, and he was hit hard and flattened on the grass. He lay there for several minutes staring at the sky and thought to himself, "I really don't want to waste a beautiful day doing this." So, he quit the team and never played again.

It's a great story, I think, perfectly suited to some Beat ideal, and it's ironic in the light of what became of my younger brother, the third Joe Spagna. Joey grew big young, thick necked and tree-trunk legged. We measured his quadriceps, and from the time he started high school, each was bigger around than my waist. He was so big that the local high school football coach cornered him in eighth grade at the fellowship hall at Our Lady. Here he was, a boy in a house of women, who'd had to announce when he was ten years old that he never wanted to hear about menstruation at the dinner table again. Did he want to play football? Of course, he wanted to play football!

And he did. He played on the offensive line, as center usually, through high school and two years of college until one day, as a sophomore, he fumbled the snap and took a helmet hard in the knee, severing three ligaments at once. Just like that. The doctors said they'd only ever seen such an injury once before, after a train wreck. They considered amputation before attempting surgery that left him a twelve-inch Frankenstein scar and a limp for life. Joey still loves the game. He watches every weekend and is already teaching his young daughter, Elena, the rudiments of the game, the same way my dad taught me. The same way I taught him. As kids, Joey and I watched the college games on Saturday, and sometimes pros on Sunday; then we took the Nerf out onto the front lawn at halftime to scrimmage. I told myself if I didn't teach him, there'd be no one else to do it.

A couple years ago at Christmastime, while Joey and I were standing outside on the porch on Burnside Court, he asked me to be Elena's godmother.

"Sure," I said. Why not? I figured. I loved my new sweet curly haired niece, and it was an honor of sorts, but I hadn't attended Catholic Mass since college.

"Why me?" I asked.

"Because you have good values and stuff," he said and swigged his beer. "And because you're the only person we know who actually made it through confirmation classes."

At thirty, Joey has inherited my dad's penchant for melding philosophy and practicality with a shrug.

"Okay, then," I said. We gazed out together at the city-lit night sky.

. . .

A short block up from Ristorante Ideale, on the corner of Grant and Vallejo, I stumbled upon Café Trieste, perhaps the only business in North Beach, other than City Lights Bookstore, that survives from my father's era. The small café was crowded with people, not Rolex types, but a more casual crowd, many wearing shorts, some sitting at outdoor tables in the brisk morning air. Photos of musicians, accordion players mostly, and writers plastered the walls. A crooner sang in Italian on the jukebox. As I took a place in the long line at the counter, I wondered if there wasn't some comfort for my dad in coming to this neighborhood that was not only self-consciously literary but also so very Italian. Here he could be both a radical and a man of the old country. Even Jack Kerouac, though French Canadian, was the son of immigrants and a failed football prodigy to boot. I pictured them pontificating all gruff and unenunciated like Marlon Brando, like my little brother, probably like my father.

I was easily the youngest person in the room. At thirty-eight, that says something in a city once known for its youth. Most of the customers looked like they *were* those youth, the children of the sixties, now in their sixties, but still long haired and slow moving. It was Columbus Day, the celebration of the takeover of the continent, for better or worse. A generation ago these folks took over the city, and my dad was, for a time, among them. I inched toward the front of the line and ordered a cappuccino from two slender young Italian men in tight t-shirts.

The Cloven Hoof

"Ever heard of a bookstore on Grant called the Cloven Hoof?" I asked.

The younger of the two, with neatly trimmed scruff on his chin, sprinkled cinnamon on my steamy cup with one hand while pouring water in the espresso machine with the other. He was not unkind, but he wasn't chatty either. He shook his head.

"Know anyone who might've?"

"Sorry."

. . .

When I was a teenager, Lisa and my mother fought regularly, sometimes daily. They waged a decade long civil war over issues as predictable as an afterschool special on TV: grades, clothes, curfews, drugs. On the shelf at home sat a copy of *Weed: Adventures of a Dope Smuggler* by Jerry Kamstra, a book that mentioned my father's name in the index, as one of the cool cats on North Beach. For most of my teenage years, that book provided ammunition for Lisa. Look, she'd cry. Dad smoked pot, too! Down the hall, where Joey and I lay on the bedroom floor poring over the liner notes to Beatles albums, we'd turn up the volume on the stereo, trying steadfastly to ignore Lisa's indignant cries. If Dad was here, he'd let me, she'd say. I wanted to kill her. Don't bring up Dad, I'd think. Don't you dare drag him into this. I hated that book, *Weed*, with a passion.

So I hesitate when Clay Barbeau suggests that I track down Jerry Kamstra. He says the author of *Weed* hung out at the Cloven Hoof, but I don't want to write to him. The mere mention of his name—Jerry Kamstra—makes my stomach muscles tense. This, I realize, is not my current self, but my teenage self roiling with disapproval. I went to church and got straight *A*s. I did not smoke pot, not once. During the frequent screaming matches in the living room, I took Joey to Baskin Robbins, where often enough he ordered a hot fudge sundae even though we both knew such rich food made him throw up. No matter how I tried I could not hold things together. When I think about Jerry Kamstra, I can feel that seam-stretching frustration. But I tell myself: that's the past, this is research. I try to chase him down to no avail, but I find Jerry Kamstra's books easily enough online, and order *The Frisco Kid*, an out-of-print tribute to the 1950s hipsters of North Beach published in the early 1970s.

"Remember," Clay Barbeau says, "The Beat movement was not literary, but spiritual. It was a revolt against dehumanization and mammon and materialism."

I know what he means: the Beats were into mysticism, into a wholeness of experience. "I want God to show his face," Jack Kerouac once proclaimed. Kerouac himself converted back to Catholicism during a weekend retreat at a cabin owned by Lawrence Ferlinghetti in 1960, but it was Catholicism of a decidedly conservative bent. ("I'm not a beatnik," he famously said a month before he died. "I'm a Catholic.") Gary Snyder, the Zen Buddhist poet, described the Beat philosophy as apolitical, essentially existentialist and pacifist. The problem is that what my dad did in Tallahassee requires a kind of proactive selflessness that I don't see in the Beats, even those with a religious bent. Not, at least, in Jerry Kamstra.

I struggle desperately to make it through *The Frisco Kid*, a book full of drugs and sex, musty books, salty sea air, and cheap wine in jugs. I even try to get in the spirit of things by pouring myself a healthy mug of boxed Franzia. I figure I should be able to relate. I went through a Beat period of my own after college when I was jobless and aimless. I read most of Kerouac one winter sitting upstairs in the Seattle Public Library, watching the ferries come and go through the fog on Puget Sound. I took the Greyhound south to Riverside, spending one lonely Christmas night in the Oakland bus terminal, reading *Mexico City Blues*. But it's no use. The disregard for women, the stealing, the drug dealing: this was a spiritual movement? My dad had inherited money from his football-playing father, who had become a successful steel engineer in Philadelphia. If my grandfather ever knew his only son squandered his inheritance on a bookshop with a vaguely occult name, I suppose he rolled over in his grave.

And squandered, I think, was the right word. Clayton Barbeau writes that "people he trusted to watch the store for a few minutes or a few hours took advantage of the position to pocket some of the proceeds, but Joe never mentioned it, and I watched him give more than one book away. So I was not surprised when the time came that he decided he had to close the place."

That's why he moved out to the cabin on Muir Beach. It was a makeshift place with an unobstructed view of the wide blue Pacific to the west and of the larger, more affluent homes to the north. He hitchhiked to the city on the weekends for dinner or to stay the night with the Barbeaus, like Thoreau leaving Walden to mooch off the Emersons in Concord, and to borrow books, one of which he returned with a strip of bacon as a bookmark. He was, Clayton explains, going through a time of reflection. Sitting by the woodstove in my own remote cabin, I reread Clay Barbeau's e-mails and think about the obvious parallels between me and my dad. I've lived in makeshift shacks on the fringe of society, off and on, for most of my adult life. By Clay Barbeau's standards, I've been going through a time of reflection for over twenty years. With that in mind, I take a swallow of wine, scratch the cat threading my chair legs, set down *The Frisco Kid*, and move instead back to my bookshelves to grab *The Seven Storey Mountain*.

Both Clay Barbeau and Joe Amato, on the cassette tape he sent from Minnesota, mentioned my father's admiration for Thomas Merton more than once. A contemporary of the Beats who attended Columbia and frequented New York City jazz clubs around the same time Kerouac did, Merton took a wildly different route: converting to Catholicism and eventually becoming a Trappist monk. Rereading his autobiography, *The Seven Storey Mountain*, I can see how much it influenced my father. Merton portrays himself as a beard growing, beer drinking, bongo playing, politically concerned aspiring writer, the kind of fellow, I'd imagine, who might have hung out in North Beach, but one who very clearly, well, hungers after righteousness. (Merton also works for a while with the poor in Harlem and later heads off to Cuba, more echoes—or premonitions—of my dad's story.) When Merton, on the brink of his conversion, decries the cowardice "which makes men say they cannot do what they *must* do," at last I begin to see a connection between my steadfast father in Tallahassee and my spiritually searching father in San Francisco.

. . .

At Café Trieste, I munched on a rich almond torte, listened to the jukebox, and studied the wall photos. Morning sun shone in on customers reading novels and typing on laptops. I stood at last to set my empty cup on the counter and to wander around the corner to City Lights Bookstore, where an entire front display was dedicated to the Beats: not books *by* the Beats so much as books *about* them. I paged through them, picked out one with a lot of photos.

"Ever heard of a bookstore on Grant called the Cloven Hoof? My dad owned the place in the late fifties, and I'm looking for anyone who might remember him from those days."

The gray-ponytailed clerk sighed. She looked at the book

in my hand, a cheesy tourist guidebook to North Beach with a photo of Kerouac on the cover, and stared at me through tiny rimless spectacles.

"Everyone who stops in here wants to talk to someone who remembers the late fifties."

She was right, I knew. Forget the past. Be here now. I walked back out into the sun, rented a bike, and rode through the city on a new paved trail along the waterfront, through parks and neighborhoods and westward toward the Golden Gate Bridge, where I stood on the narrow pedestrian way crowded with tourists shuffling along, sea wind tugging at their jackets, traffic noise muting the chatter of a dozen languages. I pedaled slowly amongst them and stopped to gaze with them out at Alcatraz, Angel's Island, the Berkeley hills cloud-shrouded in the distance, and I thought about the gay couples who had so recently lined up to marry at city hall. Even Joey, the church-going offensive lineman, said he'd watched the spectacle on TV and wept. He thought about bringing Elena down to see it, too, carrying her high on his huge shoulders, to see history in the making. He thought he might bring flowers and congratulate the couples. When he told me that, I knew that Laurie and I should have bought plane tickets and joined in. But I hadn't wanted to. I was afraid that the license would end up being no good, that whatever progress was being made would be temporary. I hadn't wanted to put so much of myself out there for so little reward. I've said it before: I'm a coward. But it wasn't retribution or violence I feared. It was futility.

When my young father arrived in San Francisco, he surely grappled with the same issue, only more so. After all, he'd actually done it, put himself out there. And what did he have to show for it? Not much. In my first letter I asked Clayton Barbeau if my father ever mentioned Tallahassee.

"Oh, yes," he replied, "he told me he was a wanted man in Florida." And he continued with the tale:

He spoke of a trial where the judge barely listened to any of the defense before banging his gavel and saying "Guilty. Six months on the chain gang." The NAACP lawyers immediately got him out on bail while they appealed the decision. Joe said "Six months on the chain gang was a death penalty. It was understood that a nigger lover was worse than a child molester. There would come a day when I would be led off into the brush and shot for 'attempting to escape.' So I thought that over and figured I had to get as far away as possible . . . I figured I had done my bit for the NAACP and they could handle the five hundred dollar loss better than I could handle the chain gang death sentence."

So there it was. My dad knew exactly what was coming, and that's why he split. I could hear the shrug of practicality in his decision, and though I still bristled at the subtle bravado in the story, at least in the way that Clayton Barbeau retold it, I was beginning to understand. Like the quitting-football story, here was a saga full of complications and nuances and raggedy loose ends tidied up neatly for the retelling, shaped in other words the way a writer would shape it. My father had no choice but to leave Tallahassee. When he arrived in San Francisco, he was left with the none-too-small task of trying to make sense, as best he could, of what had happened. And what hadn't.

In "Letter to a Young Activist," Thomas Merton faces futility head-on, urging his listener not to depend on the hope of results, that an activist has to face the fact that his work may be worthless; it might achieve no results or even achieve the opposite of what he intended. "The great thing after all is to live," Merton writes. "If you can get free from the domination of causes . . . you will be able to do more and will be less crushed by the inevitable disappointments." Merton, I'm thinking, may as well have been speaking directly to young Joe Spagna.

On the tape from Minnesota, my father's friends from Tallahassee spoke of his passion for literature, his keen eye for good work, his tireless encouragement of budding writers at Florida State. He even read his own poetry occasionally at open mics on campus. Upon hearing that he became a social worker, one of his Minnesota friends responds with mild surprise.

"Last we heard," she says, "he had gotten into a bookstore. I guess I always thought he'd go on to do something with that."

He did. He stepped out of the grainy black-and-white world where he'd been struggling and leapt full-bore into a Technicolor world on the edge of the continent, the center of a hip, new, literary world. He took all he had in the world and invested it in a place where, for a time, he could be free from the domination of causes, less crushed by disappointment, a place where he could immerse in community, then retreat to solitude, and come out with a faith that offered both solace and strength. With that in mind, maybe the inheritance money he spent on the Cloven Hoof wasn't squandered after all.

CHAPTER TEN

City of Hope

My mother needs feeding. Her hands tremor wildly, a side effect of chemotherapy or the resulting high blood pressure, no one seems to know, but the sores, open and oozing on her lips, are from the severe dehydration that landed her back here at City of Hope. She can't hold a fork or a glass. Still, the doctors insist, there is no medical reason why she isn't eating. She just won't do it. This fact scares me more, much more, than her sunken eyes or the patchy white stubble on her head. Laurie and I had shaved it at Christmastime to prevent her hair from coming off in clumps on her pillow, to tidy it up. Back then, my mother took some pride in it, proof of her valiant struggle, a badge. Back then, she looked strong. Now, she just looks very sick.

She awakens when I walk into her room. It is nearly ten, and the lights have been dimmed on the hospital hallway. It is very quiet as it's always quiet at City of Hope. At a cancer facility, there are no gurney-racing emergencies, no births, no rowdy celebrations. Just long, slow declines.

I hold my mother's hand and tell her about my trip. Tubes extrude in every direction. Tiny lights flash green from the IV monitor. Green, I will soon learn, means A-OK. Red means trouble.

"The flight wasn't bad. I was a big girl. I didn't cry or grab strangers' hands."

She tries to smile, but her cracked lips won't allow it. Her eyelids droop as I speak, but if I fall silent, if my monologue stalls, they flutter until the deep brown irises appear and find focus. Her eyes, I'm thinking, are the only part of her unchanged since October, unchanged, in fact, for as long as I can remember. They are watchful, intelligent, and guarded. Tonight they also betray something new: a trace of desperation. Don't leave me, they say.

"I will be here in the morning," I say. "First thing."

She nods, her lids firmly shut.

I wake to a break in the weather, sun through broken clouds, the squawking of birds, and more dislocation—there hasn't been so much as a peep outside my snowy cabin in months—and walk across soft, rain-soaked grass toward the hospital. I sign in at the desk, buy a newspaper, tuck it under one arm, and head up to the fourth floor.

When I enter the room, my mother points to a small alumi-num-foil package on the bed table. In it I find a Q-tip swabbed with Vaseline. She gestures, and I run the swab over her scaly blistered lips thinking: I don't think I'd want to eat either.

"How about Jell-O? Do you want some Jell-O?"

She shakes her head.

"Water?"

She shakes her head again.

"How about you try?"

This is what she used to tell me at gas station restrooms on family road trips. *How about you try?* She takes a small sip from the cup I tip toward her, dribbling ice water down the front of her hospital gown. Then she shuts her eyes and sleeps.

I settle in. Swab? Sip? Sleep. I read the *Los Angeles Times* cover to cover, work most of the crossword. My sister calls me on my mother's cell phone, which she's lent to me and insists that I use. Whassup? she asks. Not much, I say. And that's the truth. If anything, it's an understatement. Eventually I give in and switch channels between the daytime television talk shows:

Oprah, Ellen, Dr. Phil. My mother lifts one eyelid during one of Judge Judy's tirades as if to say: Turn that shit off! And I do. Water? I ask. Swab? No reply.

From this fourth-floor window, I can see past the back lots of the hospital to the 210 freeway, an eight-lane diagonal connector between outlying suburbs: Monrovia, Colton, Rancho Cucamonga. Rain, having started anew, pulses in torrents. Late-morning traffic remains steady, rooster tails spraying behind the tires of one vehicle and onto the next for as far as I can see, into the vast sprawling distance, the Pacific to the west, the Mojave to the east. As a kid in the backseat, I always wondered: Where on earth is everyone going? What's the point?

Finally I give in. I buy myself a large coffee in the lobby, return upstairs to the silent sunless room, and open my book to read, this time about the Kennedys. They are not the stalwart supporters of civil rights you'd want them to be, or at least that my mother would want them to be. Jack Kennedy took office the year she graduated from high school, and he was, for the rest of her life, the standard by which she judged politicians. They never measured up. I went through my own Kennedy infatuation in high school, too, plowing through biographies, relishing in the readerly suspense of the Cuban missile crisis, as if it were a Stephen King novel. I'd read enough as a teenager to know that Jack had refused to send troops to protect the Freedom Riders in 1961 and that Bobby had famously signed off on the FBI wiretaps of Martin Luther King Jr., but my understanding had always been couched in the biographers' admiration of the brothers' political prowess, their expert pawn pushing and power wielding. Reading the story now, from another perspective, it takes on a more troubling sheen. Refuse to send troops? John Lewis and Jim Zwerg get hospitalized with shattered vertebrae. Withhold protection for voting-rights activists in Mississippi? Herbert Lee, a community elder, the father of nine, is shot dead in cold blood for trying to register. The horror stories accumulate in a never-ending procession, like traffic on the 2 10: What's the point? I read a few pages, then rest, like an out-of-shape jogger. I can only take a little at a time. I am bothered more than the history alone demands. After all, the current president is signing off on torture at Abu Ghraib, at Guantanamo, and though I am outraged, I don't usually have to close the newspaper to take a breather. What I feel reading about the Kennedys is something closer to betrayal, something like what I felt reading *The Frisco Kid*. No, no, I keep thinking, can't they behave better than this? Can't they be *perfect*? A psychologist, I'm thinking, would have a field day with me. It's not Jack and Bobby, of course, but my father who I want to be perfect.

Whenever my mother wakes up, I begin to nag: "Do you want to do your leg exercises? No? Let's do them anyway."

Water I no longer ask about. I hold the cup to her lips, and she drinks. After a few more days of practice, I will hardly spill a drop.

In the evening, back in my small rented room, I open a cold can of beans and switch on the TV. I find reruns of *The Simpsons* and highlights from college basketball. Finally, I settle on *Survivor* until I can't take it anymore. They think *that's* survival? I call Lisa and Joey to report on Mom's progress. Very little, I say. I call my old friend Julie in Riverside. If you want me to drive out to City of Hope, she says, I will any time. Okay, I say. Maybe next week. Then I am alone, again, with my books. I stare at them on the bed table. I can't do it. Brave as my dad may have been, he never would have been able to sit all day beside my mother in that dim room. Such patience was never his forte. If I'm not exactly angry at him for not being here, I don't have the energy for it, I'm not exactly thrilled about glorifying his courage either. Not here. Not now. I switch off the light to try in vain to get some sleep. Sometime in the night it occurs to me: the only way my dad could possibly live up to my standards would be to come back to life. And that's not happening. I need to give everyone around here a break, starting with myself.

. . .

The long days are punctuated by visits from nurses and doctors, therapists and aides, a parade of humanity straight from the United Nations. A few are black, a few are white. Most are in between: Hispanic, Filipino, Pakistani, Croatian. The doctors, stereotypically, are young and Asian. Each morning they lead a procession of interns, who stand in a semicircle around my mother's bed, taking notes and muttering scientific mumbo-jumbo like white-coated witches at a séance. My mother, even at her lowest point, has an easy rapport with them: she nods and half-smiles. She thanks them, always, no matter what new variety of discomfort they've dished out: respiratory therapy, physical therapy, reintubation. She is, without fail, gracious and kind. Unless they are taking blood. In which case she screams like a petulant three-year-old. Her veins are stubborn, it's true, mostly used up, and for the chemo, she had a port-a-cath put in her chest, a direct tube to the heart. But occasionally they still need to take a sample from her hand, and all hell breaks loose. I see the needle-expert nurse heading our way with the tourniquet, and I make a bee line for the elevator. I have my limits.

. . .

Outside, in one short week, spring has taken hold. I take a quick lap through the immaculately groomed campus on my way to use one of two public computers in the patient library.

I meander through rose gardens and beneath fleshy, pink-blossomed magnolias, and everywhere I pass memorials, bricks, and plaques: dear mother, beloved son, the twenty-third psalm. They remind me of my dad's grave in Riverside. I've visited it only twice, both times as a teenager out running alone: a flat, black stone sunken in an unwatered lawn across the street from a mental-health group home. *Loving husband and father*, it reads. Not writer. Not civil rights activist. I can't help wondering what my mother's will read: *Loving wife?* That seems too sad; she's been unmarried for nearly thirty years. *Loving mother?* Certainly, but that's not the whole of it. Not by a long shot.

I sit cross-legged in the sun. Patients move slowly along the flower-lined paths; many of them are bald, and they all have cancer, every last one of them: the young mothers, the teenage boys, even the toddlers, so many of them, all the time, that hope, and even compassion, sometimes seem in danger of drying up or callusing over. I remember my parents having a fight one Easter when Dad refused to go to yet another Hollywood Jesus movie. *Why not?* my mother demanded. *I know how it ends*, my father said, shrugging, beer in hand.

. . .

"They invited me to Tallahassee for the fiftieth anniversary celebration in May," I announce one day after she has improved enough for small talk. "You could come with me after you get well."

"That would be so cool," she says.

Cool. It's a word she started using after I left home, by which time she'd become looser and easier, a teacher her students adored: tough but kind, uncompromising but flexible, a natural at meeting people on their own terms. Once when she came to visit me in Oregon, we went to the outdoor hippie market.

After a sandwich with far too many alfalfa sprouts for her taste, she took a cigarette break on a park bench. When a man with a matted beard and a drug-addled expression tottered toward her to ask for a light, I figured she'd recoil. Instead, they sat gabbing for twenty minutes like long-lost pals. My mother, I realized, *was* cool.

When she begins to snore, I dim the overhead lights and move my chair across the linoleum to read in whatever natural light can filter past the hazy L.A. afternoon, past the freeways and the parking lots, through the window into the sterile room.

In Tallahassee, as in the rest of the country, change was slow in coming. Many accounts of the boycott claim that, by May 1958, the month after my dad left town, city buses were completely integrated. That's simply not so. In 1959, a small group of A&M students tried sitting in the front of a few city buses, and though it was still strictly taboo, they had only one incident. But according to *The Pain and the Promise*, white students from FSU went along only as "observers," fearing that interracial seating was too bold a move for Tallahassee to handle. This, two years *after* my dad took his test ride! Blacks could sit up front on buses, if they dared, but they'd better not sit next to whites.

By 1960, the civil rights movement in Tallahassee hit full stride. Shortly after sit-ins in Greensboro, North Carolina, made headlines, a group of A&M students led by two sisters, Patricia and Priscilla Stephens, held a series of sit-ins at the lunch counter at the local Woolworths. They were promptly arrested and taken before Judge Rudd, the same segregationist judge who'd tried my dad.

"You knew that you were not welcome at the Woolworth store under those conditions. You knew that situation would incite trouble. You can mask [it] under the guise of Christianity if you want to, but nowhere in the Bible is there sanction of intimidation."

Judge Rudd continued the rant for a long while, lecturing the young women about the dangers of being unknowingly co-opted by communists, by "organizations that are using you." It was the same cryptic reasoning he'd used two years earlier in suspending the jail sentences of Johnny Herndon and Leonard Speed, but this time he'd face a new challenge. With nine others, including two teenage sons of C. K. Steele, the Stephens sisters marched straight to jail, heads held high, and refused to accept bail. In all, Patricia and Priscilla Stephens spent forty-nine days in jail under heinous conditions. To the adults, even those who supported the protest, this seemed ridiculous. Thurgood Marshall, the great NAACP lawyer and Supreme Court justice, had once famously proclaimed, "For god's sake, if someone can get you out, get out." But that was the logic of the 1950s, and those days were gone. *Jail, no bail*, Patricia Stephens cried. And it worked. What started in Tallahassee became the rallying cry for the brand-new Student Nonviolent Coordinating Committee (SNCC) throughout the South.

In the past, when I read about Patricia Stephens, I felt only shame about my dad accepting bail. He was not as brave as she was, I thought. Now, sitting on a hard chair in a room where my mother is fighting for her life, while in the room next door someone else is fighting for his life, and on the floor above me very small children, hundreds of them, are fighting for their lives, the competition—who is the bravest?—seems silly. Who was brave? Who deserves honor and recognition? They all do. I'm learning. I'm also sitting still so many hours a day that there is no chance to be impatient, no way to ignore the truth that change is not just slow but cumulative, that my dad and the other students who stepped forward in 1957 helped set the stage for what the Stephens sisters and other students did in 1961, just as they helped set the stage for what happened throughout the South, and the nation, later in the 1960s.

. . .

One afternoon Lisa comes to visit after school. She is exhausted, or claims to be, but she is, as usual, full of energy. She paces my mother's room, and fusses about the care she's getting.

"Why's she still on ivs?"

"She's dehydrated. It's just fluid."

"Nuh uh." Lisa charges over to the iv drips and monitors. "That one's an antibiotic. That one's the fluid, and see that yellow bag? That one's food. They're feeding her from the iv. How's she supposed to want to eat when she's got all that crap in her?"

I know it's food. I've been sitting in this room for over a week. But I don't like to argue with doctors. And I like to argue with my sister even less. Still, I know she's absolutely right.

"I'll ask the doctor to take her off it," I say.

She paces around for a few more minutes, but I can tell the boredom is killing her. She fiddles with the tv remote, reads the food menu, and shows Mom some nightgowns she's brought in case she wants to change out of the hospital gown.

"Thank you, honey," Mom says.

I'm sure she will never put one on; she's fine with her hospital gown.

"Let's go get some food or something," she says to me.

She kisses her mother on the forehead, throws her purse over her shoulder, and we are gone. At dinner, we talk over Mom's situation more—there's nothing new to report, really—and mostly Lisa talks about the time tables in the baby books.

"The baby hasn't kicked yet. He should have kicked by now."

"He'll kick when he's ready."

"Yeah, well, I'm gonna make an appointment just in case."

She talks about work, school, home, anything to distract me, and I am thankful.

"Oh yeah," she says as she's leaving. "Laurie sent this."

Laurie and I have been in touch daily via e-mail. I can't imagine why she'd bother with snail mail, so I'm afraid it's bad news. I wait until Lisa has left to tear open the envelope. No bad news! In fact, it's the opposite, a response to one of my handwritten letters, this one from Jon Folsom, one of the white men who rode the bus with my dad. His letter reads:

Your letter found the correct Jon Folsom. It arrived on 2/13 and as I read it those times began unreeling in my memory, as if I were viewing another life—50 years. Difficult to believe.

Normally I am not at a loss for words, but I am having some difficulty arranging my thoughts. To hear of his death is absolutely crushing but hearing from you is exceptionally pleasing and has taken some of the edge off my grief.

We were very close and had a profound affection for each other. It was based on our intellectual disposition and literary interests—we first met in a class on modern literature. But in the most fundamental sense it was our concern for social justice and the absolute conviction that bigotry and discrimination had no place in a civil society. The bus boycott was the starting point; merely a facet of the local civil rights movement.

It was an extremely dangerous and difficult time and a tight bond formed between Joe and myself. As idealists, we felt nothing could have been more gratifying than this just cause. We had no idea it would end in such disillusionment and cynicism—which may be why he never spoke of it.

Disillusionment and cynicism? This is what gnawed at him, the reason he kept silent about Tallahassee? This explanation among the many—fear of my mother's disapproval, grief for Aunt Rose, guilt for having left to follow his writerly dreams, or even plain disregard for the past—feels as right as it is discomfiting. Small fissures begin to reopen in my certainty. The hallway at City of Hope echoes emptily as I dial a number in South Florida. There is no answer, so I leave a message.

I pick up the TV remote, then put it down and pick up my books instead. As the years go by, the stories from the civil rights movement outside of Tallahassee only get worse. In 1963, four little girls died in a church bombing in Birmingham—it was the twentieth bombing in that city in seven years—and Medgar Evers took a bullet in the back from a braggart assassin who shook the governor's hand in the courtroom before getting off, predictably, scot-free. In 1964, Ku Klux Klansmen burned crosses in more than sixty counties, and in early summer in Mississippi three young activists, two of them white, mysteriously disappeared, setting off a full-scale Justice Department investigation that contrasted too starkly with the utter *lack* of justice for blacks in that state, ever.

Then, on Sunday, March 7, 1965—Bloody Sunday—in Selma, Alabama, John Lewis stepped onto Edmund G. Pettus Bridge. When I begin to lose hope, I try, always, to remember John Lewis, my favorite of the huge cast of heroic characters. This quiet Alabama farm-boy-turned-divinity-student joined the Freedom Riders in 1961 when he was nineteen years old, and in the four years since, he had been arrested more than forty times. He'd been elected national director of SNCC, and though he struggled with a speech impediment, he'd spoken at the March on Washington, sharing the stage with Martin Luther King Jr. On Bloody Sunday, he wore a heavy overcoat and carried a knapsack with a toothbrush and a book, necessities for jail, and led six hundred marchers east on I-85 toward Montgomery, the state capital, to demand voting rights. He'd been beaten before, plenty of times, but this time the beating was worse, bloodier, and more vicious. And this time it wasn't dealt by rogue thugs or Klansmen but by Alabama state troopers, themselves, keepers of the peace.

"This is it," John Lewis thought. "This is the end of the road for me. I'm going to die right here on this bridge." He didn't die, and the march was not futile. Within five months, John Lewis stood and watched as President Lyndon Johnson signed the Voting Rights Act into law.

. . .

After I ask, the doctors take my mother off of the IV food. They say they can't tell exactly what is wrong with her, whether it's the aftershocks of the dehydration or invisible cancer cells on the march, whether the damage is permanent or temporary. But as she improves, the doctor wants to discuss the possibility of starting the chemotherapy again. I'm aghast.

"She didn't take the first round all that well," I remind him. "What would be the danger, exactly, of skipping the chemo?"

"Well, that is very hard to say. At stage four, we try to be as aggressive as possible."

"Stage four of what?"

"Cancer. The biopsies we took in October after the surgery showed signs of very advanced cancer."

With that I am on the phone to Lisa.

"Did you know it was stage four? They told me it was preventative. I remember that word: preventative. I would remember words like 'stage four.' Nobody told me 'stage four.'"

Lisa is sitting in front of a classroom of sixth graders listening to me.

"Nope. Nobody told me about it either. You better ask Mom."

The next morning, while spooning her canned peaches, I garner my courage.

"Did the doctors ever tell you how advanced your cancer was?"

"Stage four," she answers with peach juice dribbling down her chin. "The worst it can be."

I wipe her chin with a napkin.

"But they might have gotten it all out when they took the biopsies," she says, her new gravelly voice matter-of-fact as a shrug. "They just don't know."

I stare out at the freeway.

"More peaches please," she says.

. . .

Julie arrives later that afternoon to take me away from City of Hope for the evening. We had planned to head to the ocean, but at rush hour the freeways are too crowded.

"I'm not up for it," I say.

"What do you want to do?" she asks.

"Walk," I say. "Just walk."

So we drive in concentric circles through the subdivisions at the base of the San Gabriels, looking for a way to walk up into them. Finally at the end of a cul de sac, we find a paved trail and follow it up a hillside for a quarter mile until it dead-ends at a flat spot, a house site, future or former. It's hard to tell which. A quiet spot like this, we decide, right on the fringe of the city, is probably a place for dumping dead bodies.

"When my kids ask if we went to the beach, I'll tell them no, Ana Maria wanted to walk on a body dumping road."

"At least they won't be jealous."

We sit on a block of discarded cement and look out at greater

Los Angeles, our feet in weeds, the ocean somewhere beyond
the flat-line horizon, and the mountains at our back.

"How's Laurie?"

"Okay, I guess. She's going to a conference in Utah in a
couple weeks. She wants me to meet her there then fly home
together."

"Are you going to?"

"I don't know. It's nine hours from here by car, and I don't
want to leave, but I don't know what good I'm doing by being
here."

"You saved your mom's life."

"I really didn't."

"You really did."

The sun is setting orange, the breeze cool. Below, a small
dog barks at us through a chain-link fence, but the hill is steep
and a slight wind carries his protective racket away from us.
The distant hum of freeway traffic adds to the city quiet, the
best quiet we could hope for, as the sun sets lower on the horizon, and in the moment that it drops, I see a flash of green.
I'd watched for this green flash on white sand beaches, with
Laurie, with family, as a teenager alone traveling in Mexico. It
never showed. But here on the body dumping road, here with
my oldest friend, a quick flash, unmistakably green, lights the
edge of the horizon, razor-thin neon, and then it is gone.

"Did you see it? Did you see it?" I ask.

"No," Julie says. "This time it was all you."

. . .

After three weeks in the hospital, my mother can stand
unsteadily and guide a walker to the bathroom on her own,
and the doctors are ready to discharge her. I am panicked.

"What is the next step?" I ask.

"Well, you could take her home, but she will require twenty-

four-hour professional care," says the discharge nurse. "You
might consider a skilled nursing facility for a week or so."

"A nursing facility?"

The discharge nurse is only the second white nurse I've seen
at City of Hope in nearly two weeks, and she wears, by far, the
snazziest clothes: a silk shirt and pinched-toe heels. Her nails
are impeccably manicured. Her hair is perfect. She is not only
white, I think, but flamboyantly so, like a real-estate agent.

"Yes. You can choose one in your area or we can recommend
one."

Choose a nursing home? This is the kind of thing someone
twenty years older than I am has to do. I dial my sister's number
on the cell phone and give her the news.

"I'll take care of it," she says, as if choosing a nursing home
is an everyday chore like picking up eggs and milk at Albert-
son's.

"But you have to tell Mom."

"Okay," I say.

I procrastinate for twenty minutes while my mother naps. I
rehearse the words in my mind, slowing them down, keeping
them casual. Finally, I shake her shoulder gently, and take a
deep breath.

"Hey, Mom. The good news is we're going to get you out
of here, but instead of going home right away we might try a
skilled nursing facility."

I needn't have worried. She has apparently overheard everything.

"Yes," she says. "I'll stay for a week; then I can go home."

I want to believe it, I really do. But I am unsure. Part of me
can't help thinking: *I know how it ends.* The best I can do, the
only thing to do, ever, is to be brave enough to cling to hope
in small doses. If I need a role model, I've got my young dad.

If I need a role model, she's looking me in the eye this minute, her eyes watchful and intelligent as ever, tinged this time not with desperation but with a kind of encouragement, a kind of knowing complicity, as if to say: let's just pretend. Or maybe this: let's believe.

CHAPTER ELEVEN

Folsom

The light on the phone machine at my mother's house blinks with rapid-fire insistence. No matter what, I can't ignore it. Someone may have called from the nursing home, Community Care, where things have not been going particularly well. Early this evening, Mom was running a fever, so we were told to pack her up and haul her to the emergency room. But Lisa wouldn't hear of it. She charged into the nurses' station.

"The emergency room? Uh, no. Can't you tell she has an infection? She needs an antibiotic. Now who prescribes those for her? I know it's not her regular doctor. Do you want me to call City of Hope, because I will call them right now, or if you have the doctor here, whatshisname, call it in, I'll drive over to Sav-On this minute and pick it up. I'll pay for it out of my own pocket. See? We'll help, but we're not taking my mother to the emergency room. We're just not going there."

The nurses, who had grown used to my quiet forbearance, the way I sat for hours in the dimly lit room with a big fat book in my lap, were shocked.

"She's a very sick lady," one said.

Lisa gave me that look, her faced screwed tight the way it would when we were little kids sharing a bedroom and I said something stupid, or when an adult said something stupid to both of us and we would say to each other, *No shit, Sherlock.*

"Yes she is," said Lisa, "so please help us get her some medicine."

They did. The antibiotics arrived, the fever dropped, my

mother slept—no trip to the emergency room!—and the nurses took down both our numbers and promised to call if anything changed.

Now I'm alone at her house. The yippy dog next door barks at the redwood fence. A train whistle howls over traffic in the distance. A week's worth of breakfast dishes sit dirty in the sink. I'm in no mood for phone talk, but I press the button anyway to play the messages back.

"Ana Maria?"

As soon as I hear the stranger's voice say my name, I know who it is. I grab a notebook and sit facing the boxy white screen of my mother's computer, my head throbbing, and dial the number in South Florida, hoping for a short, cordial interview. It will be nothing of the sort.

The phone rings, and Jon Folsom answers.

"Ana Maria, tell me, how are you? How is your mother?"

"She is hanging in there," I say. I have told him about her illness in phone messages and in two recent letters. "How are you?"

"I am well. I really am."

His voice is soft and Southern, slow and urgent, musical like a receding ocean wave, sand and pebbles skittering as the water retreats, then swooshing forward again as he begins to tell me his own version of the test ride story in vivid detail, a version radically different from either Johnny Herndon's or the history books'.

For starters, he insists that there was only one bus.

"Not two?" I ask. "Some books say there were two."

I am bolder already with Jon Folsom than with Johnny Herndon, less afraid of offending him, perhaps because of his regular correspondence—he has already sent two more letters of reminiscences—or his close friendship with my dad. Or maybe it's because of the soothing James Taylor cadence of his voice. Probably it's because he's white. I don't want to think about that. Not six months into this project, I'm already weary of having to think, always, in terms of race. I feel a wave of familiar shame: if I were black, of course, I'd have no choice but to think about it.

"Oh, there was just one bus. Definitely just one."

"Here's the thing," he says. "Usually all the black folks waited 'til all the whites got on, but we decided to stagger it, a black guy, a white guy, a black guy, and so on. I'm at the end of the line and decide to jerk the guy around a little. I give him two dollars and he gives me a hard look. 'Where's my change?' I say. Now the driver looked about like Don Knotts, and he was not a very bright guy. He had a little time to think about it once we took our seats and he got mad and hollered, 'You buncha nigger lovers get in the back of the bus.' I mean he just completely came undone."

Jon chuckles at the memory, and his voice grows animated.

"Well, we did nothing of the sort. Harold, Jimmy, and I went to the back and sat in a row. Then Joe and Lenny and—what's the other fellow's name? Johnny, Johnny Herndon—they sat together up front."

This split-second decision explains the division that would last for fifty years. Because Joe Spagna, Leonard (Lenny) Speed, and Johnny Herndon—one white man and two black—sat together up *front* in the white section of the bus, they would go to court, get their pictures and names in the newspaper, and end up in the history books. Because Jon Folsom, James (Jimmy) Kennedy, and Harold Owens—two whites and a black—sat together in the *back* of the bus, the black section, they became "material witnesses," sidekicks, footnotes. Their act took just as much courage as my dad's—they were *with* my dad—and it was still technically illegal, but because it presented less of a challenge to the white upper caste, it slipped through the fickle cracks of history.

"Was the bus crowded?"

"Crowded? Oh god, no. It was empty. They were all empty because folks were too scared to ride them. It was a very dangerous time, and that's why that driver, well, he just lost it."

"I see."

"So listen, we hadn't even taken our seats when that crazy driver took straight off, speeding, running traffic lights. I thought he was gonna wreck the damned bus. I mean I thought: we're never gonna live to be arrested."

I am glad to have been to Tallahassee because I can picture the scene: the bus careening north on Monroe Street, past the state capitol building, the flag waving on the rotunda, across the downtown cross streets, past brick front buildings and round-hooded fifties sedans parked by the curbsides and occasionally, surely, past a gawking bystander.

"It was a Saturday, so there wasn't much traffic, but this joker was rocking up on two wheels around the turns. He had the thing swaying back and forth. I just kept thinking: I hope he doesn't wreck the bus."

His version, I'm thinking, would make a helluva movie. I know I'm supposed to take his story seriously, but there's comedy in it, in the telling of it, and I find myself grinning, hearing the *Easy Rider* soundtrack play in my head, as Jon Folsom continues the tale.

The bus careened around one corner and then the next, and the six passengers grasped for handholds, unsure where they were headed or what might come next. Finally, it screeched to a stop in front of the police station.

"The driver just literally dove out the door, and the cops jumped on. 'Ya'll boys is under arrest,' they hollered."

"Were they cordial?" I ask.

"They weren't so much cordial as perplexed. This whole situation, well, it had totally gotten away from them. They didn't want to make an issue of it because the city council didn't want to change the law."

They were locked up in cells, integrated but separated: Herndon, Speed, Spagna in one cell, Folsom, Kennedy, and Owens in the other. Already the haphazard choice about whom history would forget was being made. Even Johnny Herndon didn't remember Jon Folsom. Or maybe there's a reason Johnny Herndon didn't want to remember him.

"I was a real smart ass," Jon Folsom says. "I started running my mouth at that police station, but I told myself I really better shut up. I mean, hit a cop, you're looking at a year."

He is clear on this point, that at times in Tallahassee he was sorely tempted to be violent. It was because of Korea, he explains. He was a vet, just out of the psych ward at Walter Reed, attending FSU on the G.I. Bill like my dad. But unlike my dad, Jon Folsom had seen actual combat, and those memories haunted him.

"We all agreed to maintain nonviolence, and it was a highly personal thing for me. I had fought in the Korean War and I had to fight in retreat in '50 and '51. I spent almost a year in a hospital."

When the conversation drifts back to Korea, Jon's voice grows softer—sometimes he is difficult to hear—and more desperate because, like Johnny Herndon, Jon Folsom has a message, something he wants me to understand.

"You see, Ana Maria, it isn't the fear. Anyone can be courageous. You see that on the battlefield all the time. You've either got it or you don't. Like reflexes. I saw guys lose it you'd never in a million years think would lose it. But the horror. It's the horror that stays with you, the things you see. My mother, she didn't even recognize me when I came home."

He is silent, breathing fast. Through the curtains I can see only the yellow glow of the streetlights on Burnside Court.

For a moment, I wonder if I have made a mistake making contact with someone who is, perhaps, unstable.

"See your father. . . ." He clears his throat. "Joe really kept me from coming undone because I was . . . I used to have to go to the hospital. He just made a critical difference."

He is quiet now, composing himself.

"I was just a little bit suicidal."

Within moments, he returns to the Tallahassee story. But the bravado, for now, is gone.

"That bus ride didn't amount to much. I was of the opinion we should not let up for a minute. We should call a general strike. Blacks drove the garbage trucks. They were the nannies, the maids, the laborers. The city would just stop cold. How could we lose? But it got contentious between me and the black leaders. The only support I got was from Joe. The challenge wasn't just to segregation, but a way of life. This, what we wanted, would require a complete change of attitude. Nobody found that the least bit agreeable."

"What about Johnny Herndon and Leonard Speed? Didn't they agree with you?"

"Lenny was a funny guy. He really didn't want anything to do with white guys."

I recall how hopeful I'd been in Tallahassee about meeting Leonard Speed. How would it have turned out if we had met?

"His dad, Dan, now he was the most loveable guy you'd ever know, give you a bear hug every time he saw you. I still have a fondness for that man. . . . But, see, your dad and I, we thought we were in a fight we could win."

"And you didn't win?"

"No," he says, "we didn't. Did you get the article I sent you about Andrew Young?"

A newspaper clipping he'd enclosed with a letter announced the former civil rights activist's new position as the public-relations spokesperson for Wal-Mart. Jon Folsom presumes this piece of evidence can stand alone in explaining to me his own disillusionment with the current state of the nation. And he's right.

"Yes," I say. "I did."

From here, he drifts into warm memories of their friendship. He calls my dad Giuseppe. Giuseppe loved good pasta, and Jon fixed a mean fettuccine. Giuseppe loved to discuss books, and Jon did, too. They shared an apartment with wisteria vines braiding over the balcony, and they'd stay up night after night talking.

"I don't think we slept more than two hours a night for two years."

I'm not sure what to make of that. Best, I think, to ignore it for now.

"What did you guys read?"

He snorts. "What *didn't* we read? The classics. The contemporary stuff. I mean I thought I'd lose my eyesight. You didn't dare blink. We went to the library for lit journals—Joe was just extremely literary—he wrote to Ferlinghetti for a copy of *Howl* and when he read it, he just brought the house down."

The night is getting late. I hear calls clicking in, but the calls will have to wait.

"We were in an American and British literature class, and I happened to sit next to him. One day the prof, who was a snob, a buffoon, said something about T. S. Eliot, and Joe stood and talked extemporaneously about how to read poetry, on "Prufrock" mostly. There wasn't a sound in the room," he says. "I mean you could hear a pin drop. The class was spellbound.

When he was done, everyone applauded. I told him to write it down, the whole speech, but I don't think he ever did."

I lean in toward the computer screen, shifting for comfort. Because I have no telephone, my mother has had to adopt e-mail. She, who changed banks rather than use an ATM card, who only recently splurged on an automatic transmission, forks out fifty bucks a month for DSL. The computer sits in exactly the same place where the color TV sat on the last night I sat with my dad watching. Now the TV is in the living room, and the plaid couch we shared, the one Mom reupholstered in a night class, is long gone.

"What about his family? Did he ever say anything about his family?"

"He never mentioned his mother, not even once. He mentioned his father but nothing of consequence. Joe favored the story 'Christ in Concrete.' Do you know it?"

"I don't."

"It's about an Italian immigrant family and a building that collapses, and it seems like Joe's father was a steel worker or something in New Jersey."

"He was an engineer in Philadelphia."

"That sounds right. Well, Joe didn't like to talk about it. But he could recite Dylan Thomas's 'Do Not Go Gentle Into That Good Night.' Do you know that poem?"

"Yeah, I do."

I know the poem well. I remember the first time I read it distinctly, in a literature textbook in a high school classroom before the bell for class rang:

And you, my father, there on the sad height,
Curse, bless, me now with your fierce tears, I pray.
Do not go gentle into that good night.
Rage, rage against the dying of the light

I read the poem under the classroom lights, and I began to shake. All fine sentiments, I thought at age sixteen, for someone whose dying father was still around, but mine was gone, and he hadn't bothered to fight, he'd preferred to run. The only rage left was my own.

"Sometimes I thought that's why Joe couldn't get it together to write. I always tried to get him to, you know, but he'd always say 'I'll get around to it.' It had to do with his father. There was something unrequited there."

I think of my younger self in the too-small desk shuddering hard from a feeling she couldn't precisely define. Unrequited is as good a word for it as any.

"What about his aunt? Did he ever mention his aunt?"

"Not often."

They hitchhiked together to St. Petersburg from Tallahassee a couple of times, Jon Folsom and my dad.

"I asked him, 'Aren't you going to visit your aunt?' I mean, it would've been nice to taste a little of that Italian home-cooking."

But my father wouldn't go for it. They slept on a beach instead.

"The family thing," Jon says gently. "It just didn't work out for him."

I had already known this, had known my whole life, but it was still hard to hear it.

Call waiting clicks in again, repeatedly. We've been on the phone for well over an hour. Now might be a good time to say goodbye. It could, after all, be the nursing home calling. But there is no stopping Jon now. He is spinning from Korea to T. S. Eliot to St. Petersburg and back again.

"Shot my car to pieces."

"What? Who?" My mind had drifted, and I had missed something critical.

"Things had gotten stinky in Tallahassee, and see, those crackers had a special feeling for me because I was a Southern boy. I grew up in Florida."

"So they shot your car?"

"They shot it to bits, a couple dozen times, but it didn't do that much. I bought some seat covers, and it still ran, so I drove it around town that way."

"Well, that took guts."

"It beat walking," he says. "One cop used to hassle me. He stopped me in that car. 'What do we have here?' he says." Here Jon takes on a heavier accent, overdrawn. "I says, 'even a hick cracker like you know what a bullet hole looks like.' That cop got a little panicky. He cursed me, called me a nigger lovin' son of a. . . . Those cops, you know, they were a little dumb but not exactly vicious. Nothing you could do about that."

His voice shushes now like river water over gravel, silty and steady, unstoppable, like a criminal confessing to a stranger, or sometimes like a small boy who has gotten away with mischief. But it turns out his story amounts to something far more serious than mischief.

"After that, I told Joe: I'm going to move down to Blacktown for a while. I moved across the tracks, and I told him not to come. And those cops they'd come by and curse me.'"

He rants about Medgar Evers, about Emmett Till, about Korea. He confuses eras, but the thread is the same: violence, retaliation.

"It was in the war I realized this. A sniper took a long shot at me, see. . . ."

I'm having trouble making connections. I'm gazing at the dry-erase board I bought for my mother to keep track of appointments, which doctor is for what, which friends are available to drive where and when, but I can't keep track of Jon's story. I want to. But I am so very tired. Try, I tell myself. Try.

"I borrowed Joe's car, an old Studebaker. I'd decided, see, I wasn't for all this. I drove to Jacksonville and bought a sawed-off shotgun and birdshot. I went into a wooded area in Blacktown and stayed there. I knew they would come for me, and on the second or third night, they did. They came by in a stake-bed truck, you know what a stake truck is?"

"Sure."

"There were a bunch of white guys in the back of this stake-bed truck, come looking for me. I opened fire and shot out the tires, blew out the window to the cab. The shootout lasted maybe three minutes, tops, forty rounds. They knew who did it, of course, so I had to leave. It was over for me."

He left then, driving south, away from Tallahassee for good. As he traveled the road, through the straight pines, he got to the bridge over the Suwannee River. An engraved sign, green and coppery, marked the spot with the words to Stephen Foster's "Old Folks at Home," the state song of Florida: *Way down upon the Swanee River, far far away.*

This, Jon thought, was as good a place as any. He opened the door to the back seat of the shot-up car, pulled out the sawed-off shotgun, and stood alone on the bridge, watching the river flow wide and green among the live oaks. Then he tossed the shotgun over the rail and into the water.

"I left it all behind," he says. "I went home."

"I understand," I say.

The conversation stalls. I can hear a distant siren. It's hard, despite my admiration for the steadfast nonviolent Freedom Riders, for Rosa Parks and C. K. Steele and John Lewis, not to admire Jon Folsom, too. Maybe the stand he took wasn't morally pure or strategically effective, but it was honest and human and moving as hell. And who knows? Maybe his actions scared the thugs away from my father. Or maybe they emboldened them to do worse deeds.

144

"I hated to leave your dad behind. I really did. I didn't feel he was safe."

He went home to Miami, and in the summer of 1957, he says, my dad followed him. Together they hung out on the beach watching girls. "Fanny gawking," he calls it.

"I had a certain charm, but Joe had an attraction that females really liked."

Here, I think, is a good place for me to cut in, to tell him I have to go, that I am afraid the nursing home may be trying to call with news about my mother. He is kind and asks after her. I ask if I can call him back, and he agrees, but he is stalling, though we have been on the phone for three hours.

"I wanted to talk to you about your book. We didn't get a chance to talk about your book."

I had sent him a copy with one of my letters.

"I have to tell you: your thought patterns and mannerisms are his exactly. It is nearly spooky. And you see, he had a real feel for good writing and the confidence to express it. Well, I want you to know, he would be delighted."

I hang up, switch on the television to college basketball, and open a beer. I am trying not to think—just watch the game, I tell myself—but the thoughts come swarming uninvited. I wonder why memory, like hope and health and so many things in the past few months, has turned out to be so very unreliable. Who's right? The scholars of history who sometimes spell my father's name with a *t*—Stagna—and occasionally identify him as a black man? Or one of the two eyewitnesses, one black and one white, whose stories are wildly different? I take a swallow of beer and stare at the television and think about the too-simplistic way I used to understand history: that right prevailed, usually, after a struggle, that if a case went to the Supreme Court and the law was obviously ridiculous, as was Ordinance 741, laws changed. I hadn't thought about case after case butting up against the bench, like wannabe ball players dreaming of the NBA. It's not the ones who have the most natural talent who make it, but the ones with the best connections, or the right timing, or plain dumb luck.

I drift in and out of sleep thinking about sitting by my mother's bedside, struggling daily, sometimes hourly, with my small act of selfless forbearance, and I wonder which I would have chosen back in the day: nonviolent resistance or self-preservation. Finally, I fall asleep on the couch with the television on and the lyrics running through my mind the way I remember them from grade school: *Way down upon the Swanee River, far far away, that's where my heart is ever turning, down near the old folks' home. . . . All my life is sad and dreary everywhere I roam.* In Riverside, there were nursing homes on plenty of corners, and that *was* where we were always turning, and they *did* seem sad and dreary. Later I'll learn that the song was long interpreted as slaves longing to be back on the plantation, that the original lyrics call them "darkeys," and that civil rights activists detested the song, detest it still. For now, on the couch in the living room, images of a lush green river alternate with visions of my mother at the old folks' home, until the phone rings again and startles me awake long after midnight.

I race to pick it up.

"Are you the skinny one with the book?"

"Pardon me?"

"This is Alice over at Community Care."

Now I get it. Even on the telephone, the nurses are afraid to talk to Lisa.

"Yes. I'm the one with the book."

"Okay. Your mom, she's fine now. No fever."

"Thanks so much," I say. "Thank you for letting me know."

CHAPTER TWELVE

Community Care

I'm running at dawn as daylight floods the wide streets of my hometown. I pass the retirement apartments under construction in the vacant field where we rode bikes as kids and the senior center where my mother had taken to playing bridge before she got sick. I am losing myself in a decadent trance, breathing air steeped in eucalyptus and diesel, watching shadows of palm trees flutter over sidewalk cracks, when the cell phone in my shorts pocket rings. I answer, breathing heavy, afraid that something has gone wrong again at Community Care.

My sister is taken aback.

"What are you doing?"

"I'm on a run."

"You're carrying a cell phone while you run?"

"Yeah."

"That's messed up."

I laugh thinking about the file folder stuffed full of letters I wrote to elected officials last year in opposition to telephones in the small mountain town. Now I'm running with a cell phone in my pocket in Greater Los Angeles. Times change.

"What's up?"

"Nothing," Lisa says, and goes on to tell me in detail her plan for the day, how the traffic is moving on the 91, what the students in her class will be doing, when she might stop at the nursing home, while I stand on Central Avenue catching my breath.

"Also, the baby still hasn't kicked."

"What did the doctor say?"

"He said he'll kick when he's ready."

"I told you so."

I am feeling good, so I decide to run farther than I had planned. I run past the spot where my dad fell, and farther west toward a neighborhood frequented by gangbangers, onto hard-packed dirt littered with broken glass, then looping back, past my nursery school, my elementary school, the paint-faded MacDonald's where Mom took us as a reward for good report cards, and finally, by the huge Sears parking lot, walled by cinder blocks, where she taught me to drive a clutch, gritting her teeth, grasping for the dash, laughing, sometimes, aloud, as we crept around the lot in the Datsun, bucking and lurching, stalling out.

The phone rings. It's Lisa again.

"One more thing," she says, "I think you should think about going home. Laurie misses you and there's nothing. . . ."

"I've got to go," I say.

Within an hour, I'm sitting beside my mother watching highlights from March Madness on a wall-mounted TV when suddenly she vomits. This is not the first time she's vomited at Community Care, not by a long shot, but it's the first time she's done it while waiting in line for physical therapy. I grab a towel and wipe her face, her lap, her wheelchair, and I release the chair brakes to wheel her back to her room.

"No," she says. "I want to walk."

"Are you sure?"

She nods, her head bowed, her hands shaking on the blanket in her lap.

I know what she's thinking: therapy is the road to recovery. Blue Cross will pay as long as there are measurable gains being made, and the measurable gains mostly consist of walking. When the time comes, she stands on wobbly legs and she leans heavily on two therapy aids, big guys, former high-school athletes. She makes it twenty-five feet before she collapses.

Back in her room, the phone rings, and I answer.

"How far did she walk?" Joey asks.

"Not real far."

"I'm thinking of coming down next week to take over from you for awhile. It will be spring break. And you really ought to get home."

"Listen," I say. "I gotta go. Can you call back later?"

I feed my mother ice chips, and talk to her softly, and when finally she sleeps, I stare out double glass doors at a cinder-block wall. I wonder how long I could stay in a room with such a view, no view really, not a single tree in sight. Not long. My mother, for her part, claims not to care. She prefers almost anything to being outdoors: playing solitaire with a deck of cards, or Tetris on the computer, or competing with the dimwits on *Wheel of Fortune*. When we were kids, the family took long road trips and frequented national parks, where we read placards and snapped photos, but we never camped. Not once. We always landed back at a cheap air-conditioned motel where the swimming pool was all the nature any of us cared much about. How I ended up as Nature Girl, my mother always marvels, she'll never know. She says it, usually, with an admiring shake of the head. I stare out at the cinder blocks. This stint, I realize, is the longest I've been away from big trees in nearly twenty years.

In the afternoon, there's another battle for antibiotics, and then another one over the procedures for irrigating her new bladder. The battles come in waves. They come more often at Community Care than at City of Hope, and they are louder. Tension is building. She has been here a week, and progress has been negligible. In the hallway, waiting for the second walking session of the day, I sit beside my mother on a small stool. The place is noisy, conversations like the kind you overhear at a beauty salon: television politics and physical ailments, double coupons and grandchildren. My mother is silent and seemingly content, but she is shaking like an aspen tree in the wind.

An administrator storms up. I'd met her when we checked Mom in. She had seemed at first intensely earnest, overwhelmingly so. "Your mother," she'd said, one hand on my shoulder "is a very special lady." Now her concern has morphed into something new and sinister. She drags me by one arm into her office.

"I hadn't noticed the tremor before. That is quite dramatic."

"She's sick today," I say.

"She's sick quite often. Do you know why?"

"No, I don't. Do you?"

"Have you spoken with her oncologist?"

She waltzes around the subject with leading questions, exaggerated patience, and a pseudo-Socratic method that grates on my nerves. I know where this is headed. She believes it's no longer the after-effects of chemotherapy but cancer encroaching that is making my mother so sick. As if I haven't thought of that already.

"You need to call her doctor," she says. "And we need to have a meeting, with your sister. Right here. At three o'clock."

At three, we sit in gaudily upholstered chairs listening as the administrator outlines the future: hospice, home nurse, pain control. She clearly supports the position that I would have taken a few months ago: get Mom off all drugs, take her home, let her die in peace.

"It would be best," the administrator says, "if someone in the family could take her in."

Lisa lives in town, but since she is newly pregnant, she's not the one. Joey's not here, and his wife, we've learned, is now pregnant with their second child. So it's not him either.

The administrator stares at me, big-eyed and expectant. I tell myself to grow up. I tell myself: this is it, the story isn't about being courageous, it's about doing the right thing. I am already designing a cabin addition and a wheelchair ramp in my mind when my sister jumps in.

"My sister lives way out in the boonies. My mom doesn't want to live that way. You can just forget about it."

Lisa's voice is loud, and people are taking notice, and normally I'd be embarrassed. Instead, I am flooded with relief and more than a little pride. Visitors carrying vases of flowers bow their heads and quicken their pace. Secretaries turn to face cubicle walls. Only the residents stare unabashedly, glad for a little entertainment. I sit back and wait while the administrator retreats into medical speak and insurance jargon to make her point. The gist of it is this: if we can get a terminal diagnosis, we're good to go. Everything will be covered. If not, all costs will soon be out-of-pocket.

"My mother is not dying." Lisa screeches, her indignation reaching a fevered pitch. "How do you know she's dying? You're no doctor. You have no right to speak to us this way. Come on Ana Maria. Let's get out of here."

. . .

At home I call Jon Folsom again. Compared to everyday life in Riverside, there's restfulness in the way the conversation meanders and the stories pour out, alternately filling in gaps in the history and prying open new ones.

"Did you testify before the Johns Committee?" I ask.

He did, he says, but not because of the bus situation. He had published some articles in a small student paper in Tallahassee that captured the senators' attention.

"I was fundamentally a Marxist," he says.

Maybe so, but he was also a twenty-five-year-old college

student and war veteran. He presented no grave security threat to the state of Florida.

"All the black folks came out for the hearings," he says, "and they were eating peanuts and drinking Coca Cola. I tried not to sound like a smart aleck, but I'm afraid I didn't succeed. It was a regular circus."

This is not the picture I'd had of the hearings, but it might make more sense. Maybe my dad's *yips* and *nopes* were neither laziness nor insolence but a little smart-alecky showmanship.

"After that I sat on the beach for a while. Then I went to Cuba and stayed almost a year, built a school in San Fuegos. The FBI never stopped looking at me."

I've written to the FBI, sending along a photocopy of my father's death certificate, and requesting his file under the Freedom of Information Act, and they've put me off for three months. I had begun to think that maybe he didn't even have a file, but talking to Jon Folsom makes me wonder anew. I make a mental note to pester the justice department in the morning.

"But it was troubling me that I had left my country. I really wanted to be involved in something like this in my own country."

"And you thought civil rights might be it?"

"I did. But then it ended."

His disappointment sounds like lostness, as if his bread crumb trail back home had petered out. He brings up Martin Luther King Jr., calling him one of the "top five Americans of all time." He tells me, not for the first time, how he shook King's hand once. He tells me how he never imagined, ever, how it all would end, and my teeth clench.

Why do these discussions always end in past tense? Aren't there still battles to wage? What about gay rights anyway? What about immigrant rights? Did the possibility of challeng-

ing injustice die with one man? King's assassination has been
a given my whole life. I was not yet one year old when he was
killed in Memphis. It's the mainstay of the story of civil rights,
the denouement, like Lincoln's assassination and the Civil War,
like any half-decent Shakespearean tragedy. *I know how it ends.*
Without that kind of History Channel hindsight, I suppose, the
assassination becomes something utterly unforeseen, something
you never get over, something like my father's death was for
me.

Jon Folsom tells me he organized some lifeguards on the
beach into a makeshift labor union.

"So they sacked me," he says.

He sold some photographs and paintings, he wrote an art
column for a newspaper in St. Petersburg for a few years.
Finally, a friend who was the head of the pipefitters local got
him a job, and he traveled all over the country in a job he kept
until retirement. I do not typically think of beatniks and Marxist
agitators settling into the blue-collar mainstream. I can't for
the life of me picture Maynard G. Krebs or Clayton Barbeau
as, say, a machinist.

"Were you involved with the union?"

"The labor movement is about like organized crime," the
old Marxist says. "But pipefitters are good straight-laced, hard-
working people."

I like Jon Folsom better all the time.

During the day, I try to tell my mother about Jon Folsom,
but her mind is elsewhere. Even when there is not a physical
therapy session or a phone call or an emergency, life at Community Care is busy. It's easier for my mother's friends to visit
now that she is closer to home, and they arrive in droves.
There's a retired doctor who provides acupuncture at a free
clinic, a middle-school teacher who commutes to inner-city
Los Angeles, and a prison chaplain who has, for years now,

ministered to Charles Manson. No one else, apparently, would do it. One close friend of my mother, a former nun, now works part-time as a New Age healer. Before Mom's surgery, she performed a series of healings, including blowing a didgeridoo over her abdomen. The world has changed in the last thirty years as much as it ever did, and these stalwart boomers shrug and go about their good deeds.

Many of Mom's visitors were members of the community at Our Lady when I was a kid and Father De was there. Father De himself left the parish years ago to become a counselor for AIDS patients. These days he's living in another nursing facility across town, battling late-stage diabetes. He calls regularly, and his conversations with my mother sound like old war buddies commiserating.

"Father De says we're the elders now, but the young people don't listen to us," she tells me after one call. Her voice is still gravelly, but her mind seems sharper than it was a week ago.

"I listen to you."

"You're not so young," she says.

I laugh. She's sharp all right.

A few years ago, we threw Mom a birthday party and I stood among these good people and felt humbled to admit that the best I could do for this troubled world was hide in the woods, doing as little harm as possible. At the party, Father De sat in the center of the room, stooped over a cane. I hadn't seen him in twenty years, but he seemed to remember me, as my mother's daughter at least, as part of the fold. I tried, but failed, to think of something appropriate to say. I held his hand tightly for a moment, and then he pulled me close to peck my cheek.

"You're a good girl," he said.

I didn't believe him.

At Community Care, I am beginning to. I am telling myself that there's legacy in the family of doing the right thing, and that for the moment at least, staying at my mother's side is it. At night, an e-mail from Laurie awaits, asking if I'll be able to meet her at the conference in Utah. There's another from Julie offering to take a couple of days off of work to drive me there. I know I need to reply. Instead, I pull out my notebook and call Jon Folsom again.

After the skirmish with the stake truck thugs, and before emigrating to Cuba, Jon had moved home to Miami, and my dad had moved with him for the summer. It was between terms. The case was making its way through the courts, and my dad had another year to go at school to get his English degree. Jon got a job as a lifeguard, and he says my dad was driving a Canada Dry beverage truck, hard physical labor in the humid Florida summer.

"I didn't know how he was doing it. He never seemed tired. So one day he tells me 'I hired a black helper.' I said, 'You did what?' See, I was interested in Marxism, and the theories, and here he is hiring a black guy to do the heavy lifting. 'Hey,' Joe told me 'he's making first-class wages.'"

I consider again how my dad melded philosophy with practicality in ways that, from fifty years on, seem contradictory.

Jon says they went fishing and mostly chased girls.

"The funny thing was that Joe was not that sociable, but when he had to be, if he cared to, he could turn on the charm."

"He just had a way with the women. I mean, Ana Maria, I'm going to tell you some things about your dad, and you're going to have to sort them out. I don't mean to offend you."

"It's okay," I say. "I'm a grown-up. You can go ahead."

"Well, he had this girlfriend in Tallahassee who was a knock-out. I told him, 'You have to promise me you won't drool on her.' You just would not believe how beautiful she was."

They'd driven south to Sopchoppy, a small rural town in the

woods southwest of town where they entered a black church for a mass meeting of some sort. I could picture the church from my trip to Apalachicola in January: the white clapboard, the dirt lot, the marquee in front. The music, the spirit, he explained, was overwhelming, and he and my dad were welcomed into the fold, and the preacher's daughter's name was Honey.

"Giuseppe went right up and started talking to her, and next thing you know, there was a whole lot of driving to Sopchoppy going on. Sometimes he'd sneak her out of the house down there and drive her up to our pad. I'll tell you sometimes I could hear banging on the walls. I admire that kind of passion."

Maybe I do too, but it's hard to hear it about your own father.

"I told him, 'Giuseppe, you're going to get yourself killed. That girl's father is going to come for you, and he's a preacher. He's got friends up here, people you don't want to get into it with.'"

I'm still not getting it.

"You mean Honey was black?"

"Why, yes, of course. Her skin was honey-colored, Ana Maria. And her father, well, he certainly did not approve. And he was, of course, not the only one."

I'm stunned. What if my father's bravest step toward integration wasn't sitting on a bus but this passionate affair with a honey-skinned preacher's daughter from Sopchoppy? God knows it was more dangerous than sitting on the bus had been. Not as dangerous as a black man sleeping with a white girl, but then, that depends on the girl's father. And it sounds like this girl's father would have been plenty mad.

"Was that why my dad had to leave Tallahassee in such a hurry? Not because of the court case but because of Honey?"

"I don't know. It could have been."

How could I follow this thread? The histories would be no

help, and anyway, I wasn't sure I wanted to know about it. The affair clearly endeared my father to Jon Folsom, this kind, sad, intelligent man, but it bothered me. I hadn't been freaked out by the letter telling Johnny Herndon to go back to Africa or by the fact that Jon Folsom opened shotgun fire on a bunch of hooligans, but learning the details of my dead dad's sex life? I don't want to stretch my imagination to relive this particular chapter. I want to let my father have his own story, separate from mine, full of secrets he surely never meant to share. I just want to let him go.

. . .

"He can't say if it's cancer or what," Lisa tells me later in the evening after the oncologist returns her call. "But he's still thinking about more chemotherapy. It'll be an easier program, he says, two drugs instead of four."

I'm silent.

"We don't have to decide now. It's just, if she gets better enough, she should try it," Lisa says. "She can keep living at Community Care while she gets the treatments if we pay for it."

"Okay. Yeah." I stare at the e-mail queue on the screen in front of me. There are twenty-five messages from Laurie on this screen alone. "Joey's coming down this weekend, and I think I'm going to go ahead and go."

"That's a good idea," Lisa says.

CHAPTER THIRTEEN

A Real Difference

Snow has drifted down to the foothills, and the Southern California sky has lightened to a thin translucent blue, like a screen fading slowly to white, as Julie drives me up over the San Bernardino Mountains toward the desert and the empty spaces beyond. Before I made enough money to fly, I drove out of this valley annually with the stereo blaring, and the journey never failed to feel, somehow, like victory, like landing in the soft mattress on the far side of my backyard high-jump pit and glancing up to see if the bar quivered. Sometimes you didn't know if you'd cleared the bar until you landed.

My mother had been sitting upright and alert when I arrived early this morning to say goodbye. I'd be headed to Utah for a week, she knew, and then if things remained stable here, unchanged, I'd fly home to Washington with Laurie. Mom didn't want me to go. She was putting on a show of strength that she wasn't quite up to, I knew, but I appreciated it.

"Maybe," she said. "I can still go to Tallahassee with you."

"I hope so," I said.

I ran my hand over her soft white skiff of hair and kissed her on the forehead.

"Love you," I said.

"Love you, too."

And then I left.

Now Julie and I pass the time with small talk, gossip about high school acquaintances and siblings, opinions about politics, books, movies—anything, anything but cancer—as we creep between two camel humps of snow and descend to flatness. Somewhere past Barstow, where the interstate straightens to bisect the sand, I give in to silence. Once on a family road trip across the desert, I'd lain in the way-back of the station wagon staring at the sky and noticed a small bi-plane following directly above and behind us. When I pointed it out, my dad slammed on the brakes, and at the next rest stop he handed me a ten dollar bill—the most money I'd ever held in my life—for saving him the speeding ticket he surely would have gotten from the highway patrol in the air.

We cross the Mojave and climb into the Virgin River canyon, where snow on the canyon tops draws streaks on the horizon, separating blue from red, and the expanse feels like hope, like a tow line on my chest. We watch for bighorn sheep on the road, but there are none. We listen to John Denver on the iPod until it peters out. John Denver, apparently, is not meant to be. Not today.

I tell Julie about Jon Folsom.

"They were really close friends," I say. "Maybe they were lovers. Who knows? There's a chance at least."

"What makes you think so?"

"He said that when they lived together they didn't get more than two hours sleep in two years."

"Not exactly conclusive evidence."

"He says I'm a lot like my dad."

"Are you? I never knew him. We met right after he died, or when he was sick, maybe."

"I don't know. I didn't used to think so. He was outgoing and opinionated and there were all these people at his funeral, like at a rock star's, but now I'm not so sure."

I tell her about two photographs of my dad I discovered long after I left home. I'd swiped them from my mother's house and saved them in a beat-up envelope. One was of him outside the cabin on Muir Beach with building tools in his hands. I'd known about the cabin before, but I hadn't necessarily thought that he'd *built* it. The other was of him mountain climbing in old-timey gear, like Edmund Hillary. I had never imagined that he'd cared about mountains. The mountains were my realm. The photos, once I found them, were blurry reminders that I owed at least part of my nature to him.

"Why was that a surprise?"

"I don't know. Maybe because I worked so hard to leave home and become something all my own, something completely different from my parents, you know."

"And he didn't?"

"Good point."

We drive in silence again, and tiny flecks of snow begin to gather, windblown on the road shoulder.

"It's snowing. What should I do? I've never driven in the snow."

"Well, it doesn't matter much, as long as you're going reasonably slow."

I glance at the speedometer, and I start to laugh. She's going nearly 100.

"I guess you might slow down."

Just before dark we arrive outside Capitol Reef National Park. I leave the car door ajar to take two steps at a time up to the second-floor motel room where Laurie awaits. She swings the door wide, and we hug.

"How's your mom?" she asks.

"She's hanging in there."

"And you? Are you doing okay?"

"I'm doing better this minute."

The three of us share a wildly celebratory finger-food dinner: hummus, fresh parmesan cheese on rice crackers, avocado, salami slices. Then we drive out under the moonlit canyons, dark against the star-streaked sky, to the dead end of a slot canyon road. The road surface when we emerge is red sand and snow, both the same texture, and in the dark, indistinguishable. The canyon walls swoop upward into slow-formed cubbies and coves. I try to run up one pretending to be a teenaged skateboarder. Laurie lies curled in another. Julie sits on the still-warm car hood smiling at the whole too-big spectacle. The temperature is seven degrees. Tomorrow morning she will call from the road to my motel room to let me know that she's made it back out onto the empty icy interstate, passing not one car, getting no cell phone reception for miles, retracing our journey, creeping south toward Vegas and, eventually, to Riverside, and to Community Care, where she will visit my mother every day for the next two months.

. . .

During the day, Laurie attends the conference about the maintenance of historic fruit orchards. Back home in the mountains, she battles elk, bear, aphids, weeds, and drought to keep hundred-year-old apple trees alive and to nurture young ones as a park service orchardist. The trees are her passion. Once, years ago, we'd been at a party where a psychic was reading palms with astonishing accuracy. When he got to Laurie, he held her calloused hands and couldn't come up with a thing. Until he noticed her feet. He cradled them in his hands—the first palm reading of feet the young psychic had ever done, he said, or ever heard of for that matter—and his face betrayed something like awe.

"You are very connected to the earth. Very. Someday you will figure out how."

At the time, Laurie seemed plenty connected to the earth. She'd worked on trail crews. Like me, each summer, she slept on the ground as many nights as not. But it turned out the psychic was right. When Laurie started caretaking the orchard a couple years later, she found her true calling. She did it her own way, shunning convention, building calluses. Here at Capitol Reef she is well known and respected among a small group of historic orchardists from across the country.

For a few days, I stay happily ensconced in the motel room catching up on my online work, reading, watching sunlight trace the tops of the canyons. I feel like I'm recovering from a long illness. My dad's courage buoyed me while I held my mother up. Now that I've let go, I feel lost. Outside of the park, unpaved roads of red cinders roll between the rock uplifts, swelling and dipping, like a slow-moving dancer. I watch them from my chair by the wall heater, staring out at where I lose sight of them in the distance. Then one day I decide it's time. I put on headphones and go running, jogging at first, then picking up the pace to run very fast, faster than I usually like to, as fast as my lungs will allow in the frigid air. The sky soaks up loss like a sponge, invites it, and I try to think about moving on.

. . .

My dad left Tallahassee sometime in the early spring of 1958. Whether he left because he was warned by his lawyers or because he sensed the coming trouble—the Supreme Court loss and the subsequent jail time in a segregated jail—or because of the honey-skinned girl, he left in a mighty hurry. His FSU transcript lists his graduation date as February, not the end of a term, not any normal time of year to graduate. His final credits are a couple of D's from Dartmouth tacked on for credit. It's clear enough: he had to skedaddle.

So he moved to San Francisco, owned his bookstore and sold his bookstore, built his hermit cabin on the beach and left it, and one day, with his pal, Clay Barbeau, he hitchhiked to a local Trappist monastery and converted back to Catholicism. Within a few months, he met the radical priest who later frequented our guest room in Riverside and headed off to Mexico with a group of students from Berkeley calling themselves Amigos Anonymous.

Later yet, in 1963, he moved to South America and met my mother, and together my parents spent the formative years of the sixties, from Kennedy's assassination until Martin Luther King's, south of the border, first in Venezuela and later in Colombia, where they learned about injustice on the grand scale, and liberation theology, and broad-sweeping socialist reforms, sometimes corrupt.

When they arrived back in St. Louis in 1968, they moved into a mixed-race neighborhood at the height of urban racial tension. They were the only white folks on the block. On the television in the thick, wet heat of a Midwest summer, Mom watched the 1968 Democratic convention in Chicago, only a short day's drive away, thinking only: *I should be there. I should really be there.* But politics had, by then, taken a back seat to raising a family. She had me at home, a precocious toddler who preferred to answer to my made-up identity as "Mrs. Johnson," and she had to watch out for me. Given half a chance, I'd throw a pretend purse on my shoulder, give a quick wave, and be headed down the steps, looking for a new place.

Twenty years later, I'd be at it again.

A few months after graduating from college, I received a call.

"There are only eleven employees, and it's eighty miles to town. How do you think you will deal with the remoteness?" the interviewer, a career park-service naturalist, asked.

"Well, I don't know," I answered. "I've never tried."

"Do you think you'd like to try?" the naturalist asked.

"Yes," I said. "I would."

I drove south through Oregon, then east across Nevada—U.S. 50, the "Loneliest Road in America," with road signs to prove it—and finally into Utah, fifty miles off a two-lane state road, into the Needles district of Canyonlands after dark. I pulled out my sleeping bag and laid it out unceremoniously in the sand, and I awoke to a horizon wider and bluer than any I'd ever seen, and red-orange rocks alternately lifted and eroded, worn by wind and water into odd protrusions and depressions, and silence prevailing, no running water, no rustling leaves, and I felt unexpectedly, inexplicably elated.

. . .

In the evening, in a crowded small-town school auditorium, a genteel Southerner speaks on heirloom varieties of apples, how and why to maintain them. He's the keynote speaker at the conference, and he is Laurie's hero the way John Lewis has become mine. I watch her listening, her fixed, eager smile, her eyes wide and expectant, her note-taking pen unused in her lap. She can't help it: she is star struck. He tells the crowd to teach five other people to graft, to pass on the skill, to keep it alive, and his passion feels like church-inspired faith.

Later that night, Laurie persuades me to go out with some of the other conference participants. I am hesitant. It's been many weeks since I attended a social event of any sort. I've been lolling in introspection, but I figure it's time, so we walk across the empty highway to meet up at a pizza joint on the canyon rim. We order pitchers of weak beer—only 3.2 percent alcohol can be served legally in Utah—and crowd around Formica-topped tables. Like us, like anyone who works outdoors alone most of the time, the guys are shy at first, but slowly stories begin to leech out. One young Hispanic man plans to replant an orchard the Jesuits cultivated at a mission near the Arizona/Mexico border in the 1700s. He will try to maintain not only particular fruits—apples, peaches, quince—but particular fruit varieties, strains of DNA that are lost in the monoculture demanded by a modern economy. A Native American man in his fifties spends most of his time as a park service ranger talking with European tourists. Top-working ailing fruit trees is, for him, a reprieve.

"They always want to know: are you a *real* Indian? They ask: are you related to Chief Yellowhorse, the guy who sells jewelry on the road outside of Grand Canyon?"

We laugh. A clandestine bottle of tequila appears and gets passed under the table to supplement the weak beer.

I am happy among these people. I never could be an activist like my dad. It's not a matter of courage so much as, well, nature. The people in the political realm live too easily with shifting ironies and complications, labels and prejudice, wealth and poverty, power and injustice, black and white, gay and straight. These sun-weathered people in work boots feel like my tribe.

One fellow, another featured speaker, is quieter even than the rest of the crowd. He is clean-cut and Midwestern, the father of teenage girls, and he is perhaps the single-best keeper of heirloom apple varieties in the nation. But he can't make a living at it. Instead, he repairs heating and air conditioning systems for money, and grafts two hundred fruit trees in his spare time. Hope takes a thousand different forms. I try to think what I believe in. I believe in the wide, clear horizon, achingly cold. I believe in truth.

Whatever that may be.

The next morning I decide to call Jon Folsom again. Honey or no Honey, there is still more I want to know. He skirts around the bus incident but covers much familiar ground: literature, Korea, the summer in Miami. He tells many stories that, like his version of the bus story, are mighty entertaining. I may have no idea which stories are true, but each gives me insight into my young father, so I listen patiently, sometimes greedily. Only rarely do I speak up.

One night during that summer, he says, Tennessee Williams gave a lecture. During the Q&A period, my dad stood to ask a question about a more obscure short story, and the famous playwright was impressed enough that afterward he invited the two young beach bums out to Key West.

"I told Joe I wasn't going, but I said, 'Why don't you go?'" Jon Folsom repeats his own line with the false innocence of a playground jeer, "and he said 'Kiss my ass.'"

"So why didn't you go?" I ask, mimicking his false innocence.

"Why Tennessee Williams was just a raging homosexual."

"You cowards," I say.

I am assuming he will take it is a joke. I mean it as one. But he doesn't find it funny.

"I wasn't going out there," he says.

So much for my theory about the two of them being lovers. There's at least one part of my personality that's mine alone. I let the conversation drift back to Miami, the jazz clubs, the cultural life. I enjoy his reverie, and when I try to hang up, he stalls, as usual, for time.

"I don't want to lose touch with you," he says. "My feelings for your father have never left me. What I mean to say is that your father was very good to me. He made a real difference in my life. I would have these nightmares."

He pauses.

"He held me," he says, breaking down. "He just held me."

Here in the off-guard moment when, for once, I'm not combing for evidence of heroism or restlessness or latent homosexuality, I see my father plainly: gentle, selfless, loving.

Did my father hold me? I'm sure he did. I've seen photographs of him holding me. But I can't remember it. I remember play-fighting, teasing, wrestling, the race to the front door when the Pinto pulled into the driveway. *Dad's home! Dad's home!* I picture him holding Jon Folsom, and I know for a fact that, had he lived, my father would have been able to sit by my mother's hospital bed. The thought breaks my heart. She deserves that much, I think. I've been a stand-in, a poor second choice for the last few weeks and for most of my life. I know this, and I know that competing with my dead father for my mother's attention, even if in only one mind-swirling moment, is, well, messed up.

"I'm glad he did," I say.

On the last day of the conference, I call Jon Folsom back with one last question. I want to know about James Kennedy, the third white rider on the bus. I had been trying to track him down.

"I wrote to a couple of James Kennedys in Sarasota since the newspaper said he was from there, but I didn't get any answer, and it's a pretty common name. Is that the guy? Was he from Sarasota?"

"Yes, that's where his family lived. Sarasota."

The attitudes of the era have crept so insidiously into my consciousness that I need to know that James Kennedy, too, was from Florida. If, like Jon Folsom and Johnny Herndon—like all the riders other than my dad—Kennedy was a native South-erner, then the whole outside-agitators argument holds no water. They weren't communist operatives; they weren't pawns; they were young men who saw injustice and wanted to do something about it.

"Do you have any memories of him?"

Jon Folsom pauses for a long moment.

"Jim Kennedy," he says, "was a really interesting guy, a brilliant guy, a mathematician."

"So you knew him from school? From Florida State?"

"Yes, and he wasn't there on the G.I. Bill. He was there on a full-ride scholarship. That's how smart a guy he was."

"That's funny. Everything I read calls him as a state roads employee."

"That's what he became while we knew him."

"He flunked out?"

"He dropped out, Ana Maria. He couldn't take it. He just didn't want any part of it. The officials at Florida State were about frantic, the math department people, the physics people. They offered him about everything to stay, but Jimmy said, 'I don't want anything from this state.'"

"Because of segregation?"

"Because of the injustice of the situation, yes. Jimmy was a little unstable, you see, and he just couldn't abide the hypocrisy."

"So he dropped out and got a job as a roads laborer?"

This pattern is starting to sound familiar. Jon Folsom left the movement to become a pipefitter, my dad built that cabin on Muir Beach, I moved into the woods to work on hiking trails. I'm beginning to feel like part of a club.

"Not at all. This is a good story. Jimmy set up an inventory of the state roads department equipment using IBM punch cards long before computers. His system was ingenious, and it really worked."

So much for being part of a manual laborers' club. I couldn't design an inventory even with a computer.

"Well, when he was going to get involved with us on this ride, I told him, 'Hey man, if you wanna be a part of this, you're gonna lose your job.'"

"Did he?"

"Not at first. See, they didn't have anybody else who understood that punch card system. If they sacked him, they'd be in real trouble."

So James Kennedy rode the bus and became a material witness, got his name in the paper, and received the same hate mail and harassment the rest of the boys did. Then a few months later, he did lose his job.

"It had nothing to do with the bus. This is what happened. His inventory system discovered that thirty percent of the state equipment was being used for personal purposes. Thirty percent! Well, when he brought that into the light, they fired him straight away. When he told us that story, he'd laugh until he about threw up."

"Do you know where he might be now?"

Jon pauses again.

"You know, Jimmy was a great guy, a great saxophone player. I remember parties at our pad, and there would be jam sessions. I mean, the guy was amazing. When I think about what happened to him, I could just about cry."

I'm confused. I thought losing his job was a funny story. The motel room windows have darkened with clouds, and flecks of snow skitter past the red rock canyons and settle on sagebrush. I walk to the sliding doors, phone in hand, and onto the small balcony to see if the snow makes the air smell like sage the way rain does. It doesn't.

"Do you know have any idea where he might be now?" I ask again.

"I think he's gone. I mean, I think he committed suicide a couple of years after we knew him."

"You think he did?"

"He did."

I sit down on a plastic chair in the cold, staring out at the desert. I wonder about the courage the act of suicide took and if it might be related to the courage it took to ride the bus. Jimmy Kennedy wasn't the only one struggling with mental health. There was Jon Folsom himself. And I remembered the story of John Boardman, the grad student who'd invited three black students to a Christmas party shortly before my dad's ride. The blacks were foreign-exchange students from A&M, it turned out, and he had invited them to a party for international students sponsored by Florida State. Boardman told reporters that he'd received permission from officials at both schools. The officials denied it, and in December 1956, he was expelled.

Doak Campbell, the president of Florida State University, described Boardman as part of "a little group of ten FSU students who regard themselves as the saviors of the world." He called Boardman "a brilliant scholar as far as mathematics is concerned" but "unstable otherwise."

"That boy is sick and needs help," Doak Campbell told the press.

"What about John Boardman?" I ask Jon Folsom.

"He was a little bit reclusive, but he was Jim's pal and we always liked him. He fit right in, you know. There was a group of eight or ten of us, and we weren't exactly easy people to deal with."

Doak Campbell would have agreed. When, at a committee meeting, the president of Florida A&M suggested that the black students at his university considered Boardman something of a hero, Campbell replied that, on the basis of profile reports on the FSU students sympathetic to integration—my dad's little group of friends—he found them all, like Boardman, somewhat "erratic or lacking in their backgrounds."

In that context, I've never been prouder to have my father

called "erratic." I can tell Jon Folsom thinks the same thing, and it brings some levity to a difficult conversation. Maybe craziness is required, I think. If you can see the faults in yourself without flinching, maybe you can see them outside yourself, and maybe you're just crazy enough to do something about it.

CHAPTER FOURTEEN

Orchard Burning

Smoke from a dozen piles of burning apple limbs obscures the view of Lake Chelan. A light mist settles on my bare arms, one gripping the idling chainsaw, the other yanking a cut branch free of the tree. The day is gray and cold. On the low flanks of the mountains, this small midslope clearing allows the lake to show only partially, above continuous forest below. The water looks dark and menacing, the fir tops like acres of thick, prickly stubble. This is not the orchard that Laurie maintains but another, more neglected orchard, near a friend's property. As a favor to the trees and to the aging owner, our friend asked Laurie and me to help him prune, and we were all too glad to oblige. The work is simple and satisfying. The orchard has not been pruned in a decade, and it has been battered by snowfall and hungry black bears. Just removing the dangly dead limbs will take most of the day. At lunchtime we sit drinking strong cowboy coffee brewed on the embers, saying little, not having much to say, glad for the quiet, and glad, mostly, not to be back home in the cabin where sadness hangs heavy as a winter inversion and seems to be getting heavier all the time.

. . .

On the day I arrived home, finally, in the tiny mountain town, after three weeks in Riverside and one at Capitol Reef, a neighbor pulled me over on the road.

"Have you talked to the ranger?"

"I haven't talked to anybody."

Orchard Burning

"Kevin Herrick committed suicide."

I didn't know what to say. I'd been told about death before, plenty of times, knew the bottomless nothing that can swallow you whole, the swooping heart-drop like a carnival ride and how you catch your breath to pad the conversation with platitudes: *I'm so sorry. What can I do? How's the family?* But this was something entirely new. I'd never known anyone personally who'd killed himself. *Did not!* I wanted to cry. *Wrong guy!*

"Kevin? Are you sure?"

She nodded. I felt blood-rush panic. Too-bright sun shone in my eyes.

"Thanks for letting me know," I said.

At home I greeted Daisy, the cat, scooped her into my lap and held her there while she squirmed in protest. In the hours that followed I dug out snapshots and pinned them by my desk. I e-mailed mutual friends and tried to sort through feelings. I'd known Kevin since we both began working in the woods. I'd dated him briefly before I met Laurie. Together we'd hiked into the mountains and swam naked in backcountry lakes. We'd even talked once about heading to Mexico to lie on the beach all winter, drinking margaritas. Even at the time, it seemed like such a fantasy was beyond his scope. He ironed his t-shirts and hung them on hangers, my first clue that we were, perhaps, ill suited for each other. After a few years, he moved to New York and went to work on Wall Street. He was, in every way, a success. He was, like me, thirty-eight years old. If I had made a list of every person I knew and ranked them in order of most likely to commit suicide, Kevin would have come in pretty close to dead last. And that was part of the problem. If Kevin were crazy enough to kill himself, anyone could be.

I scoured obsessively through the details of Kevin's life, the last time he'd visited, the last time he'd written, always with the irrational subtext that if only I'd known, I could have stopped

173

it, and I thought about all the other people I knew who might be capable of such a horrific act. Among them was Jon Folsom. I wrote to him about my grief and how much I hoped it he would not consider suicide again, and his reply was swift and lyrical and heartfelt, if not necessarily comforting.

> I grieve that your friend ended his life. . . . Suicide, I feel, is the conclusion of a compelling one word statement or question. Enough? We can't know why he said "yes." We seldom notice when we begin to move out of the light. A word may drive them to the darkness; a word may bring them back—the mystery of the human heart. Crushing.

I reread the letter over and over, crying harder each time, and I thought again about Jimmy Kennedy. I'd been wrong about his courage, wronger than wrong, dead wrong. I mean, I knew Kevin had been brave. I'd crossed ice fields with him wearing crampons; I'd sat beside him on rock ledges staring down thousands of feet below our dangling legs. But he'd used his bravery wrongly, squandered it, and left a long, messy path of grief and unfinished business in his wake. Whatever demon had haunted Jimmy Kennedy, I decided, it's not what made him sit on the Sunnyland bus. He did the right thing despite his illness, not because of it, and afterward, he simply could not take any more. Enough? Enough. Crushing.

I thought about my father, too, and how he must have struggled with these same feelings, this same agonized confusion, while comforting Jon Folsom, while grieving for James Kennedy. After he finished graduate school in St. Louis, he went to work as a psychiatric social worker, the career he'd stick with until his death. As a kid I hadn't the slightest idea what that meant: social work. I couldn't even say it properly. So-So Work, I thought it was, which made some sense. Compared to what a fireman or a policeman or a doctor did, his job was nondescript, hard to explain; as far as I could tell, it was pretty so-so. He put on a suit and tie, left in the morning, and came home at night tired. I didn't see it, back then, for what it was: a way to act on compassion, to do something, anything real, to rage against the omnipresent dying of the light.

. . .

At the orchard, after lunch I walk toward a tree and begin again to saw off any wood that seems superfluous, any wood at all, to let nutrients flow, let the light in. There is almost nothing I can do, at this point, that would hurt the tree. The cut limbs hang up, and I yank them down. After a few trees, I shut down the saw to haul limbs to fires, where as the piles burn down, a fringe of unburned ends surrounds the hot ash like the rays of the sun on a small child's drawing. I pick up the ends with my leather gloves and toss them in the fire. By the end of the day, even in forty-degree drizzle, I am wearing only a t-shirt, flipping burning sticks over with my gloved hands, getting nonchalant, when the red-hot tip of one singes the inside of my arm, sticking long and letting off a sickening smell. I race to a nearby creek and douse my arm in the freezing water; there's no pain, only the white fleshy hole. I'm thinking: well, this is serious. I'm also thinking: as long as it doesn't hurt I can keep working. I stay by the creek for a while, get a Band-Aid and some antibiotic cream from my first aid kit, then return to working, without saying a thing.

Back home I check e-mail messages to see how Mom is surviving. Not bad, says Lisa: no infections, no dehydration. Not bad, echoes Julie: she's eating and walking. I try to take it all seriously, to take preventative measures, like the twice daily antibiotic cream and athletic tape I put on my arm, to be attentive to healing and believe that things will look up soon. Instead, it becomes clear that the cat, Daisy, is very sick. She has wanted to drink water every fifteen minutes for a week, and now she vomits daily. When we take her to the vet, he tells us her kidneys are failing. We can feed her special food and be vigilant about ensuring that she drinks, but we won't change the essential fact: she might have two months to live or two years. If it weren't so tragic, it would be funny: so much grief at once.

One day a package from Jon Folsom arrives in the mail. The contents spill out onto the floor: organic tomato seeds, catnip for Daisy, and a dozen used paperbacks. Kafka, Sartre, Tennessee Williams, Nathanael West. I sit cross-legged and page through them, lingering on phrases, rereading paragraphs. There is also a brand-new minicassette player that I assume is intended for sending him voice messages in the absence of telephone conversations. But I am wrong. His six-page letter explains, in part, that the recorder is for capturing ideas that come in the middle of the night. He's nurturing my writing career, in a fatherly way, and he suggests that I should consider writing a play. And, in a daughterly way, I think: *No way. I'm no playwright. What is he thinking?* For my part, I'd tried suggesting that he attend the fiftieth anniversary celebration with me in Tallahassee, and in the letter he is unequivocal: "Tallahassee is another time," he writes. "That is over and I see no reason to either celebrate or commemorate. Only Armageddon would interest me."

I am disappointed, but I understand. Jon's distaste for the political arena gives me freedom to hold onto a grain of cynicism that may come in handy. Organizers of the boycott anniversary celebration have been inviting me to give a very short speech, off and on, for weeks, and I'd resolved that I should do it, but each letter or e-mail has mentioned me speaking less often until there was no mention at all. "There is still a lot of controversy surrounding the boycott," they wrote gingerly.

Now, after Jon Folsom's letter, I decide maybe I ought not to go at all.

When the final revised schedule for the anniversary celebration arrives, I lie on my bed and flip through the pages disinterestedly. C. K. Steele's sons will attend. Patricia Stephens Due will speak. Events will culminate in a black-tie gala on Saturday night. A gala? That's no good. If I thought I was underdressed at Bethel Missionary Baptist, how would I look at a black-tie gala? But it's not because of clothes, or even disillusionment, that I convince myself not to go. It's because I'm afraid there's nothing new to discover. I look at the three Taylor Branch books, the trilogy that chronicles the era of Martin Luther King Jr., sitting by my bedside. I am closing in on the last of the three, the one that ends in April 1968, and I feel like my dad did when he didn't want to see the Jesus movie: *I know how it ends.*

Nevertheless, lying on my bed in the middle of the afternoon, I turn the final page of the schedule to see that on the last day of the celebration, on the Sunday before Memorial Day, there will be a Freedom March from the Steele statue at the bus depot to Bethel Missionary, where the keynote speaker will be John Lewis. I read back over the page. Do they mean *the* John Lewis? They do, of course. I get up and turn on the computer to read, again, about John Lewis.

In the years the years that followed Selma, when Vietnam splintered the country in general and the Left in particular, the young leaders of the civil rights movement took different paths. Some championed black power, some sold real estate, some moved to Africa, and others taught algebra. Only John Lewis, the stuttering farm boy, the least likely candidate from among the charismatic activists, moved into politics. He campaigned for Bobby Kennedy and worked in Jimmy Carter's administration, and in 1987 he ran for the House of Representatives, where he's served ever since. His creed has never changed. He believes in the civil rights of all people, and he fights for them: immigrants, single mothers, the disabled, the disenfranchised—especially the disenfranchised—and, yes, gays and lesbians. In 1996, when Congress was considering the Defense of Marriage Act, John Lewis stood to say this: "Marriage is a basic human right. You cannot tell people not to fall in love."

A good decent thing to say. And he didn't stop there.

"I have known racism. I have known bigotry," he said. "This bill stinks of the same fear, hatred, and intolerance. It should not be called the Defense of Marriage Act. It should be called the defense of mean-spirited bigots act."

He'd been my hero before I knew all this, for months already, but once I did, he came closer to being a god. Now I may have the chance to meet him in person? My hands turn clammy. And I think about Mary Decker.

In spring 1978, just before his heart surgery, Dad bought us tickets to see Mary Decker run at UCLA. At the time, I was obsessed with runners. I memorized their world record times with the same meticulous attention I paid to the Top 40 each week as Kasey Kasem counted it down. So I knew all about Mary Decker, who'd shattered the record for the women's 800 meters at age fifteen. I knew her name and her story like I knew the names of Babe Didrikson and Wilma Rudolph, all the great women runners of Olympics past. I didn't know that women had not been allowed to race farther than a mile and a half until 1972. I didn't know the first women's Olympic marathon wouldn't be held until 1984, when I was sixteen. I didn't know, in other words, that my dad's enthusiastic support of my interest in sports, the subscription to *Young Athlete* magazine, these every-weekend jaunts to track meets, was anything cutting edge, anything out of the norm.

After her race, Mary Decker climbed into the stands to chat with some friends only two rows in front of us in the bleachers. The day was hot. I clutched the meet program in my hands, head bowed, memorizing times.

"Go ask for her autograph," my dad urged.

"I can't."

"Why not?"

I didn't have the words for how I felt: afraid that she'd be unkind, but afraid mostly that she wouldn't be what she was supposed to be. There's no way she'd live up to what she was on the track, rounding the curves, pulling ahead, her stride steady, her will unwavering.

"I'm too shy. Let's just go home."

He was annoyed with me, I could tell. He pulled off the Irish driver's cap he'd taken to wearing, light white cotton instead of wool, and ran his hand over the last balding strands of his hair.

"Give that to me," he said.

I handed him my program, and I watched as he stepped over the bleacher in front of us.

"Could you sign this for my little girl?" he asked.

Off the track, Mary Decker, at twenty, still looked the part of the quintessential teenager, bony and surly, one hip jutted to the side. The look she gave my dad was full of disdain—he looked scrappy and still slightly overweight, too-Riverside for this glitzy L.A. scene—and I felt a jolt of recognition. I knew that sometimes I looked at my father exactly the same way, and I was ashamed of myself.

He brought the signed program back to me, grinning widely, seemingly oblivious to Mary Decker's disrespect. Or mine. I stood and hugged his waist.

"Thanks, Dad."

Now I stare down at the program for the fiftieth anniversary.

I've got the chance to meet John Lewis, maybe even to get his autograph, I think, and I'd better do it myself. If it's not the best reason for flying across the country, it's not the worst one either, and after solid months of hard grief, any reason to get out of bed is a good one. I write to Cynthia Williams and tell her I am booking a flight from Wednesday to Monday, and that I am looking forward to meeting her. Then I lace my boots and drive half an hour to the one satellite phone in town to talk to my mother myself.

She picks up on the second ring.

"How are you, Mom?"

"I'm okay."

"Are you walking?"

The satellite phone has a long delay, during which neither party can speak. Communication starts and stalls and sometimes buzzes with otherworldly static, so that it's more like playing on walkie talkies than actually conversing. This time my mother's voice comes through loud and clear.

"Every day. I never skip a day. I went out in the courtyard yesterday."

"Are you eating?"

"Sometimes."

This is not good news, but it's not bad either. It's certainly better than during the last round of chemotherapy. I feel as though I'm braced and teetering, waiting for a fast, hard fall. I need to do something to prevent the unpreventable, or at least to give her hope.

"Do you still want to come with me to Tallahassee?"

This time the line goes silent for several seconds. It's not the connection; it's just the truth, and we both know it. She can't come with me. There's no way she could miss a chemotherapy appointment. And, anyway, strong though she may be, able to walk out into the courtyard is not the same as able to fly across the country. She simply can't come. I stare out at the lake, dark and glassy, and wait for her inevitable reply.

"You go, Honey. You can tell me all about it."

"Okay," I say, "I will."

With that, it's decided: I'll be returning to Tallahassee alone—Laurie cannot abandon the orchard this time of year—and as a spectator.

"What about Portland?" Laurie asks.

A book-release party for an anthology I'd contributed to has long been circled on our calendar. It'll be in Portland, Oregon, a two-day drive away.

"I'm not going. How can I go? I can't go."

"Why not?"

"Because of Kevin, I guess, and my mom and Daisy."

Laurie stares at me hard. "So?"

With that, once again, it's decided. Mother's Day weekend takes me south on I-5 among the tall firs, the green rolling hills, and the speeding trucks. May in Portland, like May anywhere, is sun-drenched and lush. There are half a dozen friends I could stay with in town, but I rent a motel room instead, not ready for that much company. Before the party, I iron my shirt and paste a large Band-Aid on my inner arm, and then I head out. The party, on a downtown rooftop, features local wines and small-time editors and writers. I like the crowd and I like the wine, and I like watching the sun on the wide Willamette, barges moving slowly north to the Columbia, to the Pacific. Partygoers I hardly know approach and politely ask what I'm working on, and at first I try to avoid the conversation, but after awhile it's no use. I set my wine glass on a railing and launch into the Tallahassee story: Jakes and Patterson, C. K. Steele and Dan Speed, the whole makeshift movement, the desperate hope in the air. And finally my dad. My listeners nod politely. They think they already know the story, that it's old news.

"Was he in SNCC? Did he protest Vietnam?"

"No, see this was before Vietnam, before SNCC even. He was at Florida State on the G.I. Bill and somehow he got involved, and it was almost unheard of before that for a student to do such a thing, especially a white student. . . ."

I can see them glance away across the Portland skyline. I know I am rambling, gushing, conversation-hogging, the way Laurie does, sometimes, when she talks about bridge-grafting old apple trees, the way I used to do about maintaining trails: trying to explain the intricacies, the fact that though there's some romance, sure, mostly it's hard work that someone has to do. Now I am trying to convince anyone who will listen that, in the civil rights movement, there's only glory in hindsight, that at the time, mostly, it was hard, but someone had to do it. I'm in the middle of a long-winded explanation of Ordinance 741, when one listener excuses herself, as did the one before her. All night I watch as partygoers smile absently and step away, moving on to mingle and leaning close to one another to whisper: *What's with Nature Girl?* I am perversely pleased with myself.

In the morning, I wake alone in the motel room, the ironing board still set up, my road clothes strewn on the bedspread. I dial Community Care, and the phone rings a dozen times before I hear my mother fumble with the receiver and pick up.

"Happy Mother's Day," I say.

"Huh?"

This is a land line, not a satellite phone. The delay is real, and I know immediately that this is it: the hard, fast fall I've been dreading.

"How's it going Mama Sue? It's me."

"Who?"

The conversation does not last long before I call Lisa to

tell her something has gone terribly wrong. She's unsurprised. It's bad, she says. Bad? How bad? Real bad. I protest that everything seemed fine, just fine, only a week ago. What went wrong? Nothing. And everything. The oncologist did watch carefully, did check the blood, every time, did put her on IVs for liquid when necessary. To no avail. Friends and neighbors have been driving her to City of Hope twice weekly for appointments, and they can't handle it any more.

"It will turn out okay," I say, but I don't believe it. It happened so fast: in less than a week, my mother slipped from walking and eating and chatting on the satellite phone to lying groggily in bed, severely dehydrated, unable to function.

"And my baby hasn't kicked yet."

"He will," I say, though I'm not so sure about that either, and right this minute it's not my first concern.

"Listen, I can come drive her. I'm supposed to go to Tallahassee next weekend for that anniversary thing I was telling you about, but I can cancel the trip. I'm in Portland now and I can maybe even catch a flight from here and head straight home." Home. I realize as I say it that I just called Riverside "home."

"Don't do that. Please go. Please. For all of us."

It's the first interest she's shown in my project, and I'm taken aback.

"There's not any reason, really, for me to go, Lisa."

"We want you to go."

"Okay."

I call Delta Airlines to change my flight: Seattle to Tallahassee to Los Angeles.

When I return home, I find yet another note from the organizers asking me to speak on Wednesday evening. I double check my arrangements; I won't arrive until Wednesday, and I can't face changing the flight again. I have already spent a small fortune on the trip. Though I could, perhaps, say a few words, I explain, I cannot commit since so much depends on the travel logistics.

I try to compose a short, tidy speech. But it's no use. I sit at the computer, the cursor blinking, scratching Daisy behind the ears. It's not about courage anymore. Maybe it never was. It was about grief, common as dirt. For twenty-five years, I'd scripted a story for myself: my dad ran away—from home, from Dartmouth, from Tallahassee, and eventually from us—and then I ran away from Riverside, from the problems of the world, from any place with a telephone. I'd been angry about the former and guilty about the latter for too long when all along I knew the truth: my dad's life, like mine, was pretty much the same as anybody else's. You do hard things. You live the best way you know how. You experience grief, and hopefully, you experience joy. If you're lucky, you share them both.

Every single time I've spoken with Jon Folsom, and in several letters, he has returned to the same day, the day my father stood to give an impromptu speech on T. S. Eliot in the English class. I've sometimes gotten annoyed with his obsession with this unimportant day, frustrated at the way memory enlarges some moments while ignoring others. But there is something in the particular way he retells it, slowing to capture every moment, working to get it just so, that feels comforting, endearing. Real. I shut off the computer and pick up his letter to reread the section over and over.

We walked back to the apartment in silence—it wasn't far—and we both felt depressed. We took a couple of long gulps out of the wine jug—it didn't work. Joe went to sleep on the balcony and I flopped on the couch.

It had been a good day. That is certainly the way we felt—generally good days, better, and from time to time really super. We were idealistic, optimistic, curious, and enjoyed trying to understand who and what we were.

Maybe that's a better goal, I think, than running a marathon or finding out the truth of my Dad's story: to be idealistic, optimistic, curious. I cradle the last Taylor Branch book in my lap, ready at last to read through to the end, looking up occasionally to watch Daisy slurping water at the kitchen faucet and Laurie transplanting honeysuckle in the yard.

Part Three

FIFTIETH ANNIVERSARY

CHAPTER FIFTEEN

Every. Single. Day.

The plane hits the tarmac, wheels skid on asphalt, and at the very moment when I'd normally be pocketing my rosary, grateful just be on the ground, I'm checking my watch. I have ninety minutes before I'm to offer remarks on my father's behalf at Tallahassee's First Baptist Church. I have tried to guess if the crowd will be big or small, black or white, formal or informal. I don't have a clue. I spent days composing a half page of words. Now I've reread them so often I have the short speech memorized. The plane taxies toward the gate in a sultry orange haze. Passengers shift in their seats, dial cell phones, then stand, at last, to grope in overhead bins as I sit silently reciting excerpts to myself: "By the time he arrived in Tallahassee to attend Florida State on the G.I. Bill in 1956, my father was well acquainted with grief. The grief, painful as it must have been, gave him perspective, a sense of priorities, and a quiet courage."

So much has changed in four months. My dad's story has melded with the larger civil rights story, the family drama unfolding in California, the hard, relentless grief in my own life. His was a small gesture, I've decided, in a world of small gestures. I haven't traveled three thousand miles this time to do more research. I'm here to honor those who made the gestures. I am here to listen to their stories. I am here to meet Johnny Herndon and Jon Folsom, to thank them for their courage fifty years ago and for their kindness in the past few months.

And I am here to let go. I want to be done living in the past. I want to say a humble and respectful farewell and move on.

Inside the terminal, already it's clear: letting go will be no easy task. The airport buzzes with history. This was, after all, the site of a Freedom Ride showdown in 1961 when a mixed-race group of nine clergymen, volunteers from across the nation later known as the "Tallahassee Nine," were denied service at an airport restaurant, arrested, and sent to Judge John Rudd for sentencing. Like my dad and so many others, they appealed to the Supreme Court to no avail. Three years after the incident they were obliged to return to serve their sixty-day jail sentences in Tallahassee. Immediately upon their release, in a sweet ironic victory, they were able to eat together at the very same airport restaurant where they'd been arrested. Change, by that time, was coming so fast that you could serve time for breaking a law that was already obsolete.

I'd like to ask around, to see the exact location of that restaurant, but the airport looks recently renovated, and anyway, time is short. I poke around long enough to notice one concession out of place. I'd noticed it on my last trip through town. With cherry wood desks and cushy living room furniture, it looks like the office of a swanky insurance brokerage. This time I see the sign: Florida A&M University Hospitality Suite—it must be a recruiting office of sorts or an alumni lounge—and above the entrance hangs a banner: *50th Anniversary of the Tallahassee Bus Boycott*. I stop in my tracks and step into the small room filled with museum displays. There's C. K. Steele, Jakes and Patterson, and there on the cover of The *Florida Star*, in an enlarged photocopy of the photograph over my desk at home, stand Johnny Herndon, Leonard Speed, and Joseph Spagna. My pride swells. I look around for someone, anyone, to tell—*Look! That's my dad!*—but travelers scurrying toward

Every. Single. Day.

baggage claim show no interest in the past. It's time to move on.

Outside the airport, road construction hogs one lane, a row of orange cones stretching toward the horizon. Rush-hour traffic creeps, stop and go. The rental car idles. I drive slowly past the state capitol building, where the same gray-bearded man that we saw in January sits in solitary protest of the Iraq War. By the time I reach the motel, I have ten minutes to shower, dress, stumble out in high-heeled sandals, and hurry into a church foyer where I stand alone sweating in my best dress, clutching paper, looking around for someone to announce myself to—*I'm here!*—but it's too late. The congregation is seated, and a large all-white choir has begun to sing. I can't parade up the aisle and interrupt the service to whisper to a stranger that I am ready to speak these scrap paper words. Instead, I enter the sanctuary, light and cool and largely empty, and slide onto a pew.

Well-dressed black people crowd together in a half-dozen front-row pews. White couples huddle along the sides. By looks, they're all over fifty. A lively gang of white teenagers in shorts and flip flops line the midchurch pew closest to mine. Youth group. I'd recognize a youth group anywhere. They're game for this, game for anything, game mostly for each other. They jostle and giggle and tease. Elsewhere, scattered about the congregation, four single white women each sit alone dressed like me: proper but unglamorous, short-haired. At a Catholic church they'd be former nuns. Here, I suspect, they are the quiet backbones of their own churches: smart, private, dependable. The service has been billed as an ecumenical unity service. I've known this word—ecumenical—all my life. My mother's uncle, Charlie, the archbishop of Kansas City, had served on the panel for ecumenicalism in Rome during Vatican II. Each Passover the Spagnas shared a Seder meal with members of the Riverside synagogue: the bitter horseradish, a sip of wine, gamey lamb, the solemn incantations. In this large church of awkward factions, I feel oddly at ease.

The hymn ends, and Bill Proctor, a Leon County commissioner, stands to make general welcome remarks. He is a solemn black man in a solemn black suit, but his eyes sparkle with mischief. He sports a tidy afro—Michael Jackson circa 1972—and light freckles are sprinkled over his cheeks.

"God is good," he cries.

"Yes he is," reply the black folks up front.

He welcomes everyone to the historic event. His rhetoric is bland, but Proctor effuses it with enthusiasm and hyperbole.

"Tonight we worship together, something new, something that has never happened in our community before."

Never? Surely blacks and whites have gathered to worship together before in Tallahassee. The crowd, the blacks at least, indulge him with the half-smile head-shaking tolerance usually reserved for the antics of a younger brother.

The white pastor of First Baptist Church stands to welcome us again, and he reads aloud the prayer of St. Francis.

"Make me an instrument of your peace. Where there is hatred, let me sow love; where there is injury, pardon; where there is doubt, faith; where there is despair, hope; where there is darkness, light."

"Blessed," he says in conclusion, "are the peacemakers."

By "peacemakers," I'm pretty sure he doesn't mean the guy with the placard in front of the capitol. He means something more bland and palatable, more like the smoother-overs, like Rodney King saying "Can't we all get along?" I understand why Jon Folsom doesn't want to be here. He does not want to get along. He thinks getting along is what stalled the movement, the revolution, what stalled justice itself, forty years ago. And he may be right. "Only Armageddon would interest me now," he said. I am not as angry as all that. I am just a little bored. My attention wanders to the youth-group kids flirting shamelessly midsermon. I think about my father falling for a honey-skinned woman in a church in Sopchoppy. I think about my mother in her single bed at Community Care. She should be sitting here with me.

There are more hymns, more scripture readings, and then a black bishop takes the pulpit to deliver the sermon. He starts plainly and builds in a slow crescendo to warn of racism cloaked in Christianity, in the past, yes, two hundred years ago during slavery, fifty years ago during segregation, and, he cries, even now, everyday hypocrisy lives on. The crowd sits in silence. No one bristles at his hard message. It is, at least for those who've ventured here tonight, too obviously the truth. But the bishop lets us down easy, telling a joke about a kid who learns at Sunday school that he should live in a Christian family and cries all the way home from church.

"But I wanted to live with you guys," the kid howls.

The bishop's delivery is pitch perfect, and the crowd laughs heartily.

Suddenly, a voice booms from the back of the church, powerful, slow, and unwavering. The voice is black and male, but it's not what we expect. Not folksy, not bluesy. It's an operatic baritone carrying the weight of contrasting cultures—African and European, secular and religious, slave and free—with authority. And while the congregation takes a collective breath—where is that sound coming from?—a similar voice answers from the other side of the sanctuary, deep and rich, loud and perfect. This is call-and-response unlike I've ever heard, unlike any of us has ever heard, I suppose. We crane our necks to see two black men, tuxedo clad, process slowly toward the front of the church, slower than a bride on her father's arm, slower than a funeral procession. They sing as they walk, a medley

that begins with slave spirituals, slides into gospel, and culmi-
nates in the familiar anthem of the civil rights movement: "We
Shall Overcome." By the time the two men reach the pulpit,
the congregation, to the one, is singing along. The youth-
group kids sing loudly and off-key. The folks up front sway
and harmonize. In front, one lone white man in a choir robe
tries to join in by picking the strings on his violin. That this
is supposed to mirror progress, powerful, inevitable, painfully
slow, is clear as day. Even the goofy white guy trying gamely
to fit in seems appropriate.

. . .

After the service, I approach the most approachable man in
the church: Bill Proctor, the garrulous county commissioner,
who promptly whisks me by the arm toward the fellowship
hall, introducing me to people as we go.

"This Ana Maria Spagna. All the way from Seattle, Washington. Her father, uh. . . ." He turns to me. "What was your
father's first name?"

"Joseph."

"Her father, Joseph, was the Florida State student arrested
during the boycott."

I meet Reverend Foutz, the local SCLC leader, and his wife.
I meet two of the single white women, Barbara DeVane and
Karen Woodall, neither of whom, it turns out, is a churchy
matron as I'd assumed; they're liberal political activists, pow-
erhouses in fact. So much for first impressions. Finally, we find
Cynthia Williams holding a napkin of cookies and a paper cup
of punch. She wears an elegant linen pantsuit, and she has the
bespectacled look of a former schoolteacher with no tolerance
for nonsense. When I ask about Johnny Herndon, she grows
elusive.

Every. Single. Day.

"He came to one event early in the week. He's very private, you know."

"I'd like to meet him. That's part of the reason I've come so far. I hope he attends."

"He may attend on Sunday. He enjoys a good church service."

It's Wednesday night. Sunday sounds like a long time from now. I had planned on calling him sooner than that, maybe even this evening.

"He was very kind on the telephone. I'd like to meet him."

She nods and smiles wanly as a large white man in a suit approaches. He is a long-time member, he says, of First Baptist Church.

"You came all the way from Seattle to attend our church?"

"I did."

We chat about travel and weather. Then he launches into a story, and a small group of stragglers leans in to listen to him.

"In 1965, our church voted by five votes to keep Negroes out."

I look around at the boycott organizers and try to gauge their reaction. Part of me wants to pass judgment. I can't help thinking that I would have trouble attending a church that, in 1965, voted to keep blacks out. Then I realize: I've attended plenty of churches where gays are not welcome, not openly at least. I wonder how I'd be treated if Laurie were here with me. I banish the thought. The night has been a celebration of slow-moving change. It's not MTV. Not the History Channel. Just earnest people trying to breach the gap. These folks, all of them, are well dressed and weary, out for a midweek event in a week chock-full of midweek events.

"They saved the vote for Wednesday prayer service and got

195

the best turnout ever for a midweek event. Fifteen hundred people."

Everyone laughs, and I realize that this man is neither bragging nor apologizing. He's witnessing. He's telling it like it was.

"Change is slow," he says.

. . .

In the morning, I go running and sweat-soak my shirt in two Florida minutes.

Back at the motel, I open a special fold-out section from the previous Sunday's *Tallahassee Democrat* dedicated to the boycott. The biggest news is that the publishers of the *Democrat* are apologizing, now in 2006, for having supported segregation in 1956 and beyond. This is yet another small gesture, one that cynics could easily dismiss as too little, too late—*fifty years* too late!—but celebration organizers last night were nearly ecstatic. If it's worth remembering who took risks, it's worth remembering who failed to do so.

I sip my coffee and page through now-familiar photos and sagas. I stop to study a timeline of the boycott and feel familiar discomfort. Here's the problem: the timeline shows that the boycott began with Jakes and Patterson in May 1956 and ended with victory when the Supreme Court ordered Montgomery to integrate city buses in December 1956. That makes Dad's role a little difficult to explain, since he rode the bus in January 1957, *after* the Montgomery order, because the boycott was flailing *after* the supposed victory. The problem isn't that my dad's role gets ignored. His name is listed alongside Johnny Herndon's and Leonard Speed's in the fold-out on the "honor roll" of those who made the boycott a success. The problem is that, once you start explaining exactly what my dad and his friends tried to do, you come close to suggesting that, well, maybe the boycott wasn't such a success.

The fold-out section states in small print that Ordinance 741, the bogus save-segregation law they tried to prove uncon-stitutional by sitting together on the Sunnyland bus in 1957, was never actually repealed. It stayed on the books in Tallahas-see until 1973, when the city took over bus service from the private company. Of course, I know that lousy ordinances stay on the books everywhere. Every so often someone puts out a list of ridiculous laws (no parachuting for women on Sunday in Florida) and obsolete laws (no washing a mule on the sidewalk in Virginia). But those laws weren't challenged all the way to the U.S. Supreme Court. People didn't risk their lives to chal-lenge them. The fact that Ordinance 741 was never repealed feels to me, personally, like a slap. The fact that I can walk a mile south across the railroad tracks right now, in 2006, and see segregation thrive feels like something worse than that.

I remind myself that I haven't come to Tallahassee this time to worry over such things. I'm not here to figure anything out. But I have a few hours on my hands before a scheduled luncheon, so like an addict backsliding, I head to the library archives at FSU to read more interview transcripts.

The first I find is with Dan Speed, the grocery owner and boycott leader, who discusses, among other topics, the test ride. The interviewer asks him if he had encouraged his son, Leonard, to take the test ride.

"No, I'll tell you what happened along that line," says Speed. "We had a meeting, and in that meeting we came to a decision that we needed (lost transcription). . . . We didn't have anyone in our group who was willing to go and, of course, one of the boys from FSU said 'Well, I think that I can serve as one of the persons and help solicit somebody.'"

"Joe Spagner (sic)?" asks the interviewer.

"Yeah, that's the guy. He said he could assist in doing it and I said I can help get somebody to work with the blacks and of course this is how that really got moving."

"They just got on it and sat down in front?"

"Oh yes. It was understood. They knew what we wanted and they performed in that respect."

"And of course they were arrested. I mean the bus driver called the police?"

"They made pretty good rounds at first, and they had enough money to keep riding and I think they got tired of . . . (lost transcription)."

The interview stops cold, the photocopied text trailing off into oblivion. Like the missing copies of the *Tallahassee Democrat*, this is beginning to seem suspicious. Were they hiding the truth from the Johns Committee, trying to keep the bus driver's behavior off the record, protecting my dad for some reason, or protecting all of them? Or was Dan Speed's voice simply difficult for the transcriber to hear on the recording? More to the point: Did the boys ride one bus or two or more? Were there three riders or six? I'll never know for sure.

As the week goes on, mention of Dan Speed, the architect of the carpool and treasurer of the ICC, the bailer-out of jailed protestors, will be rare and grudging at best. History, it seems, is changeable. But some characters are utterly predictable.

The next interview I find is with none other than Judge John Rudd, the municipal judge who tried my dad, who tried the Tallahassee Nine, who tried Patricia Stephens Due, who never failed to lecture the defendants with thinly veiled disdain. The same bitterness permeates his comments twenty years after the fact, in 1978, once the civil rights movement was, for the most part, a done deal. He does not mince words.

About activists: "These people, they grab a little placard and bound up and down public streets. What are they accomplishing?"

About blacks: "I haven't done a damn thing to them except support them. And they haven't been victimized by me and my generation worth a damn. I don't owe them anything."

The interviewer begins to lose patience and steps in.

"Of course you know that the blacks come from slavery, and after the Civil War for 200 years, they were second class citizens."

At this point Judge Rudd, as Jon Folsom would say, comes completely unglued.

"Well, now, I'm sick and tired of that theory and philosophy and that's just a new approach to get further sympathy and something for nothing."

I can live with the fact that change is slow. But the intentional slowing of it, the purposeful and wrongful manipulation of justice, can still enrage me.

. . .

I'm late for lunch.

I'd found the community college campus and parked the rental car before I realized that I didn't know where, exactly, on campus the event was to be held, so I call Cynthia Williams's cell phone from a pay phone in the student union.

"Where *are* you?" she cries.

Turns out they're holding festivities awaiting my arrival. This I did not expect. I wanted to be a spectator, not an honored guest. I had gotten the distinct impression the night before that was exactly what I would be.

"In the student union," I say. "I'm wearing a pink shirt."

"Okay," she says. "Reverend Foutz will be right there."

Through double glass doors, I can see three men in suits walking fast, three abreast, across a wide nondescript lawn toward me, so I hang up and scurry out so they can get me where I belong.

"How are you this morning, Sister Spagna?"

And so it begins. For the rest of the week I will be Sister Spagna, which sounds somewhere between a nun, a radical lesbian feminist, and an honorary black woman. The name sounds silly enough that I nearly giggle, but it rolls from their tongues easily and is effused with warmth. They don't mind that I'm late. They're glad that I'm here. They whisk me into a large conference room where I shake hands and make apologies—*So sorry, thank you, glad to be here*. I can see immediately that I am underdressed yet again, and that I'm one of perhaps three white people in a room of a hundred or more.

"This is Sister Spagna," Reverend Foutz says and seats me at a table up front with administrators from the community college.

This luncheon honors Carrie Patterson and Wilhelmina Jakes, who sat on the bus in 1956 to start the boycott, though neither is in attendance. Jakes, a retired schoolteacher, could not make the long journey. Patterson is dead, strangled to death in 1969 at the age of thirty-three, likely in a domestic dispute. No one mentions that fact or the fact that no one was ever convicted of the crime.

On the dais sit ten prestigious black women including Patricia Stephens Due, the activist leader, the first to say: *jail no bail*. They are here to honor, in addition to Jakes and Patterson, women throughout Tallahassee who supported the boycott, many of whom are in the room, all of whom were brave and selfless and steadfast.

One of the women, a college professor, steps forward.

"God is good," she says.

"Yes he is," the crowd responds.

Every. Single. Day.

By the time the next speaker stands to say "God is good" I won't miss a beat.

"Yes he is," I will say.

I'll never get to the point where I yell "Amen." But Barbara DeVane does. She is white as can be, and she yells it louder than anyone in the room. She sports dangly bracelets and bright red lipstick, and she's the first on her feet for every ovation, the loudest in every response. She is utterly unselfconscious and apparently effective. Later, I'll Google her name to find her involved in every cause there is in Florida: women's rights, civil rights, workers' rights. When I crane my neck to see her, she smiles, winks, and waves, her forefingers flapping toward me playfully, and I relax.

After several speakers, Patricia Stephens Due stands last to address the importance of remembering history. The room grows still. She is a formidable presence with the dark glasses she's had to wear continuously for forty-five years, ever since her eyes were damaged by tear gas during a 1961 protest right here in Tallahassee. Her voice is low and slow and unyielding. And her favorite phrase is "foot soldiers," meaning those who actually hit the street back in the day, those who *did something*.

"Stories live forever," she says. "But storytellers don't. Listen to the foot soldiers while you can."

She could be speaking to me.

"If you don't tell your story, someone will tell it for you, and they will get it wrong."

After she finishes, a reporter approaches and asks me to tell my dad's story. The administrators politely stand to get in the food line, scooting behind my chair to pass, as I tell the story as honestly as I can: my father did his part, then skipped town.

"It was too dangerous," I say, "for him to stay."

The reporter scribbles fast.

I tell him how the family didn't know, how I came in January, how I admire Jakes and Patterson, how I am here to learn and not to be honored. Like a ballplayer after the big game, I try to say the right things. But I fail.

The administrators file back to their seats with plates of food.

"So you've come all the way from Seattle?"

"Yes."

"And your father got arrested during the boycott?"

"Yes."

"Then he went to Washington?"

"No . . ." I start to explain that he went to California and then to South America.

"But he jumped bail, right?"

"Right."

I try to explain that he had graduated, that he was encouraged to leave by his attorney. I list the same bogus excuses I've found inexcusable myself for months now.

"He could've gotten killed in jail," I say finally. "It was just too dangerous."

The conversation, already chilly, freezes hard. The woman's chin jerks upward slightly, defiantly, one eyebrow lifts over eyeglasses.

"Now you know. That's what it was like for my people every day," she says. She slows to enunciate: "Every. Single. Day."

"Yes," I say too fast and eager, staring down at my unused napkin shredded in my lap. "You're right. You're absolutely right."

From what I can tell, maybe a third of this room was alive during the boycott—they might remember it—and the rest, I'm guessing, don't need a special occasion to remember discrimination.

I stand, last in line, to fill my plate with baked chicken.

Every. Single. Day.

Rev. Foutz's young daughter, Yolanda, passes me as I make small talk with another woman, balancing my plate on one hand, to shake with the other.

"Yes, I came from Seattle. Thank you for having me. I am honored to be here."

Yolanda pauses beside me, and reaches over in a one-arm hug, and pulls my collar straight. She pats my shoulder and smiles as if to say: you're doing just fine.

. . .

Patricia Stephens Due signs a copy of her book for me: "To the daughter of a foot soldier from FSU. Remember, the struggle continues."

Laura Dixie, a woman who was spurred to action by bus discrimination in the late 1940s and had been an activist ever since, approaches.

"I never knew your father, but I certainly knew of him. We appreciate what he did for us. Thank you for coming."

"It's an honor to be here."

Just as I'm preparing to leave, Reverend Foutz puts a hand on my shoulder, to lead me toward the head table to meet C. K. Steele's sons and, with them, Carrie Patterson's son, up for the day from Tampa.

Derald Patterson reaches out for my hand with both of his.

"Your mother must've been a very brave woman," I say.

He smiles, head bowed, so two gold molars show, and shifts his neck to the side, adjusting the collar of his suit coat.

"I didn't know her well," he says. "She died when I was so young." He gestures toward the podium where her portrait is displayed front and center, right beside Jakes'. "I'm only now beginning to understand."

"I know what you mean," I say.

. . .

Back in my room, I e-mail Laurie to tell her I made it safely,
and I call my mother at Community Care.

"How's it going? How did the appointment go yesterday?"

"Well, we decided to stop the chemotherapy." She is slur-
ring so much I'm not sure that I heard her right.

"What?"

"The blood counts were no good."

She sounds groggy and far away.

I guess I won't be driving Mom to her chemo appointments
when I get to California. I'm not sure what I'll be doing.

"It's a relief," she says.

"I'll bet it is."

But it doesn't feel like a relief to me. Even though I didn't
want her to start this round in the first place, even though I
hate the chemo with a passion, hate the whole hair-falling-out,
kidneys-shrinking, puking mess of it, quitting still feels like,
well, quitting.

"I'm going to get out of here soon and go home," my mother
tells me.

"Yes, you will," I say.

. . .

In the evening, I attend a town hall meeting. I walk to the
wrong church, Bethel Missionary Baptist, early, and then finally
make it to the right one, Bethel AME. I skulk in and take a seat
next to Barbara DeVane who smiles broadly, her lipstick red.
I'm late, but I haven't missed much. A sociologist from A&M
is giving a PowerPoint presentation outlining problems in the
black community: high incarceration rates, low home ownership, and appalling education statistics. Forty three percent
of black ninth graders do not finish high school. Nearly half!

Every. Single. Day.

None of these statistics is worth writing down because none say anything new. I am trying to listen, genuinely, but I am also distracted by an older black man stooped over a cane in the corner. It might be Johnny Herndon, I'm thinking. It could be.

A long row of A&M students sit straight-backed and serious in the row of folding chairs in front of us. No flip flops here. No hippie flirtations. But it doesn't seem to make a difference. These kids are up against it. More than one speaker rants on the wrongness of rap, and hip-hop culture, and boys with their undies showing. The college kids look weary, their lips tight, but they sit still and silent, and they do not lose eye contact with those on the podium, not for one moment. They listen to the endless incantation: Martin King. Martin King. Martin King.

One black woman stands in the back to say she used to run an early-childhood education program and when she called A&M she'd get five or six volunteers, but when she called FSU she'd get fifty. Another speaker asks dramatically about passing the torch and there is no answer. Who will take up the mantle? How these dozen college students take this beating without flinching, like John Lewis bowed over under the police baton, I don't know. I'm not one of them, but it's making me mad.

They try to defend themselves. One well-spoken recent graduate says she was watching a video about the four little girls in Birmingham and her roommate didn't know what it was, that too many young people don't know their own history, their own legacy.

"They should be learning it at church," one speaker snaps.

"Some people don't feel like going to church. Some of us don't feel welcome."

Finally, a small group of students stand to announce that they can't stay long but that they are planning a march in protest of the death of Martin Lee Anderson, a young black man who recently died in a juvenile-detention center, a boot camp of sorts.

An NAACP leader replies—impossibly!—that his organization opposes the protest because they don't want to put college kids in danger. Didn't college students start the movement? Didn't they carry it along? Weren't they the foot soldiers? These contradictory refrains are older than fifty years. Protect the children. Let the children lead. What's wrong with the children? The mood in the room is this: exasperation.

The evening drags on an hour too long, while the group tries, democratically, to consider a motion to eliminate the FCAT, the statewide test that adds exponentially to the number of black kids who can't graduate high school.

"Amen," cries Barbara DeVane. "Let's do it!" She is on her feet beside me fists pumping.

A white lawyer standing in the back dampens the mood.

"The FCAT isn't the problem," she says. "It's getting the kids the skills to pass the FCAT."

The audience seethes. The tension pulls taut, tauter than it's been all day. But no one stands to rebut.

A state senator tries to explain more practically that with a Republican state senate, house, and governor, no motion from this piddling town hall meeting will change the FCAT or anything else. He says this gently; he knows how not to offend constituents. But he also says this: "I knew more about politics when I was in college than most of the people in this room know now. That's sad."

I glance behind me. Could-be Johnny Herndon is leaving, cane walking to the door.

The frustration in the room is palpable, like the burned-coffee smell of a church hall, an AA meeting, earnest people striving then failing, Humpty Dumpty style, over and over.

Every. Single. Day.

Sometimes in trying to right heinous wrongs, you run the danger that all you see is the wrong, all you feel is the cold, hard seat and the slow clock hands turning. God knows, I would like to go back to my room this minute to e-mail Laurie and watch TV. I have my own family to worry about. I am tired. Who here isn't? *Now you know what it was like for us.*

A woman stands to say she brought her thirteen-year-old tonight.

"I told her she had to come because that's how it was back in the day, when people brought their children to mass meetings, when sometimes children brought their parents to mass meetings."

The thirteen-year-old, for her part, looks miserable. To say I feel her pain is an understatement. I look at her mother, my age probably, and like me, I'm guessing, the child of activists. For a moment I think: how could she do that to her kid? Then I realize: if I had kids, I'd probably drag them here, too.

The woman suggests that maybe the *Brown v. the Board of Education* decision to integrate schools was not such a good thing. Maybe she's right. Here we sit on cold chairs, among many more empty chairs, in a dimly lit room, watching a PowerPoint presentation, listening to rhetoric about dead Martin King. The sameness weighs heavily. Something hasn't worked.

"You know, if we had our own schools. . . ."

Barbara DeVane crosses her arms on her chest and rolls her eyes. She doesn't buy this self-deprecating crap for one second. Put John Rudd in a room with her, and he wouldn't stand a chance. But here tonight Barbara DeVane is not the only one who's at wit's end.

Cynthia Williams stands. She is a small woman—diminutive, a historian might say—but instead of speaking in place, standing amongst the rows of cold metal chairs, she strides forward with fierce restrained dignity toward the front of the room, where the all-male panel parts like the Red Sea to make room for her at the microphone, where she wants to speak, unscheduled and off the cuff, as a self-described former school-teacher. Standards, she says, are written for middle-class white kids. Class size is too big. She is right, and she is angry, and she is articulate, and Barbara DeVane, nearly teary with relief that the self-deprecation is over, stands to cheer and pump her fists:

"You tell it, Cynthia. That's the truth, Cynthia."

But even Cynthia Williams breaks off a piece of blame from distant powers-that-be and sets it down hard in the somber room.

"Our kids are up against kids who are read to in the womb," she says with bitter enunciation. "In. The. Womb. It's up to each of us to take responsibility at home, to do what's right."

CHAPTER SIXTEEN

Tarpon Springs

The war had left scars on Jon Folsom, I understood that. Not so much scars as unhealed wounds ready to crack open and ooze each time our conversations skirted anywhere close to Korea, as they did regularly, because of the current war in Iraq and because of his refrain: that courage is not the point, that what he and my father did during the bus boycott was scary, sure, but courage is something you are born with, that in war you see this all the time. Some people can deal with fear, some people can't. Now, in Florida, a few short hours from meeting Jon Folsom in person, I'm thinking I must be in the latter group, because after all the late night calls and intimate handwritten letters, I'm still a little scared to meet him.

What do I know about him, anyway? That he worked as a pipefitter. That he swims two miles a day. That he is, by self-definition, a big guy. And because he would not be coming north to Tallahassee for the anniversary celebration, I'd planned to drive six hours to see him, alone, some three thousand miles from anyone I know well enough to call for help.

I'd be more scared if it weren't for the conversation I had with him from the Seattle Airport as I waited for my flight to be called.

"Did you hear that?" he said.

"Hear what?"

I thought I'd heard a background noise, a television perhaps.

"That was my wife, Vita, giving me a kiss."

"Your wife?"

This was the first I'd heard of her.

She took the phone and apologized that their place was small and they could not accommodate me overnight.

"Oh, no. I would not expect you to," I said.

"I knew your father, too," she said.

"Well, I'm looking forward to meeting you," I said.

. . .

I left Tallahassee at five on Friday morning with an ambitious plan to drive six hours south, visit the Folsoms, and return the same day. Now I follow the interstate, driving I-75, listening to ubiquitous classic rock, looking at ubiquitous scenery: chain stores and gas stations and restaurants and thick, green trees. When I cross the Suwannee and see the musical notes now painted white on the green interstate road sign—*Way down upon the Swanee River far far away*—I try to picture Jon Folsom standing here, chucking a shotgun off the shoulder of the interstate before I remember that in 1957—duh!—there was no interstate. Right river. Wrong freeway. I stop twice to look for a pay phone. No luck. Even at a rest area that advertises telephones, the phones are out of order. When I find one at last and call from a booth in a pavement-cracked corner of a seedy gas station, Jon gives me precise and detailed directions.

"You'll see the truck in the driveway," he drawls.

I picture a battered Ford with a gun rack.

I drive another hour west and then pull into the driveway behind an older Ford Bronco in front of a small, flat-roofed house, white with turquoise trim, on a hot, unshaded lane of small, well-kept homes without lawns. A large turquoise seahorse adorns the garage door. A lime tree droops from the weight of a thousand fragrant blossoms. Flowering shrubs line the walkway.

I park the rental car and step into the sun. And there on the porch stand Jon and Vita. He is heavyset and white bearded, barefoot in shorts and a t-shirt, more Santa Claus than Hell's Angel. Vita is elegantly gray and gracious. Not for the first or last time this week, I chide myself for my ridiculous fears.

They hustle me inside the cool house, where there is evidence everywhere of their left leanings: NPR on the radio and posters of native wildflowers. The texture and mood of their home feel immediately familiar, like the homes of my friends. They live on social security, they explain, but they sit me down to feast.

"What do you want on your sandwich?" Jon asks.

"Anything is fine."

"No," he insists. "What do you *want?*"

He has ham and gruyere cheese, deli bread and bleu cheese-stuffed olives, pickles, and a full refrigerator shelf of Old Milwaukee beer.

"We read in *Consumer Reports* that it's the best one."

These are luxuries, I know, purchased for my sake. I do not want to be rude. I don't think it's past eleven in the morning. On Pacific Time, from which I've yet to adjust, it's not yet eight. But this is, clearly, a special occasion, so I sip from the icy can.

"It tastes great," I say. And it does.

Jon putters around the kitchen while Vita and I sit at the kitchen table.

"When your dad and Jon came down to Miami, you know, I had my own place," Vita says. "You could do that in those days." Afford it, she means. "And there was this little group of guys, free spirits, beatniks. They wanted to be writers, and I was drawn to them."

Jon sits at last at the table with us. He is more vulnerable in person than on the telephone, almost shy, his blue-eyed gaze earnest behind wire-rimmed glasses. He doesn't look like a pipefitter, nor does he look like an intellectual. He looks like someone's grandfather, as I suppose my dad would by now. I'd never allowed myself to imagine it, but at age seventy-five, my dad would be gray and bald and heavyset; he'd be kindly and ornery in equal measure. And like Jon, I imagine, he'd be an enthusiastic storyteller.

Jon launches in.

"We'd been living in fraternities, you know, and it's a good thing Joe came along, because he hated it about as much as I did, so we got this apartment together. It had this great balcony with wisteria growing over the railing, and Joe loved to sit out there and read—he was always reading—and one day he was sitting there when a flying squirrel came and landed on his chest."

My dad befriended the squirrel, and the squirrel came back. Day after day. So eventually, Jon says, my dad bought him a wheel to run on. This story is drenched in artistic license—who ever heard of a flying squirrel on a hamster wheel on a balcony?—but it's a good story so I listen, and he says again that my dad would be ecstatic to know that I am a writer. He repeats the word: ecstatic.

"He was never without a book," Jon says. "Never."

Vita chimes in. "Whenever he left, instead of 'goodbye' he said one of two things. He said: 'Read.' Or he said: 'Be.' That was one of his favorite sayings: 'Don't seem to be, just be.'"

Sounds like an arrogant twenty-five-year-old, I think. But I say nothing.

"He was a good person," Vita says.

I nod and stare out sliding glass doors toward plants on a shaded patio, the lush greenness, simple and varied, pots and trellises, and beyond that, in the blinding sun yard, a small citrus tree struggling.

"Your letter brought all those memories flooding back," Vita says. "It's funny. We can't remember yesterday, but we can remember years ago."

"But they're rich," I say.

Leaves flutter on the patio. Postcards and scrap paper mementos overlap on the refrigerator door.

"What?"

"Your memories are rich."

"Yes, they are," she says, but there is something unsaid in her voice, a sadness without wistfulness, not something to be indulged, but something to be steeled against. After lunch we retire to the living room, where I give them a bottle of Washington wine and show them snapshots of the family when Dad was alive, of Daisy, of Laurie and me and our cabin. Jon is taken with one photo of Laurie and me in work clothes at our half-finished house. Our grubby exuberance interests him far more, it seems, than the suburban staidness of my dad on the couch in a gaudy 1970s sweater vest, his collar askew, my sister and I in our Easter dresses in his lap, my mother looking tan and young and beautiful. And this annoys me. I want to linger on this photo, earth-toned and blurry, to say to Jon: See, this is really him; sure, he's bald and overweight, distracted by the camera and the three wiggly kids with unfashionable clothes and too-long sideburns, and yes, a tic. He's not exactly The Man, but he is a grown man, everyday, fallible, middle aged. Not a warrior. Not even a writer. Jon barely glances at it and laughs instead at Laurie and me caked in sawdust, and I know the reason. He didn't know that man in the photo. I did. I knew that man.

He gives me an embarrassing shower of gifts, some of them Florida souvenirs—a set of dog shark teeth, a sand dollar, a shell—and some more personal—my father's copy of *Paradise Lost* and a wineskin, a leather bag with a hand-painted bullfight scene on the side with a plastic squeeze nozzle at the top.

"Joe and I had one just like this. We took it full of red wine everywhere, to class sometimes. Joe could spray it across the room so I'd catch the wine in my mouth."

His eyes sparkle with boyish mischief, and I'm a little afraid he's going to tell the story of that one day again, the T. S. Eliot day. But he steals a glance at Vita, who returns it with a look of strained tolerance. I can tell she is thinking the same thing I am: not that one again. Please. We exchange a small smile, Vita and I.

The three of us settle into talk, deep real talk, of religion, for starters, and they are eager to speak of their own feelings, their measured skepticism. Jon cannot believe my father ever took what he calls a leap of faith, but he tears up when I tell him about the community at Our Lady taking care of us after his death. Whether he is moved by the goodness of our church friends or grieving, still, for the too-young death of his old friend, I don't know. He removes his glasses to wipe his eyes with an index finger and a thumb.

They talk about the hopefulness they had in their youth, about Dr. King and nonviolence.

"No one talks about these things anymore," Jon says.

"Everyone in Tallahassee is talking about those things," I say. "This week."

They won't argue, but they don't believe me. And I know they have no interest in being there, so I don't want to push the subject. But I can't help it.

The talk turns to greed and materialism, how everyone is for only themselves.

"Even the college kids," Vita says.

"Not the ones I saw this week in Tallahassee," I say, and I begin to describe the A&M kids that I had seen the night before, how much I admired them, but as I speak I can see that I have lost them. This is not the point.

"How is your mother?" Vita asks.

"She's fine. I mean, she's okay."

I explain as best I can, that she's in the nursing home, that she's just had to stop chemotherapy. The story sounds even worse when I tell it aloud, a regular conversation stopper. Vita listens intently, her gray eyes clear and intense.

"Some people can say 'I understand.' Others can say 'I know.' Do you know what I mean?"

I nod.

"Believe me," she says taking my hand, "I know."

In the past year, she tells me quietly, she's lost both her sister and her sister's son to lung cancer. And this, suddenly, is the point. This is the source of the raw sadness: not the shortcomings of our national leaders, or our apathetic teens, but the cold hard fact of grief.

"What about Daisy?" Jon asks. "How is Daisy?"

"She seems to be hanging in there."

"We had this beautiful cat, all white, named Harvey, you know, for the Jimmy Stewart movie. When he got sick and we had to put him down, I went to the vet and held him. Just held him," Vita says. "I can't do that again. We just can't get another cat."

"I understand. I mean, I know."

Vita smiles, but a pall has fallen over the room.

"Let's take a drive," Jon says.

. . .

As we creep through neighborhoods, lush and green, Jon talks about growing fruit trees. The local soil, limestone, he explains is good for grapes but ironically lousy for wine. He tried growing a peach developed at the University of Florida but has had no luck. Just last year he had a grapefruit and a lime tree die because, he thinks, of a canker.

"I couldn't stand to cut them down. It broke my heart," he says. Then he grins. "I was waiting for the trail crew to show up and do it for me."

"Where's the saw? I'll do it."

"I did it myself. I had to."

We drive along the wide blue gulf to Tarpon Springs, a nearby tourist town. It's a Greek town known for sponges, with a full-sized statue of a sponge diver, and small shops, and fishing boats docked in the estuary of the lazy Anclote River.

"Look, it's open," Jon cries.

He takes a hard left into a seafood restaurant parking lot.

"We wanted to take you here, we'd planned on it, but then we found out it was closed. But now it's open!"

I am still stuffed from lunch, but before I can say as much, he's leapt from the car and is marching up the steps to hold the door open for me, ordering a table for three.

"Have a beer," he says. "We're buying."

"You don't need to do that."

"Please. We want to. What do you want?"

I scan the chalkboard menu over the bar, and choose a Blue Moon. I can sense awkward surprise from my hosts and think I've offended them by ordering an expensive microbrew after raving over the Milwaukee's Best at home. But that, I soon see, is not the problem at all. The frosty pint glass that arrives is filled with liquid both murky and bright colored, not beery at all. I take a sip and cough a bit.

"It's a Florida special," Vita says and laughs. "Beer and orange juice mixed together."

"It's not half-bad," I say. But I'm lying, and they know it, and there's more laughter.

When the waitress arrives, Jon orders half the menu—fried oysters and calamari and crab cakes—even though I've already eaten, and it turns out, Jon can't eat much because he's been recently been to the dentist.

"Now," he launches in again. "You should really think about writing a play. . . ."

Outside sea birds perch atop piers. A half-submerged sponge boat lists in the blue water. I drink my Blue Moon and eat fingerfuls of calamari. Something about the outing feels giddily like childhood, the fried food, the sweet specialty drink like a Shirley Temple, the exuberant urgings to eat, eat, eat. It's odd that I've never met these people before, and I wonder if this is what it's like for those who take pilgrimages back to Europe to meet distant relatives, the celebratory mood, the delight in connections across space and time, the sightseeing and hospitality, even the banter.

"But, Jon, I told you: I don't want to write a play."

Vita chimes in on the authenticity of art, how an artist must do what an artist needs to do, and the relationship of Vincent Van Gogh and his brother, and another hour passes easily, and before we leave, Vita orders a huge piece of coconut cake to go.

The early sadness has dissipated completely. Until we get in the car. On the way home, I am feeling so comfortable that I grow talkative and launch into the story of the night my dad died, how he went out jogging even though he wasn't supposed to, how I sat on that couch waiting, how I was watching reruns on TV. It's my most private memory, and here it is spilling out from the cramped back seat of a two-door Bronco.

Jon and Vita are silent.

It's too late to take it back. These are strangers after all, and all my anguish might be too much for an afternoon drive amongst the trinket shops of Tarpon Springs.

The silence grows long.

"Well, Joe always was hard-headed," Vita says at last. "He taught me the Italian word for it, stubborn. I can't remember it exactly."

Meanwhile, Jon has taken a right turn on the highway. Despite his silence, he wants to expand the tour, to continue the celebration. But the sun is setting on the Anclote. If I left this minute, I wouldn't get to Tallahassee before midnight. Now he is driving slowly south, the wrong direction, away from their house.

"Where are you going, Jon?" Vita asks.

"I'm looking for that pizza joint we like."

"We can't have pizza. We're stuffed, Jon, and besides, she has to get back."

Vita is gentle and persistent. I try to picture my parents still married at this age, and I wonder if Jon and Vita have kids, or ever had them. I haven't asked. Whether it's premonition or cowardliness, I'm afraid to.

Jon pulls off into the parking lot of the pizza joint, an old railroad depot, and sighs. Vita turns toward me and her expression is easy to read. It says: you have to tell him.

"I really do have to get going," I say.

"You're staying in a hotel up there?"

"They're putting me up. I'm riding on the coattails of your brave act, Jon."

He hesitates, and then looks at me in the rear view mirror, his blue eyes watery again.

"That's a very kind thing to say."

"It's the truth," I say.

"Next time you'll have to bring Laurie with you."

"I will," I say.

He puts the Bronco in reverse to begin his reluctant U-turn.

Back at the small house, Jon scrambles into the garage as I collect my things to load into the rental car.

"Wait. I have to show you something."

"She has to go," Vita hollers.

"Just a minute," he says.

He wants to show me paintings he's been doing, he says, because of my inspiration. What inspiration that might be, I can't imagine. The inspiration of memory, of his old college pal brought back into focus? Or my interest in art, in literature? Or my admiration for his courage? I know it's simpler than that. I've taken the time to listen to his stories. Maybe that's enough. And the paintings, when he pulls them out, tell yet another story. There is one of the Phoenix rising, angular and sly; one of an alligator winking; one of a spectacular polluted sunset. The paintings are large but subtle and playful, boldly colored and boxy. They are, in a word, hopeful.

"They are amazing," I say.

"You really think so?"

"I love them. You should do more. Really."

The large canvases lean against the couch back in the darkening living room, reminding me of those half-carved wooden busts in our garage on Burnside Court, my dad's last stabs at artistic expression. I glance again at my watch. It's after seven.

"I've really got to go."

"Just one minute. One more minute." He shuffles out to the garage again.

I can't stay any longer.

"He'll keep you for an hour," Vita says. "He is bad at good-byes. He does this to my sister. You just have to go."

Vita takes my hand firmly and walks me into the yard before he returns.

"Read," Vita says squeezing my hand. "Be."

I ease out of the driveway in reverse and then crane my neck as I shift gears, hoping for one last glimpse of him. There's only a dark shadow against the canvases on the couch. I wave anyway, hoping he might notice.

CHAPTER SEVENTEEN

Not Forgotten

The activist grandmas. That's who I'm among this morning; it's an honor and it's a hoot. We sit side by side on a hard, splintery pew in a historic church, a pretend church, really, at the Tallahassee Museum, clapboard sided, old-timey, with a potbelly stove, and most noticeably today, no air conditioning. My pew-mates are community pillars, some of whom had been on the dais at the luncheon on Thursday wearing frilly hats the size of cafeteria platters. Today they're wearing matching boycott anniversary t-shirts and they joke freely with me and with each other, mainly about the heat. Organizers have distributed fans to the crowd, popsicle sticks topped by cardboard with the fiftieth anniversary emblem on them, and the activist grandmas flutter them with aplomb.

Up front sit eight panelists who will offer so-called historical perspective on the boycott. Among them is ninety-year-old Stetson Kennedy, a white man who once infiltrated the Ku Klux Klan, and, again, as the only woman, Patricia Stephens Due. The others are scholars whose work I've read. I take notes diligently on competing sociological theories, biographical tidbits, critical nomenclature, as the t-shirt grandmas nudge me good-humoredly. They don't need theories. They lived it. They *are* the historical perspective. Still, they listen respectfully. Many speakers acknowledge the importance of student involvement in the boycott, how it set the stage for later activism on campus throughout the South. One speaker mentions the FSU students who supported the boycott, and Reverend Foutz in the pew directly in front of us turns and smiles wide. I am slipping into schoolgirl mode, listening and not listening, writing longhand across the wide-ruled lines, the heat getting hotter and the boredom getting more boring, when a speaker missteps.

"Remember," he says, "no students went to jail during the boycott."

I try to give him the benefit of a doubt. Maybe he's using that typical timeline that puts Johnny Herndon's and Leonard Speed's arrest after the official end of the boycott in December. Then again, he's been studying the movement for fifty years, and I've only been at it for one. Even if my dad weren't involved, all I'd have had to do would be to read the Sunday newspaper fold-out to know that students *had* gone to jail. I wonder if this is what organizers meant when they told me in their letters that there was still controversy surrounding the boycott. I glance around to see that no one else seems bothered. Though it'd be hard to tell. Most people in the little church are fluttering their fans and peeking at their watches. They are ready to be done.

When we emerge into the breezy courtyard, I corner Barbara DeVane. I'm worried about my dad's legacy, sure, but I also have more immediate concerns.

"What should I wear to the black-tie gala? I mean, I only have one dress. I don't think I should go."

"Oh, honey," she says, "they know you're white." She throws back her head and laughs. "You'll be fine," she says patting my arm with something close to pity.

A quiet, stately woman approaches, a woman I've seen at several events. She introduces herself as Barbara Black, and she says was a faculty member at A&M on the day in 1956 when students took over the buses, though she does not look old enough. She says the excitement in the air was positively electric.

"I'd never experienced anything like it," she says.

"Have you since?"

"No. Never."

She also wants to tell me the story of Reverend Metz Rollins, though I've already learned much of it. In 1953, Metz Rollins arrived in Tallahassee, not yet thirty years old, to serve as pastor of Trinity Presbyterian Church, a new black congregation in a traditionally white denomination. He was to minister in an elementary school while they waited to build a new church with money donated by First Presbyterian, the larger and grander white church downtown. When Rollins got involved in the boycott—as a board member of the ICC, no less—the white Presbyterians promptly yanked the land for the new church. At that point, Rollins was ready to leave town, but his tiny congregation wouldn't stand for it. They admired their brave young minister and gave him a unanimous vote of confidence.

Eventually, in 1958, Metz Rollins did leave Tallahassee. He moved to Nashville, where, in 1961, he joined the famous sit-ins and was chosen to be among the first Freedom Riders, though he was unable to make the trip. And that was not the end for Metz Rollins. Not by a long shot. His name pops up at every juncture in civil rights history. In demonstrations following on the heels of marches in Birmingham in 1963, he was beaten bloody on Easter Sunday. In 1964, he traveled as part of a tiny delegation of Presbyterians to Hattiesburg, Mississippi, where he coordinated a revolving picket line for voters' rights for six months. And, of course, he was in Selma.

Still, for some reason, his name does not appear on the honor roll either here at the museum or in the fold-out section of the *Democrat*, though Barbara Black's does. This slight seems much worse than the fact that the speaker this morning failed to acknowledge my dad's ride. Here was a movement leader, a career foot soldier. History, I'm realizing, is full of slights, big and small.

Barbara Black and I walk together across the courtyard to a museum exhibit that has been designed for the boycott anniversary. We pull open the heavy doors and enter the room, eyes adjusting to the light, and there front and center stands a Klansman. Not a real Klansman, of course. A mannequin wearing a Ku Klux Klan robe, but the sight of it chills me, unnerves me even, unnerves everyone who enters, you can tell. The mannequin is about my size, and the robe is well worn, trademark white, with a hand-stitched patch. Who sat and painstakingly sewed such a thing? Who donned it in the night? Where did he go? What did he do? The robe fit a very small man, figuratively as well as literally. Knowing as much doesn't dampen the effect.

"Spooky, isn't it?" Barbara Black says.

"Yes it is."

I roam the room to see tributes to Jakes and Patterson, to C. K. Steele, to the icc board members and carpool drivers, and soon I stand with a crowd gazing at the small display that describes my dad's role in the boycott. A placard tells a succinct history-book version: that an integrated group of six students had boarded a bus to ride together, and when three moved, those three were arrested.

One of C. K. Steele's sons, Derek, comes up behind me: "Getting arrested for doing something right? Now that's something to be proud of."

"Maybe we should be the next generation," I say.

"Yes, we should."

I can see a photo of C. K. Steele on a wall behind Derek and the physical resemblance is so close it's unnerving. I can see how he admires his father, how he longs to be like him, and I can't help thinking how unlikely it is that he will ever live up to that. It's my story, too, I think. And it was my dad's story, too. Maybe, in some ways, it's everyone's.

A serious young black man standing behind us in a t-shirt interrupts testily.

"The problem now," he says, "is so many of us are being arrested for doing nothing."

All Derek and I can do is nod in agreement.

. . .

"Your dad was one of those FSU students in the movement, right?"

John Due, the husband of Patricia Stephens Due, is a very tall black man with a small ponytail at the back of his neck, an iconoclast and an accomplished civil rights lawyer, a foot soldier in his own right, who nobly sits up front each time his wife speaks, a first husband of remarkable grace in this crowd. He's caught me just as I'm heading for my car.

"You should study the culture of the 1950s," he says. "You know, the James Dean movies, Camus and Sartre, the whole scene."

"You're right," I say. "My dad was into all that stuff."

He tells me about a football game he attended at A&M when he first arrived at college.

"I came from Indiana, and the South, you know, wasn't like up there," he says. "Everyone wore suits and ties even to a football game. But then here comes Patricia wearing a crazy outfit with ten white guys in shorts and sandals following after her like the Alpha. You know what Alpha personality means?"

"Yeah," I say. "Top dog."

"Those white guys were disillusioned, see; they were searching. They came to the movement looking for something," he said.

I stand stone-still in the doorway. Somehow it had never

occurred to me that Jon Folsom and my dad *came* to the movement disillusioned. The story I'd heard all my life was the one Jon Folsom tells: that the world went to hell in the late 1960s right around the time I was born. A helluva message for a kid: you were born too late. Now I know I can't be the first child to have heard this message spoken or unspoken. My father was born shortly after the stock market fell, at the height of the Great Depression, my mother at the height of World War II. We're all born at precisely the moment the world went to hell. We start out disillusioned and searching. The trick is to overcome it.

. . .

At seven sharp, Karen picks me up for the black-tie gala. Karen is a freelance lobbyist, a political consultant, who juggles a dozen liberal causes at the state capitol: health care, women's rights, migrant workers' rights. She says that even though she is employed by several different organizations, she can hardly eke out a living. The rest of the state lobbyists, most for corporate interests, make salaries exponentially higher.

"Do the lobbyists really effect change?" I ask.

She looks at me wearily, as if she does not have time for someone as naïve as me.

"Don't fool yourself. Lobbyists effect all change, my dear," she says. "Every single drop of it."

She drives a fifteen-year-old convertible vw Rabbit, a small car plastered in stickers for now and No Nukes. I like the idea of arriving at a black-tie gala in such a vehicle. We arrive at the brand-new multimillion dollar athletic club at Florida State, where fifty years ago black people could not step foot on the lawn without risking arrest or worse. Now the sports heroes whose photos line the walls, including a recent Heisman Trophy winner, are, of course, nearly all black, as are most of the attendees of the gala.

Karen hands me a stole to throw over my shoulders, to gussy myself up a bit, and I clutch it like a toddler playing dress up. As soon as we're inside, I can see that it doesn't matter a whit. Sure, people are dressed to the hilt: frilly hats and dresses, tuxedos even for the smallest boys, but they are gracious and kind, welcoming, and in the mood for a celebration. All week, Bill Proctor has been bragging about the dancing that will go late into the night.

"We're gonna shake it down!" he'd say, grinning. And the listeners would roll their eyes and shake their heads, all except Barbara DeVane.

"Amen," she'd holler. "Yes we will!"

The very large room—ceilings higher than a gymnasium, wood floors fancier—is decorated to commemorate the boycott anniversary with posters and photos and, most noticeably, elaborate fabric banners with the silhouette of old-style buses. Cynthia Williams ushers me to a seat beside a white man, Lance Block, the lawyer grandson of a Jewish lawyer who put up the money for bail for students during Patricia Due's era, and earlier too, he thinks.

"Lance's grandfather could have been the one who put up the bond money for your father," his wife suggests.

It's certainly possible. It makes a lot more sense than the NAACP posting bail for him since there would be no paper trail, no official memory of such a gesture. White folks, as Johnny Herndon so gently put it, had to work behind the scenes to avoid "retaliatory measures." Sitting beside the Blocks, I feel as though maybe the loose dangly ends of history can, after decades, weave back together. Maybe that's the whole purpose of events like this, even if, at times, all the pomp and circumstance is a little much.

Speakers speak. Preachers pray. Once again I stand to be acknowledged, the white daughter of a foot soldier among many black public officials: black judges, black bankers, black mayor, black city and county commissioners. The dais, once again, is full, and among those seated there are a handful of A&M students who served on the planning committee for the anniversary celebration. Talk about young people getting involved! Well, I suppose, it depends how you define getting involved. I try to picture my dad in a tuxedo on a dais at twenty-five. Not a chance. Even C. K. Steele, in the enlarged photograph propped in front of the podium, looks out of place. The fire in his eyes, the hunger for righteousness: how does this mesh with salad and dessert forks? I am trying again, trying always, to keep my cynicism at bay, when the keynote speaker, Congressman Kendrick Meek, stands.

I've been hearing the name all week, but I am surprised when I see him. He is my age, but he looks younger, handsome and smiling, and when he stands to speak, he is, in a word, dazzling. He pulls out his U.S. Congress voting card and holds it high in one hand, with his mother's U.S. Congress voting card in the other. He says they are only the second mother/son combination to go to Congress. He carries both cards in his wallet, he says, to remember where he came from. He talks about how we must remember the unsung heroes and sheroes of the Tallahassee boycott, of the movement in general, and finally, he wonders how C. K. Steele would be accepted here. Steele was not accepted in his own day, not as he should have been—he's still not accepted, really, Meek says, not to the extent that he should be—because he went against the grain, because he told the truth. This is precisely what I'd been thinking five minutes before when I scolded myself and banished the thought. See? I remind myself. It's not cynical to tell the truth.

When Meek steps down everyone at the table repeats their

favorite story about him, one I've already heard a half dozen times tonight: how he and Barbara DeVane once staged a twenty-four-hour sit-in at Jeb Bush's governor's office, protesting a plan to terminate affirmative action programs. They ordered a bucket of fried chicken delivered for dinner after the government offices closed with a cell phone smuggled in amongst the legs and wings. Soon the media had the story and within days fifty thousand people showed up in Tallahassee to march in support of their cause. Lobbyists, it turns out, are not the only ones who can effect change.

Finally, it's time to dance. The music is loud and soulful, and I am a little tipsy from nerves and one glass of wine. Twice I try to line dance, and though an A&M student tries to show me the simple steps, I stumble before bowing out to sit alone at a nearby table and watch. I've never felt whiter in my life.

As I sit alone, a very large woman, dressed in a stunning white gown, charges toward me.

"I'm so glad you came," she says. "Let me give you a hug."

I am positive that I haven't met this woman yet this week, and I am confused, but I stand and accept her hug.

"I'm on the anniversary celebration planning committee. Cynthia read us your letter months ago, and we just cried and cried. I'm so glad you came. You must be so proud. Aren't you proud now?"

"I'm honored to be here."

"And you're proud of your dad, right?"

I nod and smile. So this is what all the fuss is about, why they put me up in a hotel, and have me stand to be acknowledged, over and over. Like Johnny Herndon, they want me to believe. To believe in my dad. To believe in the cause.

"I'm so glad." She leans forward to hug me again. "You should take one of these banners. Really."

She points to one of the fabric banners with the bus silhouette.

"I'm going to get you one," she says.

"That's okay. Really."

"No. I'm going to get you one."

She goes and confers with Barbara DeVane, who smiles this time with her eyebrows furrowed, and sends my new friend into a back room. She returns, not with a banner, but with a poster with a collage of photos: Jakes and Patterson, C. K. Steele posing, bow-tied, with a charred cross, Metz Rollins, Dan Speed. And in the corner, a copy of the photo from The *Florida Star* that Cynthia Williams sent me months ago of three young men outside a courtroom: Herndon, Speed, and Spagna. The poster reads: *50th Anniversary. Tallahassee Bus Boycott. Time passed, but not forgotten.*

I stand beside her, arm in arm, and hold up the poster as one of her friends snaps a photo. As we pose, another woman approaches and introduces herself as Tella Marie Norwood, the daughter of Ed Norwood, also a founding member of the ICC. She, too, hugs me, and we pose together with her brother and with Derek Steele and his family. I am humbled. The Steeles remember the crosses burned in their yard and their home being bombed. Their father died of colon cancer not long after my father did, leaving his six kids with little security. Suddenly, the fact my father died young, victim in part of his own passion, does not seem so unique, or at least not as tragic as it once did. And not nearly so lonely.

· · ·

The next morning I stand in the air-conditioned foyer of Trinity Presbyterian and wait. How will I know him? How will he know me? In three days, I've become so accustomed to being the only white person in the room that I have forgotten that I might stand out. When I called Johnny Herndon, hoping to make a plan to meet him here, it was too late. He was already at his own church, Bethel Missionary Baptist, his wife told me.

"Oh, he won't mind. He enjoys a good church service," she said. It was the second time I'd heard that in a week.

Now the service is about to begin, so I take a seat. A moment later, in the middle of the opening hymn, a hand touches me lightly on the shoulder from the pew behind mine.

In the photograph with Leonard Speed and my dad, Johnny Herndon is the smallest of the three, wearing a sweater vest and sporting a thin mustache. He looked, I thought, a lot like dust-jacket photos of Langston Hughes. And now, fifty years on, there's a good chance I could have recognized him from that one photo except that he appears much taller than I expected. He stands straight in a fine brown suit. He takes my hand in his and holds it for a long time.

The congregation at Trinity is very small, only about twenty-five people, and they are more subdued than the Baptists we've been with all week. From the pulpit where she stands in her choir robe, Tella Marie Norwood introduces me and Johnny to the congregation as honored guests. She asks Johnny to say a few words, but he politely declines. Instead, Tella's brother, Ed, retells a story that Johnny told at the event he attended earlier in the week. Just before he was arrested, he had bought a new wool flannel suit. When the police picked him up, he was wearing it, and for the next two weeks of hard labor in the hot sun guards made him keep it on, until it was worn to tatters. Then, at last, they issued him prison garb. The congregation gasps and applauds. Johnny Herndon smiles tightly and bows slightly, as the choir starts another hymn.

. . .

At his home, Johnny introduces me to his wife, Clara, and we sit together in the living room.

"They called us forward at church," he reports, and Clara clucks her tongue. "If I'd known they were going to do that, I probably wouldn't have gone," he says.

"I'm sorry," I say. "We could have met someplace else."

"Oh, it's not your fault," he says. "I just don't care much for all the attention."

"Will you stay for a snack?" Clara asks.

"Oh, no. I really shouldn't stay long."

"The boycott," he says, "was going nowhere before we stepped up."

When Johnny first told me this, months ago, I didn't understand, but now I do. I can see where the gaps in the history lead to this precipice, this place where the boycott nearly faded away, unnoticed, in the too-chilling face of vigilantes on the street.

"Did people support you then? Did they realize the importance of what you'd done?"

"Oh yes. Everyone knew. Everyone. But it was different for your dad. He had it worse because he wasn't supported by his own people."

I've heard these refrains before from him and others, in letters and phone calls and musty archived interviews, but I like hearing them again, like the familiar anthems of the movement that have been sung, over and over, at each event this week. I hated "We Shall Overcome" as a kid. I heard it too often as a soundtrack to black-and-white TV documentaries. Now it feels different. More hymn or mantra than soundtrack, like something that has to be drummed into me. So, too, with Johnny's stories. Tell it again, I think. Tell it again. I need to hear it.

As we sit together on the couch in the living room after church on an early Sunday afternoon, he eases further into the past. Turns out the test ride he took in Tallahassee was not Johnny's first act of defiance. He'd sat up front on a bus once before, he says, in Amarillo, Texas, in 1951. He was on his way to San Francisco after boot camp, en route to Korea in full uniform. He'd been on a military flight, but the turbulence was so bad he got off, and when he boarded a Greyhound to take him the rest of the way, he decided to sit up front.

"That driver read me the riot act. He told me never to come back to Amarillo—and I never did—but he didn't dare do anything because I was on my way to serve my country."

After that, when he returned from the war, he didn't ride buses at all in Tallahassee. Even before the boycott he refused to face the humiliation, so when the opportunity came up to take this stand, he was ready.

"It wasn't a fluke, you mean," I say.

"No," he says smiling. "It wasn't."

"And you paid for it."

"I suppose."

Clara was working as a teacher at the time—they had recently married—and school district administrators gave her a subtle warning that Johnny should cut it out. She ignored it. Even Clara's father, who had worked for the city of Tallahassee for thirty years, received a warning.

"Did that worry him? Did it worry you?"

"No. My father-in-law told them: 'He's a grown man, I can't tell him what to do.'"

I'm thinking that Johnny has it backward. He thinks it was harder on my dad because white people saw him as a traitor, but my dad didn't have a young wife, no father-in-law, not yet. He was only endangering himself.

I show Johnny a digital photo of Jon Folsom I took yesterday. "Did you know him? He was a friend of my father's? He says he was on the bus with you."

He leans in close to study the tiny camera screen.

"No." He shakes his head. "It was a long time ago," he says. "I'm sorry."

I stuff the camera in my bag and bring out a small gift of smoked salmon I've brought from the Northwest, and Johnny calls his wife in to show her.

"Now are you sure you can't stay for a snack?" Clara asks.

"Well, I suppose I could," I say.

With that, the conversation turns to fishing and eventually to reptiles. Johnny shows me pictures of alligators and water moccasins. When talk sways occasionally back to the bus ride, his refrain is constant and familiar.

"We were the spark," he says. "Immediately after the ride everyone was enthused and coming to meetings. You had to get there early to get a seat."

He met Martin Luther King Jr., who came to Tallahassee in May 1957 to celebrate the first anniversary of the boycott and to try to force more press coverage of the protest in the face of the *Democrat's* stubborn refusal.

"A celebrity like that," Johnny says, "can keep the flame alive."

And Governor Collins, of course, came like a savior.

"It took courage for him to stand up on our side. His political career would have been brighter, but he sacrificed. See, had it not been for him. . . ." Johnny's voice trails off.

"Well, he told the sheriff and the chief of police if they didn't stop, he'd call in the National Guard. If the governor hadn't stepped in. . . ." He stares out the large picture window through the green layers of oak leaves, limp in the afternoon heat, and I follow his gaze out to his pickup in the driveway sporting a bumper sticker urging, impossibly, support for the police. I want to ask about it. I want to ask about so many things.

"It would have been like Selma," he says at last.

And with the mention of Selma, he loses composure. He pulls a clean handkerchief from his breast pocket, buries his face in it, and excuses himself to go down the hall.

I sit alone in the living room and then wander into the kitchen, where I find Clara preparing a multiple-course meal.

"Some snack," I say, and she smiles. "Can I help with something?"

She has me fill glasses and set the table. Ice cubes clink. The oven door opens and shuts. Television news moans from a set in the corner of the room, something about Martin Anderson, the recent juvenile victim of the prison system.

"It's still hard for him," Clara says. "The memories."

I consider saying, "I know," but the truth is that I don't. I have not lived through what he has.

"I understand," I say.

Johnny reappears, having changed out of his suit, and sits with us among the dishes on the table: squash and corn, ham and bread, each homemade, each delicious. I find the Herndons as easy to be around as the Folsoms, about a thousand times easier than anyone at the black-tie gala. They ask about my family, and I tell them about my mother's illness. Clara offers sympathy. She, too, took care of an ailing parent.

In passing, Clara mentions Dan Speed's wife, Leonard's mother, who goes to church with her each week. I am surprised that she is alive, this woman in her nineties, and even more surprised that she has not yet been acknowledged at the events, and I say as much.

"They hardly mention Dan Speed. I don't understand this whole thing."

"People have their own versions. They've taken a kind of control of the history," Johnny says.

I know exactly whom he's referring to now, and I pause for a moment deciding whether to say anything.

"A speaker yesterday said that no students went to jail during the boycott."

Johnny freezes. I can see the briefest glimpse of anger in his tightened lips, a weary grimace.

"I'm glad I wasn't there," he says with a quick shake of the head, "because I would have walked out."

I'm not sure how to respond. Perhaps I should have walked out. Honesty, I decide, is the best policy.

"The ego in that room," I say shrugging, "was nearly suffocating."

We all laugh and return to the meal, to easy friendly chatter, until at last Clara stands to begin clearing the table.

"It's so nice that you've come," she says. It's the most courteous of hints: time to leave.

"I'm sorry that I can't offer you more," Johnny says. "I didn't know your father well. We only met a few times."

"It's okay," I say. "Really. You've shared so much. It's the story that I'm trying to figure out. I want to piece it together. I just want to understand."

"Yes," he says, looking me in the eye. He is not pleading, nor is he threatening. His voice is even, matter-of-fact, as practical and plain-spoken and unflinching as my mother's is or as my father's was.

"Someday," he says. "A historian is going to get this story straight."

CHAPTER EIGHTEEN

Heroes and Sheroes

The freedom march, such as it is, convenes at the bus plaza under the statue of C. K. Steele in stifling afternoon heat.

"Ninety-six degrees," Proctor announces, exuberant as ever. "It's not stopping us."

The crowd, by any standards, is meager. Maybe fifty people, mostly black, but a few whites. The lawyer, Lance Block, stands up front in jeans and flip-flops. The octogenarian activist, Laura Dixie, stands under the statue in the back with me. Speaker after speaker stands to say a few words. More than a few of them mention the fact that Jeb Bush, the president's brother and Florida's governor, in his mansion just down the road, hasn't shown up for a single boycott anniversary event. No surprise there.

Morris Thomas takes the microphone. His is the most famous face of the Tallahassee bus boycott, mainly because of a scheduling mishap. Thomas tells the story with good humor. He'd just returned from military service in North Africa in December 1956 and heard rumors of a mass integrated ride. He was eager to join in, but he showed up exactly one day after Klansmen had lined the streets with their hatchets and boycott leaders had called the ride off. Problem was, he hadn't heard about the cancellation. Right here on the street corner where we stand waiting for the freedom march, Thomas boarded an empty idling bus and sat in front. The bus driver promptly shut the bus off and climbed off, but not until a photographer captured an image that subsequently ended up in history books:

the disgusted white driver, the steadfast Thomas. Because of the photo, even Thomas's ill-planned gesture made a difference in the long run.

"I was born and raised in Tallahassee," Bill Proctor says, "but I was in college in Boston before I saw that picture in a textbook. That picture changed my life, changed the way I looked at everything."

The march, once it begins, is short. The politicians and preachers that lead the way are, as they were in 1956, all men. Off-key voices wade through successive verses of "We Shall Overcome." Sunlight filters lazily through palm fronds. Bored motorcycle policemen guard quiet intersections. I overhear a young black boy complaining that his feet hurt in shiny wing-tips. Next to him a young white boy asks his mother if the church will have air conditioning. Only a few months ago I would have cringed at such a march, at such a pitiful show of outmoded liberal optimism, but I can't anymore. If Laura Dixie can still believe, then I can. If Morris Thomas can still believe, then I can. I sing in my best off-key voice and keep step with the others as we wind around the block toward Bethel Missionary Baptist Church, where I'd attended the service in January, where C. K. Steele had preached for twenty years, and where tonight Congressman John Lewis will speak.

I am excited. I can't help it. I want to hear John Lewis speak because of who he once was—a superhero from the pages of a book, of many books, the pages of history—and because of who he is: a man of integrity and courage and compassion. I want to hear him speak because I trust him to tell the truth. And it looks like I'm not alone.

We climb the steps onto the white-columned porch and find it crowded with jostling bodies. I assume at first that marchers are hesitant to enter the too-hot church, but I'm dead wrong. They're out here because the church is already packed, beyond packed in fact: there's not an empty pew in the house. I enter and stand in the main aisle gazing across the room, looking for Johnny Herndon. I see waves of fluttering paper programs and sweaters flung over pew backs. I see eager faces, nearly all black, nearly all older than me, hundreds of them, but I can't begin to pick him out. A woman nearby scoots over and pats the wooden pew beside her. I sit and immediately scoot over to make room for more.

The front of the church is lined with dark-suited black ministers—representatives of the NAACP, the SCLC, the Urban League, the Tallahassee Interdenominational Ministerial Association—each of whom stands in turn at the pulpit to warm up the crowd like opening bands at a rock festival. This ritual is a page straight out of the civil rights movement, where other preachers always preceded Martin Luther King Jr. As each man preaches, the others fiddle with their suit coats or their programs, or they stare out the windows, letting out an occasional encouraging "Amen." Only John Lewis, sitting front and center, remains silent. He nods solemnly, and his eyes do not move from the pulpit. Maybe this is a skill he's learned from having been the camera-center for so long, from having been on CSPAN: to feign interest, to feign unflagging attention, to feign seriousness. Maybe.

But you can't fake the presence that John Lewis has in this room. If I'd never heard of him before in my life, I could still feel it. This must be a small taste of what it was like to be in the room with Martin Luther King Jr. or, for that matter, with C. K. Steele.

Through preacher after preacher, the audience remains steady and transfixed, patient and eager.

Then John Lewis stands.

"God is good," he roars.

"Yes, he is," we reply.

Laurie persuaded me to bring the small cassette recorder that Jon Folsom sent. She told me to record what matters, so I have John Lewis's speech on a squeaky cassette, indelible, to turn to in the months and years ahead when I slide into hopelessness, which will be often enough.

John Lewis begins slowly, with his childhood in Alabama.

"I would ask my parents and grandparents and great grandparents: 'Why segregation? Why racial discrimination?' And they would say 'Don't get in the way! That's the way it is. Don't get in trouble.' But I was inspired by Martin Luther King, by Rosa Parks, by C. K. Steele, to get in the way. When they got in trouble, it was necessary trouble."

Murmurs of approval rustle through the crowd.

"And they got in the way!"

"Yes, yes, yes. Amen."

"We celebrate the civil rights movement because it changed this nation. I don't care what people say fifty years later. It *is* better in Tallahassee. It *is* better in the South. It *is* better in America. We brought about what I like to call a nonviolent revolution. And sometimes when I travel this country young people tell me, 'Nothing has changed,' and I tell them, 'Come walk in my shoes and I'll tell you what has changed!'"

The crowd is with him. They cheer loudly, a kind of cheering that feels intimate, visceral, communal. They lived it, too, many of them. They are thinking: come walk in *my* shoes! The age of the crowd is beginning to make more sense to me. They're not just churchgoing age: they are the former fly-by-night martyrs, the former revolutionaries. They, too, got in the way.

As John Lewis begins to trace the history of the movement from Montgomery to Tallahassee, I picture Mary Decker rounding the curves, fast as a gazelle, lapping other runners. There's beauty in watching someone do what they do better than anyone, the sheer grace. But there's more: there's the example they provide, the inspiration, the possibility. *I want to do that!* That's why my dad took me to all those track meets. That's why I'm sitting here. But what do I want to do now?

"We must tell the stories over and over again so that our children and their children will never, ever forget what happened."

That's it. That's what I want to do.

"In the sit-ins in Nashville in 1960, when we were sitting there waiting to be served, reading our books, doing our homework, writing a paper, and someone would come up and spit on us or put out lighted cigarettes in our hair, or pour hot water on us. . . ."

He recites the litany of offenses plainly and without complaint.

". . . . We didn't strike back because we'd come to accept nonviolence as a way of life."

He pauses briefly. Then he is off again. There's a lot to tell, and he will not leave any of it out. He describes his first arrest, in 1960.

"The moment I was taken to jail, I felt free. I felt liberated. I got in the way. And it's time for another generation to find a way to get in the way."

"Amen."

He talks about the March on Washington. John Lewis is, as Bill Proctor has said many times tonight, the only living survivor of the dozens who spoke at the podium that day.

"There was so much hope, so much optimism," he says, "but eighteen days later, at a church in Birmingham, the Seventeenth Street Baptist church, those four little girls were killed."

Pause.

"It was a dark moment. But we had to move on."

He explains the lack of registered black voters in the South in the early sixties, the ploys and the nonsense: poll taxes, literacy tests, how one black man with a PhD failed the literacy test, how one was told to count the jelly beans in a jar. So, John Lewis explains, they decided to start the Mississippi summer project in 1964.

"More than a thousand students came to work in voter-education drives, one day three young men that I knew, two white and one black—Andrew Goodman, Michael Schwerner, and James Chaney—went out to investigate the burning of an African American church, and they were stopped by the sheriff, arrested, and taken to jail. Later, the sheriff took them from jail and turned them over to the Klan, where they were beaten and killed."

"My Lord."

"It was a sad and dark hour for the movement, but we didn't give up."

"No, no."

"And I say to the young people here today: these three men didn't die in Vietnam. They didn't die in the Middle East. They didn't die in Africa or Central or South America. They died right here in our own country trying to get all our citizens to become participants in the democratic process."

"People ask why were we so concerned about what happened in this state in 2000? In Ohio in 2004? Because some of our people *died* for the right to participate in the democratic process, *died* for the right to vote."

. . .

This shift of focus to the wrongs at home, the wrongs today, is jarring and invigorating. These days the word "heroism," at least in the media, is reserved for young men and women who go to other countries for reasons they may be uncertain about, without questioning, and risk their lives. Does what they do take courage? Good god, yes. Does that make it right? It's a harder question. What I've been calling courage for the past several months is something more than that. It's integrity. The people in this church tonight are heroes not because they served the nation but because they decided, in very personal and difficult ways, that their nation, their community—the only way of life they'd ever known—was simply wrong. They are not falsely pious or blindly idealistic but earnest to a raw and glaring fault. It is plainly impossible, even for me, a child of the age of smirking irony, to look Laura Dixie or Johnny Herndon or even Morris Thomas in the eye and not feel rightly humbled. Time and the fickle taste of politics, the warmongers, may forget them, but they don't much care. They saw it. They did what they had to do. And what they had to do was right. You look at any one of them and you can see that fifty years later they still know: they did what was right.

· · ·

"So we went to Selma."

As soon as John Lewis says this word, I crane my neck to look for Johnny Herndon.

"Selma is in the heart of the Black Belt, fifty miles from Montgomery. They had a sheriff there by the name of Jim Clark. Sheriff Jim Clark had a nightstick on his left side and an electric cattle prod on the right. And he didn't use it on cows. One day when it was my turn to take some voters down to the courthouse to try to get registered, Sheriff Clark met me at the top of the steps, and he said, 'John Lewis, you are an outside agitator. You are the lowest form of humanity.'"

Here Lewis's voice grows soft and stubborn as clay, more Southern, angrier. "I looked up at the sheriff, and I said, 'Sheriff, I may be an agitator, but I'm not an outsider. I grew up ninety miles from here, and I'm going to stand here until these people are allowed to register to vote.' Sheriff Clark said, 'You're under arrest.' A week later, three hundred people were arrested, and one young man was killed by a state trooper. Because of what happened to him, we made a decision that we would march on Sunday, March 7, from Selma to Montgomery. We didn't have guns or billy clubs; we had blankets and knapsacks. We started walking, two by two, onto the Pettus Bridge, the main bridge out of town."

The crowd is utterly silent. They know what is coming.

"The man standing beside me was my friend Hosea Williams. Hosea looked down and saw this water and he said, 'John can you swim?' I said, 'No, Hosea. Can you swim?' 'No.' I said, 'Well, there's too much water down there. We're not gonna swim, we're not gonna jump, we're going forward.'"

Lewis takes a moment to savor the suspense in Bethel Missionary Baptist.

"I was wearing a backpack before it became fashionable to wear backpacks. I thought we were going to be in jail, so I wanted to have something to read. I had two books. I wanted to have something to eat. I had an apple and an orange. And since I was gonna be in jail in close contact with my friends, colleagues, and neighbors, I wanted to be able to brush my teeth so I had toothpaste and a toothbrush."

John Lewis has told this story into a microphone, over and over, for decades. He has told it more times than the Rolling Stones have played "Satisfaction." In the next few months I will often read analyses that claim that Selma was the high point of the civil rights movement. After that day, many historians agree, the spirit of nonviolence died. I would not make that argument to John Lewis. He is not drawing a line graph of history. He's not tooting his own horn. He is trying to make a point.

"We get to the highest point on the bridge, and down below

we saw a sea of blue Alabama State Troopers, and we continued to walk, and when we got within hearing distance of the state troopers a man spoke up. 'This is an unlawful march,' he said. 'I give you three minutes to disperse and return to your church.' In less than a minute and a half he said 'Troopers advance!'"

The crowd at Bethel Missionary Baptist slips beyond silence into stillness. Not even the fans are in motion.

"We saw the men putting on their gas masks, and they came toward us, beating us, trampling us with horses. I was hit on the head with a nightstick. I thought I saw death. I thought I was going to die. I thought it was my last protest. Forty-one years later, I don't quite understand how I made it across that bridge, back through the streets of Selma, back to that little church. But I do recall being back there. And someone asking me to say something. The church was full, more than two thousand people. I stood up and said, 'I don't understand how Brother Johnson can send troops to Vietnam but he can't send troops to Selma to protect people whose only desire is to be able to vote.' The next thing you knew I was in the hospital."

"On Monday morning Dr. King came by to visit me. He said, 'Don't worry. We will make it from Selma to Montgomery and we will pass the Voting Rights Act.' Eight days later Johnson introduced the Voting Rights Act. So don't tell me—because I'm a living witness—that when people start marching, when they start speaking out, things don't change."

This is the only point in the speech when John Lewis very nearly loses it. I wonder if the secret behind his anguish is not pain or humiliation but the fact that people like me can sit back and think it's all futile. John Lewis takes a moment to compose himself, and then he hollers into the microphone.

"Things. Can. Happen."

The church erupts.

Last time I sat in this church four months ago, I anguished over what I believed. This time I know: I believe in hope. I believe in doing what's right, no matter how big or small, and hoping that it's enough. And it is. It is enough.

"Today we stand on the shoulders of C. K. Steele. We stand on the shoulders of Martin Luther King, Medgar Evers, the four little girls, the three civil rights workers. We stand on their shoulders. As we celebrate the fiftieth anniversary of the Tallahassee bus boycott, don't forget we have a bridge to cross. Don't forget those ordinary people, nameless individuals. . . ."

"Amen, Amen."

". . . who gave all they have. Don't forget!"

"Amen."

"Don't forget!"

"Amen."

"It doesn't matter if we are black Americans, or Asian Americans, Hispanic Americans, or Native Americans, or gay and lesbian Americans, we are one family. Don't let anybody turn us against each other."

"No!"

"We are brothers and sisters, and we must continue to recognize and respect the dignity and worth of all of god's children. If someone had told me when I was sitting in, getting arrested, going to jail forty times; if someone had told me when I was left bloody and unconscious on the ground of the Greyhound bus station in Montgomery May of 1961 during the Freedom Rides; or if someone had told me when I had that concussion on the bridge at Selma, that one day I would be standing here . . ."

"All right. All right."

". . . celebrating the fiftieth anniversary of the Tallahassee bus boycott, well, God is good. God is good!"

The tiny cassette tape screeches with feedback. The crowd is on its feet and will stay there. John Lewis is growing hoarse but no less passionate, no less powerful.

"Hang in there. Don't give up. Don't give in. Keep your faith. Let the spirit of the Tallahassee bus boycott, the spirit of C. K. Steele and our mothers and fathers who have gone on ahead of us, and the spirit of God almighty, and the spirit of history be our guide."

I am stunned. I have never heard a more moving speech in my life. It doesn't matter if you get the story straight. It matters that you tell it. That you tell what it means, which is simply this: *Hang in there. Don't give up. Don't give in. Keep your faith.* For most of the last several days I have kept my mother out of my mind. Now I remember and I remember the poem my young father had memorized: *Rage, rage, against the dying of the light.* I am praying for strength, praying shamelessly for her to not give up, not give in, to keep her faith. As the standing ovation for John Lewis begins to subside, Bill Proctor takes the pulpit to try to draw out the moment.

"What we have just heard," he says, "is not third-person, not a PBS documentary, but first-person, a living eyewitness."

He spurs the crowd, teasing them, taunting them. Any minute someone could pull out a lighter and begin waving it overhead, calling for an encore. John Lewis, though, has taken his seat, and it seems like time for Proctor to wind down, to offer a prayer, perhaps, and then send us out into the world. The evening is growing long; the temperature has finally cooled. It's time to go home.

"We gotta keep the flame going, we gotta remember the stories, and we have a candle here. We're going to light it for those unnamed heroes and sheroes."

A large white candle has appeared in front of the pulpit at Bethel Missionary Baptist, in the exact same place where the young women stood to be saved four months ago.

"I'm gonna ask Mother Speed, Dan Speed's wife, and Leonard Speed's mother, to come forward. Reverend Dan Speed was a leader of the movement alongside C. K. Steele, and his widow is here today. Let's welcome her."

There are murmurs of approval. This crowd remembers Dan Speed, and they appreciate the recognition at last. I crane my neck to watch a very small elderly lady in a church dress and wide-brimmed hat, walking slowly forward from amongst the front pews.

"And I'm gonna ask Brother Herndon. Johnny Herndon. Could you come forward?"

From the very back corner of the church, he walks in his brown suit, his head high, his expression unreadable.

"I'm also gonna ask Sister Spagna, who comes to us from Seattle, Washington. Her father was a student at Florida State University who stepped up during the boycott. Where are you Sister?"

On the minicassette tape, you can hear a long awkward pause.

"Come on down. Don't be afraid."

I stand to pass the side-turned knees of my pew-mates and walk slowly toward the pulpit amidst the polite applause.

"Ladies and Gentleman," Proctor says, "what you have assembled here, is the daughter of one of the three students who were arrested trying to test the ordinance of the city of Tallahassee. Ana Maria is the daughter of the late, uhm . . ."

He leans over to ask in a whisper my father's name.

"Joseph. Joseph Spagna, a white student from Florida State University, who believed in this cause, in the justice of the boycott. And Mrs. Speed is the mother of Leonard Speed who was arrested on that day. And Mr. Johnny Herndon. . . ."

He pauses for effect. "Brother Herndon is the *surviving* arrestee of that event."

Over a few surprised gasps, and a cacophony of applause, Proctor continues. "Johnny Herndon was arrested and sent to jail to make Tallahassee a better place. While their names, Spagna, Speed, and Herndon, are already demarcated in history—will always be there in history—we pause now to recognize those who were not."

Proctor hands each of the three of us a white candle, and like the parents at a wedding, we lean in, one at a time, to light the larger candle with our smaller candle. Outside, the sky has darkened with night and clouds. Inside, the crowd has settled into silent remembrance. Perhaps even sadness. The flame flickers slowly, wax melting from the wick, then it takes, and we turn to walk back to our seats. Before I do, Johnny Herndon holds my hand again tightly in both of his.

"Keep in touch," he says.

. . .

The crowd streams toward the doors, stragglers mill in the aisles, and a long line has formed to speak with John Lewis. I told myself, before I came, to get his autograph, but now that seems silly. The night is getting late. I make my way instead to thank the organizers: Cynthia Williams, Bill Proctor, Reverend Foutz. And I say goodbye to Karen, the lobbyist, who wears a lapel button celebrating Rosa Parks, a button that she explains she got when she and Barbara DeVane went to see the body lying in wake.

"A pilgrimage," she calls it. "Barbara and I went on a pilgrimage to Montgomery."

"I suppose this has been a pilgrimage for me. Thanks for

everything," I say and turn, bag on my shoulder, to head for the door.

"What are you doing? Aren't you going to talk to Congressman Lewis?"

"I can't get anywhere near him tonight. He's like a rock star."

"You've had a little bit of that treatment this week, too," she says and smiles.

Now I'm really embarrassed. No longer a suspicious character, I have become something of a mascot here, a stand-in for all the nonbelievers out there. *You're proud of your dad now, right?* I am. Without a doubt I am. Derek Steele beckons to me from the podium.

"Go," Karen says.

I climb the steps onto the stage, cutting to the front of the line, and I pose again with the Steeles, with Rev. Foutz. At last John Lewis turns to me. He is exhausted, you can see it in his eyes, and he says to me what he has said to everyone tonight.

"Don't forget."

He puts one arm around me, as Derek snaps a photo for posterity. In it, I look like an awestruck schoolgirl, grinning wide, my bottom teeth showing the way they do only in photos from when I was very young, when I was a toddler splashing in the bathtub with my sister, or snuggled tight between my parents in my Easter dress. This snapshot will become Laurie's favorite souvenir of my whole Tallahassee adventure because it captures something so unquestioning and joyful. Something the polar opposite of cynicism and despair.

While I am still lingering, collecting myself, Proctor steps in from the porch to announce that it's starting to rain. We can hear the rumblings of thunder.

When I step out, it's dark.

"Where's your car?" Mrs. Foutz asks.

"I'm over at the Doubletree," I say. "I can walk."

It's only six blocks, but she looks concerned.

"Have a good night," I say, and I begin to walk, hands stuffed in my pockets, into yellow streetlight glow streaked with rain, and back out. As I pass the fenced-in cemetery, the darkest section of my short walk, I see a bearded black man emerge fast from the iron gate on the far side of the block. For a moment our eyes lock. It would take him a few minutes to walk the circumference of the fence, so even though I suspect it's paranoia, I walk faster, then look back to see him following at a fast clip. That's it. No more analysis. I take off up three steps at a time and into the silent lobby, wheezing and soaked. The desk clerk glances up, pen in hand, and then hastily back down. I take the elevator up six floors and switch on a baseball game for background noise, unnerved in a thousand ways. It's after eleven, and I haven't eaten since noon at the Herndons', a lifetime ago, so I order a bowl of soup from room service.

The young man who brings it is in his twenties, a college kid with long hair and lashes, Ashton Kutcher style, and he stops on his way out, though he's already been tipped generously, to study the poster leaning next to the television.

"What's this about?"

I'm a little defensive. Is he a frat boy ridiculing my historical obsession? Or worse, is he a modern version of the Florida racist?

"The Tallahassee bus boycott was an early struggle in the civil rights movement. My dad was involved," I say. "There have been events all week."

"Really? I wish I'd known. I'm sorry I missed it."

He studies the poster up close, and for a moment I consider giving it to him. What am I going to do with it on the airplane? It's much too big to fit in my luggage. But I'm too selfish.

"That's really cool," he says, and he's gone.

I'm staring at the poster hard when I realize it's flawed. Tallahassee has an extra *e*: Tallahasseee. I laugh aloud. It seems fitting to have received a special gift that might have been thrown away otherwise, something that only has value, really, to me.

In the morning, I slip out before dawn, the way my father did fifty years ago: he just picked up and left the sun-soaked campus, the wisteria-vine balcony, the threats and taunts and tense courtroom dramas, the newspapers spread over the floor, his name notorious or forgotten. He booked a flight or hopped a freight or stood on the road with his hair slicked back, his shirt untucked, and his thumb high in the wind. And he was gone.

The humid air hangs heavy even in the predawn dark. I lock the rental car, drop the keys in a lock box, and make my way toward the security gate, where I place the poster into a gray plastic bin with my shoes and my sweater.

The black man behind the X-ray monitor pulls it from the queue.

"What's this?" he asks.

"That's my dad," I say, pointing.

"So he's a hero?"

"Yes," I say without a second thought. "And that's Johnny Herndon. He still lives here in Tallahassee. He's a hero."

"Well, I'll be."

Soon the other security workers have left their stations to come have a look at the poster, while business travelers grumble in the unmoving line.

Finally, he hands the poster back to me.

"Now that's something," he says. "God bless you."

CHAPTER NINETEEN

Always Go Forward

Five hours later I stand barefoot in the Pacific. Jets landing at LAX roar overhead, descending perpendicular to incoming waves, and toddlers squeal at the tide line, sand-coated and lolling. My sister stands beside me comfortably quiet while her stepson, Michael, takes a few last rides on the boogie board before we pack up her RV and head home. They've been camping here over Memorial Day weekend, and that made it easy, by coincidence, for them to pick me up at the airport. Not twenty minutes out of baggage claim, we stand, pants rolled in the surf, like we did as very small girls in bikinis, squinting at swells reflecting sun.

"I felt the baby kick," she says at last.

"You did? Finally? That's great news."

"The doctors said I'd know when it happened, and I did for sure. It hurt! It almost took my breath away."

"Better get used to it."

She grins.

Michael emerges from the water, hair matted with sand. He had misjudged an oncoming wave, half hopping, half swimming toward it, trying to get over it as it curled and broke, charging toward him, hurling him back and under, and in the froth the boogie board appeared first, and now Michael, shaking his head.

"That sucked," he says.

"Yeah, we've been there," Lisa says.

On the familiar freeway ride home, we talk a little about

Tallahassee and about their weekend at the beach. Michael and I banter about rock music: Black Sabbath or Black Flag? Nirvana or Green Day? Finally, we can avoid the subject no longer.

"How's Mama Sue?" I ask Lisa.

"Better."

"Really? Because she's off chemo?"

"Yeah, she's a lot better. But maybe not as good as she thinks she is."

That sounds to me like a good thing, to be feeling positive about recovery. Believing you're doing well is the first step to doing well, I figure. So I don't ask much more. Instead, we pass the miles heading inland, tossing out names for the baby. Something Italian: Anthony, Dominic, Marco. Anything but Joe. Too many Joes in the family already: our grandfather, dad, and brother. Even Lisa's husband's name is Joe.

"What about Geremio?" I suggest. "That's a character's name in *Christ in Concrete*. It's a book I guess Dad liked a lot when he in college."

"That'd be cool. Then we could call him *mijo*—you know, like the Mexicans do: my little boy."

She pulls her new family van up to the curb on Burnside Court so I can unload my luggage and head to the nursing home where I left my mother two months ago.

"See you at Julie's," she says. Julie has a Memorial Day picnic planned for later this afternoon, and she's hoping my mother can attend.

"Will Mom be up for it?"

She shrugs. "You'll have to see."

Twenty minutes later, I walk into the familiar front lobby of Community Care and take a hard right, the opposite direction from the way I turned each morning back in March. That side of the facility is for patients who might reasonably expect to go home. This side is for long-term patients. No therapy. No walking. The stinky side, Lisa calls it, and she's got a point, though it's not as bad as the places I remember visiting as a Camp Fire Girl to sing Christmas carols. Back then, the acrid urine smell lodged hard in my gut. Here it wafts subtly, and my empty stomach—two bags of peanuts on a five-hour flight—hardly takes note. I take a deep breath and stop at the nurses' station.

"Sue Spagna?"

The nurse smiles. "Oh, she's expecting you," she says, and she directs me down the hall.

I pass rooms already dark at four in the afternoon, silent but for the whirr of oxygen tanks and canned laughter from the televisions. I gaze through open doors at bodies pillow-propped and hunched over trays or curled to the one side, blankets twisted, feet protruding. There are no visitors. Not one. Their loved ones, I suppose, have grown accustomed to futility. You visit a couple times a week. You bring flowers and air refresher. What else can you do? When I enter the small room at the far end of the hall, I see my mother lying atop the covers of her hospital bed, fully dressed in a white button blouse and a denim skirt. I haven't seen her in street clothes in more than six months, and it's a shock.

"How's it going, Mom?"

"I'm ready to go home."

"What?"

"I told the nurses you were coming today to take me home."

I had told her on the phone that I was coming—of course, I had—but I am sure I didn't say I was coming to take her home. I'm positive of it. There's a long list of skills she'll need to have mastered before going home: bathing, cooking, brushing teeth, driving, negotiating the bathroom. I mean, only a week ago she wasn't eating or drinking. How could change come so quickly? I have no idea how she's doing physically, but one thing's for sure: she's sharp.

"You can get my suitcase out of the closet, and don't forget the plastic bag with the dirty laundry."

She swings her legs over the side of the bed and sits upright, scanning the room for her shoes. The nurses, taking her at her word, have packed a few medical necessities in a cardboard box. It looks like I have no choice.

"Mom, listen. I can't. I don't even know what you need right now. What if we go to the picnic, then come back here? I'll pick you up in the morning and spend the day with you at your house and see how it goes."

She's silent.

"If that goes well, we'll come back and pick up your stuff and you can move home."

"And you can stay with me until I'm back on my feet," she says.

This is not a question, and the fact that it's not comforts me.

"Right. That's what I'm here for."

"Okay," she says. "It's a deal. Let's go eat some hot dogs."

When Julie asked my mother for menu requests for the picnic weeks ago, before her latest decline, all she wanted was hot dogs. This would be a bigger effort than you'd think for Julie since her family turned vegan a couple months back. Her husband's cholesterol dove a hundred points. But for Mama Sue, he'll gamely grill the real deal.

"Resurrection happens," Julie says when we pull up in the driveway. She busses my mother's cheek as she climbs out of the car.

Mama Sue smiles and takes the three porch steps one at a time with her walker and then charges into the living room, where she sits on the couch with a cold drink to rest and listen while I talk about my trip.

I hold up the poster from Tallahassee and point to the picture of my dad and tell the story, in brief. Julie's kids struggle to make sense of it. They're smart kids, who know history, and to them, like so many Americans, it seems nearly fantastic that where someone sat on a bus could matter, or even if it mattered once, for Rosa Parks, that it could be a big deal anywhere else.

"It was a big deal everywhere in the South, before Rosa Parks and afterwards."

"But aren't people supposed to disobey laws that are wrong?"

"Yeah, I guess they should, we should, but that doesn't mean you won't get in trouble for it."

"Which one is your dad?"

I point him out, down in the left-hand corner: slack-jawed, hands in his pockets. I glance over at my mother, searching for signs of melancholy. Is it too hard to hear again about the glories of her long-dead husband? If it is, you'd never know it. She's not even looking at the photo on the poster; she's beaming at Julie's kids. It's the teacher in her eager to see the kids learn, and the proud mother in her as well. She loves the history lesson, and the group-ness, the family-ness of all of us gathered around this poster, and she grins at me as though I've brought home a prize-winning science project or a spelling-bee trophy.

"They called me Sister Spagna," I say.

The kids laugh and chant: "Sister Spag-nuh, Sister Spag-nuh."

"I'm so glad you went, honey," my mom interrupts.

I look at her and think about what was at stake, really, if I'd

256

gone to Tallahassee and things had taken a turn for the worse. It was, in hindsight, gamble.

"Aren't you?" she asks in the same leading tone the folks in Tallahassee used. There's a conspiracy in the works, it seems. Everyone wants me to believe in my dad, to believe in goodness and hope and courage. Everyone wants the story to have a happy ending. I suppose it's the wanting that makes it so.

"I am, Mom. I really am."

I drone on about Johnny Herndon, about Jon Folsom, about Kendrick Meek and John Lewis. I am talking more than I usually do, chattering really, getting out of hand as I had in Portland two short weeks ago.

"Come on, Sister Spagna," Julie finally butts in. "It's time for dinner."

Julie's husband has the spread prepared: tofu dogs, real dogs, potato salad without mayonnaise, chips, green salad, beer, soda. We sit at a picnic table near the backyard swimming pool. My sister parades in with Michael, keys jangling, and pulls up a chair.

"That's a cool poster she got, huh Mom?"

"It sure is."

It's my turn, I know, my line, but I have the feeling I've been stealing the show, or more precisely that my dad has. Not just tonight, but for thirty years. Sort of like the Prodigal Son. The parable always seems so unjust: here's one brother staying home, year after year, doing the right thing, and who gets the fatted calf? The one who was off gallivanting. Here's my mother who stayed home and raised us, paid the bills, kept us fed, weathered our storms, and eventually settled into her own life. Now she's fought death for months, eked out a shocking victory, and what are we celebrating? My dad's bus ride from fifty years ago? It suddenly doesn't feel right, so I keep my mouth shut, chewing on my tofu dog. This moment,

for once, is not for the myth but for my mom. But she isn't
thinking about his heroism or even her own.

"Do you remember when you learned to swim?" she asks
me.

"Not really."

It's true I don't remember, but I've heard the story a thousand times. As we sit poolside in the shade, palms swaying, my
mom retells it for the crowd.

"You were only four or five when we'd go down to the
Belknaps' house for pool parties."

I can conjure the summer evenings, not unlike tonight:
the hot wind and the cool water, kids in the pool and parents
sitting beside round cable-spool tables, legs crossed, smoking
Winstons, drinking Busch, laughing.

"You'd grip the side of the pool and scoot, hand over hand,
away from the shallow steps, and fling yourself back, splashing
through the water, dog paddling for your life. You'd sit alone
for a long time, catching your breath, then next thing you
know we'd see you creeping a little farther from the steps to
do it again."

"Yeah, and once Rollie Belknap had to rescue me when I
took a wrong turn toward the middle of the pool."

My mom will have none of it.

"I don't remember that. I remember how you stuck with it,
how you never wanted any help," she says.

"Where'd I learn that, Mama Sue?"

Everyone laughs, and the subject changes. A basketball
appears and a game of HORSE ensues. My mother jiggles the
ice in her empty glass, and I notice for the first time that her
tremor is almost entirely gone. *Hang in there. Don't give up.
Don't give in.* I thought I learned it from John Lewis, but that's
not true. My mother reaches for the mayonnaise and slathers
it on a bun, preparing for seconds, as a flock of swifts swoops

toward treetops and power lines, turns on itself and spirals toward the sky.

The next morning when I pick her up for her first trial day at home, I bring a long, detailed list of questions for the nurses. I ask them to re-explain the procedures for irrigating the bladder.

"She knows how to do it," they say.

I ask about any dietary restrictions. None. Just drink lots of water. Physical limitations? None. She can use a walker if she feels more secure with it. They hand me a long list of prescriptions to pick up at Sav-On. And that's it. We're on our way.

Once home, my mother settles into the chair at the head of her kitchen table, the seat she's held my whole life, where she reads the newspaper or plays solitaire, pays the bills, or chit chats with neighbors. She scans the table, too tidy now that no one lives here, no empty envelopes or scribbled phone messages, no empty tea mugs or stacks of coupons to be clipped.

"It's nice to be home," she says.

"I'll bet. It's been a while."

I soft-boil an egg too long, not runny enough, and set a small stack of mail in front of her, cards from well-wishers mostly, and find her a pair of reading glasses. And she's off. She takes up the mantle of normal life, easy as getting back on a bike to ride. She stays in that chair at the kitchen table and makes small talk, putting off her midmorning nap so long that I'm afraid she'll topple over. Then she stands at the sink, fills her water glass, and gulps it down, and takes off down the hall, walker-less, to do her bathroom chores and lie down. Later in the day, when she finds that I've confused one of the prescriptions, she'll grab the phone and call a pharmacist who knows her, and clear it up in a snap. At the end of the day, it will be clear: she's ready.

Mom and I settle into a routine. I replace the shower head with a hose she can use sitting on a bench. I cook meals I know she'll eat, ones I remember from when I was a kid: homemade macaroni and cheese, hamburgers, spaghetti. During the day, we go to the pharmacy or the doctor's office. We run errands, looking for cheap medical supplies, since even that kind of shopping perks up the bargain hunter in my mother. Then in the evenings I pester her to walk.

"I get too tired," she says.

"What if I bring the chair?" I say.

So I carry a folding lawn chair—a yard-sale purchase, bent up and fabric torn—through the neighborhood, and I set it down at the end of the chosen destination: four houses down one day, five the next. She sits for several minutes in the evening breeze, then places both hands on the walker and heaves herself up to begin the journey home. Some nights Julie or Lisa comes over to help. They take turns carrying the chair, or their kids do, and we march in a clump down the sidewalk, a goofy chair-carting parade. Afterward we pull out more folding chairs and sit in the driveway drinking ice water, watching the sun set over the palms, and when we do, neighbors stop by to sit for a while and wish Mom the best until sometimes there are a dozen wobbly lawn chairs set up in her driveway, and I can sit back and listen to stories and watch the evening sky. Everywhere in Riverside, everywhere in Southern California, jacarandas are in full bloom: purple flowered and stunningly beautiful against the blue. I cannot remember the purple flowers from childhood, not for the life of me. I cannot figure how I missed them.

Was this what it was like for my dad to have Aunt Rose in the kitchen, cooking with garlic? He would have been my age when she visited, or a little older. Did he feel like this? Like the parts of your life, practical and meaningful, that you thought you'd lost show back up, like tools when the snow melts away, a little rusty, but no worse for the neglect. Maybe Aunt Rose wasn't enough. Maybe he needed to reconcile with his own dad, dead and gone, before he could write. Or maybe he did reconcile by being a father, a good father, and he didn't need to write. I wish this for him, for whatever spirit of his lurks unseen or within me or my siblings or my mother. He was wrong, of course, about never going back. There's a time for it. And after three weeks, my time is done.

. . .

We sit together, Mama Sue and I, playing Scrabble, grappling for letters in the yellow drawstring bag my Irish grandmother sewed, the same one my mom and dad used when they stayed up late together, the same one we used when I learned how to play. The game passes the time as we wait for the last moments before Julie comes to pick me up to take me to the airport. We play in silence, racking up respectable but unimpressive scores, twenty points say, or sometimes only fifteen, checking the clock regularly.

"I should thank you for everything you've done," my mother says.

I tap a tile absently on the board.

"It was no big deal," I say.

"But I mean it. I appreciate it."

I fumble with my letters, trying for a five-letter word, or maybe six, even if it makes for a lousy score, to open up the board a little, to create a few more possibilities.

I glance up.

My mom stares at her tiles.

"I was glad to do it."

Epilogue

Summer came as a whirlwind and a tonic. Laurie and I climbed trails, a thousand feet per mile, to meadows where snow melted away in a circle to expose a single yellow lily. We peeked over ledges where cornices hung translucent blue, ready to crack apart, lose purchase, and chatter down a thousand feet of granite. We snapped photos of ourselves drinking from the wineskin Jon Folsom had gifted to us, and we sent him the snapshots in the mail, along with pictures of Daisy, the cat, who prowled the grass, frisky and proud. We lifted her to the faucet to drink, and maybe it was the water, or the attention, or plain dumb luck, but her recovery held steady, nearly miraculous. Hers wasn't the only one.

Mom's health improved by the day, as if she'd bolted upright like a suited casket dweller in a cheap horror film. She stepped out to summer garage sales each Saturday to buy clothes for the anticipated grandkids and went to the food pantry at Our Lady each Monday to pass out peanut butter to the homeless. In August, Lisa gave birth to a boy, Dominic Vincent, who was born prematurely, and my mom drove her to the hospital each afternoon to feed and nurse him in a role reversal so complete and so rapid that it was becoming at least as fantastic as the bus story. In September, Father De died in his nursing home, and I walked autumn-hued meadows thinking of the mantra he'd offered my mother, the one that saved her life probably, at thirty-eight, and again perhaps at sixty-four: life-death-resurrection.

No Big Deal

· · ·

Midsummer a wildfire took off in the steep, forested mountainsides a few short miles from our cabin. It erupted in a mushroom cloud, unexpected, on a clear blue-sky day, and it threatened our community, our neighbors, our cabin. For weeks afterward, the sheriff arrived on our doorstep regularly to serve evacuation notices, ranked by severity from Level One to Level Two to Level Three and back down again. We never left home. We never intended to. The fire moved and retreated, hope rose and fell, despair crept in and got squelched.

One full-moon night when the sky was speckled with orange flares and the moon rose huge and woozy over the ridges, the local amateur band played at a party and riffed for hours. *Level Four*, they sang. *We're going to Level Four.* Never mind that there's no such thing as Level Four; it was the right song for the night. Why not laugh and dance? What else is there to do? When I woke the next morning, I told myself this: there's plenty to do.

Though I'd never become an activist, after summer passed, I'd run for public office and be elected fire commissioner for a brand-new volunteer fire district, a small gesture, trying to do something to make things better. And there was more. I'd be able to tell the story of my dad's death more easily and without guilt; better yet, I would be able to talk about his life with pride, the Tallahassee story, sure, and also the whole of it: the Marine Corps and the Cloven Hoof, the beach shack and Aunt Rose, *Paradise Lost* and "Howl," family and football and more. I'd think about civil rights in a more hopeful and specific way, too. Within a year, Laurie and I would register legally as domestic partners in Washington State, the first step toward marriage, riding once again, gratefully, on the coattails of the brave acts and persistence of others. And within two years, nearly unthinkable at the beginning of my journey, Barack Obama would be elected president. As he walked toward the podium to deliver his inaugural address, he'd stop to lean toward Congressman John Lewis and say only this: "Because of you."

Meanwhile, my father's story grew distant. The FBI wrote to say conclusively that my dad had no file. I didn't know if it was true or not, but I had no way to find out. The military sent his records: he had been an aircraft mechanic—just as he'd always said—and he'd been discharged honorably. Whether he ever went AWOL in between, it didn't say. My own journey had been rich and full of surprises, but I feared that I still didn't know the answers to the questions I set out to answer or, if I knew them, they were no different than when I started out. Why'd he do it? Because it was the right thing to do. Why'd he leave? Because he had to. Why'd he never talk about it? Now there was the stickler.

Late in the fall, I landed back at the Midtowner, the same small-town motel where I'd sat jacket-bundled in the earliest days of spring staring at newly green hills nervously waiting to call Johnny Herndon. Now the hills were brown with drought or black from fire. And I was not the least bit shy about calling. The visit in May had cleared the remaining shards of formality between us. Now I sat cross legged on the motel-room bed, asking questions, a thousand questions, every question that came to mind. I asked him about Judge Rudd, whether he remembered him, and Johnny Herndon told me how Rudd had called when he was up for re-election not too many years earlier, shortly before his death, and asked for Johnny's support.

"He asked for your support?" I was aghast.

"Yes, he did." Johnny said. "He was like George Wallace. He changed."

"He changed because he had to change, you mean."

"Yes," he chuckled a little. "Once we got the vote, everything had to change."

"So did you give John Rudd your support?"

"No, I did not."

I laughed aloud, and I could hear Johnny Herndon laughing on the far end of the line.

"And what, exactly, happened to you right after you got out of jail and dropped out of school?" He'd told me that his wife had been harassed and that her father had, but I still wasn't clear on what happened, specifically, to him. I didn't want to open wounds. I just wanted to understand. "You eventually found work?"

"Not really. No one would hire me. That's why I went into business for myself."

"The taxi business?"

"No, at first I did outside sales work for eight or ten years. What I did, really, was work out of town a lot in rural areas, and mostly black areas, so there'd be no trouble."

"Wait a minute. Did you say you had to stay away from Tallahassee, more or less, for eight or ten *years*?"

"Oh, it was no big deal," he said. "What we did on the bus was something that had to be done. And we were glad to do it."

I believed him. I believed *in* him. And I knew this was my chance.

"Was it worth it? Are things really any better?"

"You wouldn't believe the difference now."

"What has changed, exactly?"

"The attitude of the people," he says. "Young people who can't remember just can't understand, people younger than maybe forty. Much more has been accomplished than I ever expected to see in my lifetime."

Somewhere in the middle of the conversation I realized I was having the conversation that I'd wanted to have with Leonard Speed, the one I'd wanted to have with my dad. About politics and life and the past and the future. About what matters. About life. I didn't want to hang up, so I found myself stalling for time, trolling for a question to ask, and I came up with one.

"Did you ever tell your kids about what you did?"

"It's funny you ask, because with all this anniversary stuff, they heard about it, and said, 'We never heard about that.' They said, 'Dad, how come you never told us you did that?' And I told them: 'It was no big deal.'"

No big deal that he risked his life, lost his job, and dropped out of college with a term to go, then traveled away from his family for eight years afterward? No big deal? I thought about that famous quote from *War and Peace*: "It is only un-self-conscious activity that bears fruit, and the man who plays a part in a historical drama never understands its true significance."

Johnny Herndon's voice turned soft and earnest again. "See, that tells you something about your dad, too."

It had occurred to me before, and now I was sure of it. My dad didn't avoid telling the test ride story because of fear or guilt, shame or disillusionment. It wasn't because of the honey-skinned girl or the FBI or some clandestine bail bondsman. It was simpler than that. It was, to him, no big deal. It was what he had to do. And, like so many others, he'd done it.

There's humility in it, I think, but there's more, too. Courage requires not just the physical bravery to step up at the moment, planned or unplanned, when danger threatens, but the strength to live the best way you can with the consequences, deserved or undeserved, of what life has dealt you. Part of what I was dealt was being fatherless. I'm pretty sure Johnny Herndon is right: if my father had lived, I'd never have learned the bus story, not the whole of it at least. I'd never have heard of C. K. Steele or Dan Speed. I'd never have traveled to Tallahassee to meet Johnny Herndon or Jon Folsom or John Lewis. And I'd never have understood the truth: that the test ride on the Sunnyland bus was, in fact, a big deal, a very big deal, that without courageous acts like it, we'd live in a very different country, a far lesser one. Truth is, if my dad had lived, I would never have taken this journey at all. Would I trade the experience to have him back? I would, of course. In a heartbeat, I would.

Short of that, I wouldn't trade it for anything.

Acknowledgments

I owe my heartfelt thanks to the many people who inspired, encouraged, and supported me on this journey.

Almost thirty years ago, in a living room in tiny Marshall, Minnesota, Joe and Cathy Amato and Bob and Posie White switched on a cassette recorder as they sat together to reminisce with the hope that one day we kids might take an interest in our father's story. It worked.

Dr. David Chappell, author of the fine book *Inside Agitators: White Southerners in the Civil Rights Movement*, convinced me that the thread was worth following.

Washington State Artist Trust Grants for Artists Program provided funding to get me out of my books and onto an airplane. Joy Tutela and Krista Ingebrestson helped to shape and promote the project. And Dan Lehman and Joe Mackall, sponsors of the *River Teeth* Literary Nonfiction Contest, finally brought this book to print.

The organizers of the fiftieth anniversary celebration of the Tallahassee bus boycott toiled for a year to bring this forgotten history into the light, to educate their community, and to honor those who struggled for change. Cynthia Williams, Rev. William Foutz, Bill Proctor, Barbara DeVane, Karen Woodall, Barbara Black, Tella Marie Norwood, and others welcomed me into the fold with kindness and warmth.

For fifty years, scholars and journalists have delved into the story of the Tallahassee bus boycott. Without their work, I could never have pieced together my father's role. My thanks to Jackson Ice, Charles Smith, Lewis Killian, Gregory Padgett, Patricia Stephens Due and Tananarive Due, and the staff of the *Tallahassee Democrat*. And to Glenda Rabby. Her book, *The Pain and the Promise*, may not be the Bible, but it is a very good book.

Clayton Barbeau sent me long, detailed e-mails. His exuberant tales of my dad's Beat years in San Francisco never failed to boost my spirits while I camped at City of Hope in the early stages in my mother's illness.

Many friends took the time to read parts of *Test Ride*. Linda Cooper took time off from her own family struggle with illness to help me out; her gut reactions, hard won, always drew me back to compassion and truth. Anne Grunsted, a friend I've never met, critiqued each chapter as it evolved; her wise and incisive comments honed the story, giving it shape and clarity. Jerry Gabriel, too, read the entire draft and gave it his unequivocal thumbs up, a much-needed blessing.

Julie Ann Higgins Russell walked with me for miles, literally, around city blocks, down beaches, up mountains, into the frozen desert, and back out again. Who deserves such a friend?

The six young men on the bus are the heart of this story. I owe my gratitude to those I never met: James Kennedy, Leonard Speed, and Harold Owens. And I owe something much deeper to the two men who answered a letter from a stranger and ended up sharing their memories. Johnny Herndon's quiet strength and humility taught me the meaning of integrity. And Jon Folsom, more than anyone else, brought my young father to life for me, a greater gift than I can ever repay.

Finally, all my love.

To my brother, Joe Spagna, and my sister, Lisa Iorio.

To my mother, Susan Spagna.

And to Laurie. Always.

Winners of the River Teeth Literary Nonfiction Prize

Five Shades of Shadow
Tracy Daugherty

The Untouched Minutes
Donald Morrill

Where the Trail Grows Faint:
A Year in the Life of a
Therapy Dog Team
Lynne Hugo

The World Before Mirrors
Joan Connor

House of Good Hope:
A Promise for a Broken City
Michael Downs

The Enders Hotel: A Memoir
Brandon R. Schrand

An Inside Passage
Kurt Caswell

Test Ride on the Sunnyland Bus:
A Daughter's Civil Rights Journey
Ana Maria Spagna

A Double Life:
Discovering Motherhood
Lisa Catherine Harper

Mountains of Light: Seasons
of Reflection in Yosemite
R. Mark Liebenow

So Far, So Good
Ralph Salisbury

Young Widower: A Memoir
John W. Evans

To order or obtain more information on these or other University of Nebraska Press titles, visit nebraskapress.unl.edu.